THE BEST OF

Catherine Marshall

Her Intimate Life

D0451718

THE BEST OF

Catherine Marshall

Her Intimate Life

Edited by LEONARD E. LeSOURD

AVON BOOKS ◆ NEW YORK

Permissions are listed on page 351, which serves as an extension of this copyright page.

AVON BOOKS
A division of
The Hearst Corporation
1350 Avenue of the Americas
New York, New York 10019

Copyright © 1993 by Leonard E. LeSourd
Published by arrangement with Chosen Books
Library of Congress Catalog Card Number: 93-1606
ISBN: 0-380-72383-2

The Chosen Books edition contains the following Library of Congress Cataloging in Publication Data:

Marshall, Catherine, 1914-1983
[Selections. 1993]
  The best of Catherine Marshall/edited by Leonard E. LeSourd.
    p.   cm.
1. Marshall, Catherine, 1914-1983.   2. Christian life—1960-
I. LeSourd, Leonard E.   II. Title.
BX9225.M3515A25   1993
242—dc20   93-1606

First Avon Books Trade Printing: July 1995

AVON TRADEMARK REG. U.S. PAT. OFF. AND IN OTHER COUNTRIES, MARCA REGISTRADA, HECHO EN U.S.A.

Printed in the U.S.A.

OPM 10 9 8 7 6 5 4 3 2 1

To all those individuals throughout the world
whose lives have been touched
by Catherine's writings

Contents

Contents

Introduction

From the time she climbed into her backyard "wishing tree" as an eight-year-old, Catherine Marshall dreamed of becoming a writer. As a teenager she began putting her thoughts and observations into journals, a discipline she continued until her death in March 1983. During her twelve-year marriage to Peter Marshall she added research skills, spending hundreds of hours in the library pursuing sermon topics for her husband.

Peter Marshall's death in January 1949 launched her writing career in a way she could never have foreseen or desired. First, a book of Peter Marshall sermons, *Mr. Jones, Meet the Master*, was an astonishing bestseller. Then came his biography, *A Man Called Peter*, a bestselling book and hugely successful movie on the colorful life of this Scottish pastor and U.S. Senate chaplain. Twenty other books followed, with total sales of over twenty million copies, and a hundred or more articles in both secular and Christian magazines.

How do you select the best writing of an author whose subject matter ranged so widely?

Catherine wrote vividly of her childhood; that had to be included. The years with Peter were filled with loving and growing. Ten years of widowhood brought pain and triumph. A second marriage, including stepmothering three small children, was a fresh challenge. This second marriage—to me—moved her into a close editorial relationship with *Guideposts* magazine, during which both of us plunged into the middle of the Holy Spirit movement.

The death of a grandchild triggered a year-long "dark night of the soul." During Catherine's deepening prayer life, a vision was given her of an intercessory prayer ministry, Breakthrough—which could prove her most enduring spiritual legacy. A book of Catherine's best writings would be incomplete without memorable segments from her novels *Christy* and *Julie*. Finally, Catherine turned the approach of her own death into an adventure to be explored in detail.

Putting all this together has revived many memories of our 23 years of marriage, with the low, painful moments in some ways more treasured than the highs. To be sure, there was great euphoria over the birth of a dozen impact-creating books, the extraordinary success of *Guideposts*, the development of meaningful family life through joining together two broken homes.

Yet the low points stand out because God was closer and more real in times of defeat and grief. Thank God for those times! Without them success would have become bland, relationships stereotyped, gratitude and joy never so savored.

By many Catherine Marshall was seen as an unblemished Christian of great maturity and wisdom. Those of us close to Catherine knew better. Catherine was flawed, thank God, or she would have been impossible to live with. Her blemishes made Catherine real. Her weakness forced her to depend on God. So long as she sought His strength, He blessed her—and her readers.

Leonard E. LeSourd
Evergreen Farm, Virginia
May 1993

SECTION ONE

Childhood: Short on Money, Long on Faith

Childhood was not an easy time for Sarah Catherine Wood. Her father, John Wood, was a Presbyterian pastor, struggling to feed and clothe his three children on a small salary. But in frugal living Catherine absorbed the basics of the Scriptures, found childhood joys and developed that special gift of her heavenly Father: creativity.

Our Father, Who Art on Earth

My early childhood was a crazy mixture of exuberant joy interspersed with moments of fear. Assorted odd things alarmed me: mice, spiders, snakes, darkness, the nuns in their flowing black habits in the Catholic school across the street, the page in *The Book of Knowledge* picturing Joan of Arc being burned at the stake. Yet as long as my father was near, my world was invulnerable.

My dad, the young preacher John Wood, was tall and slim, with black hair always combed neatly and soft brown eyes with a glint of mischief in them. And, I thought, very handsome! He was gregarious, full of good humor, fond of teasing and practical jokes.

Until I was seven, I was the only child. Then came my brother, Bob, and fourteen months later my sister, Emmy. Because Dad chose to have his office at home rather than at the church, I saw more of my father than most children do.

Often I would creep into his home office unbidden, but he was never too busy for me. Invariably he would smile and hold out his arms to receive me. "Girlie—my girlie," he would say.

Even when Father had a guest, he would allow me to sit silently on his lap while he carried on a conversation with the church officer or parishioner or the young Catholic priest who lived nearby. Dad's lap always seemed more commodious than Mother's, his arms more firm. For me, those arms were protection and reassurance, warmth, strength and nourishment. In some strange way, the love that flowed between us must have been nourishment for him, too.

The setting for those earliest memories was a one-floor white frame home in Canton, a small mid-Mississippi town. This cottage-manse was dwarfed by the red brick church sitting squarely beside it, and overshadowed by huge old oak trees. The giant oaks also lined Peace Street in front, creating a tunnel of green through which to walk or bicycle—welcome respite from the cruel Mississippi sun.

My shyness might eventually have led to withdrawal and a feeling of inferiority, for I could not easily admit people to my inner self. Fortunately, this pervading reticence was countered by the way my parents treated me. Since I had "discovered" Robert Louis Stevenson's *A Child's Garden of Verses* and enjoyed the sound of the cadences slipping off my tongue, I was encouraged to memorize my favorite poems and recite them to the family.

When Father wanted to chop down the wisteria vine all but smothering the old coal house in our backyard, and I protested loudly, he listened to my pleas. "If you feel that strongly about it," he said, patting my hand, "I'll just give the wisteria a haircut."

When I had progressed enough in my piano lessons to play simple hymns, Father would encourage me to be the pianist for small parlor meetings.

Thus, early was I given a sense of self-worth, the recognition of my individuality and the surety of being cherished.

Balancing such love and attention to us children, our parents were definitely the authority figures in our home. We were not allowed to give up easily on tasks we considered difficult. Their attitude was always, "We'll help you where help is really needed. Between us, nothing is too hard."

That included a regular Sunday afternoon session of memorizing *The Catechism for Young Children,* followed by the misnamed *Shorter Catechism of the Westminster Assembly.* (Actually, the *Shorter* is considerably longer!)

A futile religious exercise? Not a bit of it! Couched in the chiseled English of another century, these laid a right base for those all-important questions about life and death, about God and our relationship to Him.

Q. What is God?
A. God is a Spirit, infinite, eternal and unchangeable in His
      being, wisdom, power, holiness, justice, goodness and truth.
Q. What is the chief end of man?
A. Man's chief end is to glorify God, and to enjoy Him for-
      ever. . . .

That last idea was startling to me. From some of the pictures and tales in my Bible story books, the Jehovah of the Old Testament seemed stern and unapproachable—unless you were someone like Moses or Abraham. This God thundered from Sinai, demanding sacrifices. His fierce anger destroyed great cities, once even flooded the whole world and drowned everyone in it except for Noah and his family.

Yet here was the catechism telling me that God was to be enjoyed! That I would have to ponder long and deeply.

One day I asked my father, "How can I love God when I'm afraid of Him?"

"Because He loves you," came Dad's reply. "Remember that Bible verse on your Sunday school folder just last week, 'We love Him because He first loved us.' He loved you before you even knew He was there."

"But I don't see a face full of love like I see your face, Dad."

"That's exactly why Jesus came down to earth—to tell us and show us that the Father in heaven is all love, is made of love. Jesus liked to say that even the best human father couldn't be half as loving or kind or generous as the heavenly Father."

Seeing doubt on my face, Dad added gently, "Sometimes I have to punish you or Bob or Em when you've done something wrong. I'd be a poor father to you if I didn't correct you. But that doesn't mean that you're afraid of me, does it?"

Looking into those warm brown eyes, I saw only love beyond measure and, as always, a glint of humor. Certainly I could trust my earthly father. But God was still vague, up in heaven somewhere. I wasn't sure where I stood with Him.

So I went my blithe way reveling in the freedom to roam in an outdoor world of never-ending delights. In the midst of all this, the fact that our family had little money mattered to me not at all. We had each other, and we had fun together. And so, many years later, I have only to turn my memory loose, instantly to recapture the feel of a small child's fresh, sharp joy of sight and sound and touch and smell.

To others, the yard around our cottage-manse may have seemed ordinary enough. To me it was the most beautiful place on earth. How could there be anywhere a more delicious fragrance than the Southern honeysuckle that rioted over all the fences? And not only fragrance, but taste. Pick a blossom, delicately bite off the stem end, suck out the delicious honey. No wonder the bees loved it!

And what bliss in the spring to hunt for the first white bells of snowdrops among the green foliage and to bury my nose in the first hyacinths! How could my eyes absorb enough of the beauty of the purple wisteria vine I had persuaded Father to save? Had anyone before me ever really felt the enchantment of bare feet on the thick carpet of moss under the oaks?

Years later I would read the Genesis account of how the Creator looked with approval on each day's handiwork and "saw that it was good." Reading it was like an echo out of my own deep spirit. Of course it was good—every flower, every fragrance, every drifting cloud and singing bird. Not only "good," but glorious. My child's heart had known it all along.

But my private Eden also bore the unmistakable mark of my earthly father. It was Dad who constructed an outsized sandbox where my playmates and I spent endless hours building elaborate sand castles.

It was Dad who built a seesaw, sturdier and longer than any to be found in a store. Everything he built was big, enduring, meant to last a lifetime.

And the swing! Quickly we learned to stand and pump: begin slowly, bend the knees in rhythm. Make it go higher, higher, up and down. Now again, swishing through the air, until finally the jerk of the chains told us that the swing had gone as high as it could. Then "let the cat die."

There were joys awaiting me inside our home, too. As in many older, deep-South homes, the cool, ten-foot wide center hall ran the length of our house. This gallery-corridor was the favorite site for games, all revolving around my father. Pure gold were the hours he spent with us children playing Parcheesi, caroms, checkers, dominoes, Rook, Old Maid, jackstraws or jacks or putting together countless jigsaw puzzles.

For some reason, Mother could never get the hang of games, so she would mend or sew or read while Dad and I and anyone else we could pull in battled tenaciously to win. Father was a sharp competitor, never giving us children any quarter because we were small. We liked it that way, for when we won, the taste of victory was all the sweeter.

I also enjoyed just sitting on the floor beside my father, talking to him as I watched him make repairs around the house. He was a good carpenter and painter, even bricklayer and stonemason, with an adequate knowledge of plumbing and electricity.

It must have been the security of Dad's presence that made his office the most lived-in room in successive manse-homes in Mississippi, the Eastern panhandle of West Virginia and the Eastern Shore of Virginia. The study was always lined with open bookshelves floor to ceiling. A comfortable leather Morris chair with wide arms sat in the corner just within arm's reach of *The Book of Knowledge, The Harvard Classics* and Maclaren's *Expositions of Holy Scriptures*, along with novels and reference books.

It was here that the family always gathered after the evening meal while we children worked on our school lessons. Sitting in the Morris chair or at one of the pullout leaves of Father's desk or sprawled on the floor, we were surrounded by plenty of study helps. Dad subscribed to several magazines, and he always had catalogs from which we could order books, for our town rarely had a bookstore. All our *National Geographics* were saved for schoolwork and a cupboard was crammed full of past issues. We were free to cut and paste them as illustrative material for school papers.

My father had his weaknesses, of course. He could be stubborn. A case in point: the episode of the flamethrower. Fond of tools and gadgets, he was often tempted to spend too much of his meager salary on such things. Since the West Virginia house had a large yard, he treated himself to a power mower. Soon after that he saw a flamethrower advertised. Apparently the War Department had overbought and was offering these items at a discount.

Mother was annoyed when he brought it up. "What on God's green earth do you want such a thing for? You know perfectly well we haven't any money to spend on silly things like that."

Father looked wounded. "A flamethrower is *exactly* what I need for getting rid of the tall weeds in fence corners," he retorted. "And I *am* going to buy it."

Buy it he did. We still have the flamethrower in the family. We also still have the weeds.

Then there was his volatile temper. How vividly Bob remembers the time he was helping Dad string Christmas lights over the front door when Father's thumb accidentally slipped into the live socket.

Out came the thumb and out of Dad's mouth poured forth some very unclergymanlike words. Then Dad glared down from the ladder.

"Son," he said solemnly, "forget that I said that."

Bob never did, of course. Not only that, but in later years he told me, "From that moment, I loved and respected Dad more than ever. He was not too 'good' to be human."

Nor could any of us forget the Sunday morning when Bob and Em got a switching.

During the previous week the two children made the rounds of the neighborhood begging empty fifteen-pound lard cans, neglecting to report to our parents how the empty cans were to be used.

Sunday morning our preacher-father was all dressed for church—black hair slicked down, white suit, white shoes (his only pair of shoes not at the repair shop). Last of all Father went out to the garden to select a flower for his buttonhole.

A half-minute later we heard a howl. Red-faced, Father stomped into the house with a switch broken off the privet hedge to punish the culprits. It seemed that Bob and Em had filled several lard cans with water and sunk them in strategic places in the flower garden, laying twigs and tufts of grass over these homemade booby traps. That Sunday Father preached with a soaked left foot while two of his children listened with smarting legs.

But Dad was always fair in administering punishment. We knew he loved us even while he was chastising us. There was no inconsistency with what he preached from the pulpit and the way he dealt with us as the head of the house.

It wasn't that my father was eloquent in the pulpit. He was an average preacher with only a mild interest in theology. His forte was people. He loved them and enjoyed mixing with them, friends and strangers alike. He had a knack for finding a just-right conversational meeting ground with all manner of folk.

One of my favorite stories is about how Dad went down to the railroad yards near our home in Keyser, West Virginia, to seek out a new member of his congregation. In one of the Baltimore and Ohio's enormous roundhouses, the Reverend Wood found his man at work.

"Can't shake hands with you," said the man apologetically. "They're too grimy."

John Wood reached down to the ground and rubbed his hands in coal soot.

"How about it now?" he said, offering an equalized hand.

But if at an early age I knew I could trust my earthly father, I continued to resist the sermons that urged us to surrender our lives to a faraway God. What would that mean? The idea of spending all my time praying, reading the Bible and talking about God did not appeal to me at all.

When the evangelist Gypsy Smith, Jr., came to hold services in our town, I went with curiosity but little more. A huge tent was pitched on a vacant lot near the town limits—not large enough to hold the crowds that flocked there. On a platform of raw wood from which the resin still oozed sat the massed choirs gathered from all the churches. Their favorite anthem was the spirited "Awakening Chorus":

> The Lord Jehovah reigns, and sin is backward hurled.
> Rejoice! Rejoice! Rejoice!

The "rejoicings" vibrated so shrilly that they raised goosebumps along my spine. As the congregation sang, the waving arms of the music director beat out the rhythms of hymns like

> Standing on the prom-i-ses of Christ, my King. . . .

or

> Sing them o-ver a-gain to me,
> Won-der-ful words of life. . . .

Each time we collectively took a breath, the pianist would run in scales, chords and flourishes marvelous to my childish ears.

Then came the preaching, so dynamic that decades later Gypsy Smith's thundering word-pictures still reverberate in my ears. Samson, succumbing to fleshly temptation, delivered into the hands of the Philistines, his hair cut, his eyes cruelly blinded. Then that final scene in Samson's drama where a repentant Samson, his hair grown back, faces three thousand Philistines gathered in the great hall to make sport of him. With his right hand on one of the two key pillars supporting the roof, his left hand on the other, Samson bows himself with all his might. . . .

The emotion in Gypsy's preaching, mounting steadily, transferred itself to the congregation. What did Samson's story have to do with Keyser, West Virginia? Selfishness and sensuality brought only destruction, the evangelist thundered. It would always be so. Each of us had to decide which road we would travel.

Finally a hush would fall over the tent as the choirs sang almost in a whisper,

Softly and tenderly Jesus is calling, calling for you and for me. . . .

Soon, at the far edge of the tent, someone would rise and make his way slowly down the aisle toward the front. Then another person, and another, and another. . . .

What impressed me were the faces of the people who went forward. There was radiance and joy on those faces. Most seemed eager to get to the front, where they knelt and wept and prayed and "gave themselves."

At home I asked my parents about the people who had made this act of commitment to God.

"Does this mean they joined the church?" I asked.

I wondered, too: Had not some of them "gone forward" out of the emotionalism of the moment?

Dad understood my wonderings behind the questions. Wisely he answered, "Sure, most of them will join a church. You, too, will want to do that at the right time. But Catherine, joining the church is only the outward part of it. You should not join the church until it really means something. It must mean the gift of yourself to God."

I pondered that statement many times during those preteen years.

I was nine on the Sunday morning when I sat in church beside my mother—my brother and sister were in Sunday school classes—and watched my father conduct the service. My heart was full of love for him in a special way. I can never remember many things he said from the pulpit, but I felt God's love flowing through him for all of us in the congregation.

At the end of the service, rather spontaneously as I recall, Dad issued an invitation for those to come forward who wanted to accept Jesus as the Lord of their lives and to be part of the church fellowship.

And suddenly I felt a stirring inside me. Very gentle. There was no voice, no words, just a feeling of great warmth. I loved my father dearly. And I trusted him with all my heart. I loved him so much that I could feel tears forming behind my eyes.

And then came the assurance. All along God had meant for the love of my earthly father to be a pattern of my heavenly Father and to show me the way to make connection with Him.

Following this inner conviction came the sudden urge to act and the will to do it. To my surprise and Mother's, I rose from the pew and walked down the aisle to the front, joining a half-dozen or so others.

At first Dad did not see me as the group formed a semicircle around the altar. He spoke to us briefly about the step we were taking and was about to pray when he noticed me.

Full recognition flashed into his brown eyes; he knew instantly that my being there was significant. I was presenting the gift of myself, a first step in faith. The resistance to surrender had been broken.

I shall never forget the look on my father's face. Surprise . . . joy . . . sudden vulnerability. He stood for a long moment in front of the altar, looking at me with eyes swimming in tears behind his spectacles. Then he pulled himself together and had us kneel as he prayed.

It was my first encounter with the living God—my heavenly Father. The catechism had said that He had loved me first. So had my earthly father. He must have loved me even before birth while I was carried in my mother's body.

Not only that, but since I could love and trust my earthly father, how much more could I love and trust my Father in heaven, and without fear place my future in His hands?

Mother Never Thought We Were Poor

hile my father was the one to present God to me as a heavenly Father who cared tenderly about each of His children, it was my mother who showed me how a relationship with Him could change everyday situations. The lessons God had taught her were indigenous to the poverty of the first eighteen years of her life. Either she had to settle down to lack, or find God's way out of it. The creative approach He gave her has been of help to countless numbers of people, myself among them.

Leonora Haseltine Whitaker was born in 1891 and reared on North Carolina farms. When she was eighteen she volunteered to join Dr. Edward O. Guerrant's mission in the Great Smoky Mountains of east Tennessee as a schoolteacher. Her experiences there with the mountain people in the Cove would later form the basis of my novel *Christy*.

Mother was taller than average, which was accentuated (I see as I leaf through the family album) by the Gibson-girl shirtwaist dresses of her girlhood. She had extremely large, expressive blue eyes and an aquiline nose with a piquant tilt at the end. Her chestnut-colored hair was so long that she could sit on it, though she usually wore it pinned up on top of her head. Later she began braiding it, winding the braids twice around her head in a lovely natural coronet.

Soon after Leonora Whitaker got to the Cove, the mission fell into dire straits for funds. As Mother prayed about this, an idea dropped into her head. She had received an invitation to speak to a woman's group in nearby Knoxville. While there, why not call on a Knoxville businessman with a reputation for philanthropy! What followed was an object lesson in how faith and creativity can blend effectively.

For these engagements she was determined not to look like a dowdy mountain missionary who needed to beg for herself as well as for the mountaineers. She wanted her appearance to say, "I'm having fun doing the Lord's work. Wouldn't you like to have a part in this adventure, too?"

A visit to a beauty parlor was her first step. She emerged with an elaborate hairdo, curls on top, a figure-eight in the back.

Next, in one of Knoxville's best stores, Mother found an enormous black hat with sweeping ostrich plumes. It would be perfect, she decided, with her one good garment—a black broadcloth suit. But the hat was priced at $25, every penny of her salary for one month. She pondered a long time. Shouldn't the $25 go directly into the mission fund? Or would buying the hat actually be an investment in the work?

Mother bought the hat.

Her blue eyes sparkling with the fun of this feminine adventure, Mother swept into the downtown offices of Mr. Rush Hazen, a wholesale grocer and philanthropist. Heads at rows of desks turned to stare. Even Mr. Hazen stared. In fact, he all but whistled.

"You—a missionary! I don't believe it. Why hasn't somebody thought of sending out missionaries like you before? What can I do for you?"

Mr. Hazen did a great deal. Triumphantly, Mother went back to the mission with enough food and money to keep boarding students all winter, and with the promise of more money for the future. She also went back more secure than ever in the conviction that God would supply our every need if we but ask Him to show the way.

It was at this mission that Leonora Whitaker met John Wood, who had just graduated from Union Theological Seminary in Richmond, Virginia. They were married in Asheville, North Carolina, when mother was nineteen.

My parents spent the next forty years serving Presbyterian congregations in small communities, living frugally. Yet that did not dampen Mother's creativity a whit. I well remember an especially harsh period—the early 1930s. Because his church people in Keyser, West Virginia, were suffering financially, Dad had voluntarily taken three successive cuts in salary. That meant that our family of five barely scraped along.

Dad received his portion of what had been in the church collection plates on Sunday night, and it never lasted the week. The Friday grocery shopping, therefore, included an element of acute embarrassment to us children. Even now I wince at the remembrance of standing beside my father, pretending not to notice while he leaned over the counter and said to the grocer in a lowered voice, "If you'll let us have this list of groceries, I'll drop by on Monday to pay you."

During those lean years our family had no car. We children walked or bicycled. Our parents walked—for all shopping, to church, to call on parishioners.

Bob and Em and I did not mind the fact that we had to go to a neighbor's to read the Sunday funnies, since one of our economies was cutting out the Sunday paper. What we *did* mind were some of the clothes we had to wear.

I've never forgotten one brown velvet dress Mother made for me out of someone's hand-me-down. The velvet was worn in places, and the chocolate brown was wrong for a young girl. I suffered in silence every time I wore it. And my sister was mortified, she tells me, by never having a proper girl's snowsuit of her own, but having to wear an old pair of her brother's pants in wintertime.

We children certainly did not enjoy those Depression cutbacks, yet no tinge of fear about lack of money ever clouded our home. It never seemed to enter Mother's head that we were living through a period of poverty. She went through each difficult day of the Depression as though she had some secret bank account to draw from—and in a sense she did.

Though we did without many things, Mother always provided us with a feeling of well-being. Chiefly, I think, because of the ways she contrived to give to others. Out of our meager pantry she would send a sick neighbor a supper tray of something delicious she had prepared—velvety-smooth boiled custard; feather-light homemade rolls—served up on our best china and always with a dainty bouquet from our garden.

While Mother always tried to provide her family a balanced diet with plenty of fruit and vegetables, we often went without meat, and I cannot recall any luxury foods. The main course for many an evening would be French fries and hot biscuits with honey or jam, or salmon croquettes, or fried mush. But we children didn't mind the mush at all, not the way Mother made it: sliced thin, browned crisp and served with maple syrup.

Mother could turn even fried mush into an occasion by giving some of *that* away. This happened when she discovered that Mr. Edwards, our wealthy neighbor, was fond of mush. Since his wife never served him such lowly fare, he would from time to time be the grateful recipient of our hot, golden-fried mush.

Only unconsciously were we aware of it, but Mother was providing us constantly with an object lesson in giving. The message: No matter how little you have, you can always give some of it away. And when you do that, you can't feel sorry for yourself.

But there was even more to it. For Mother, giving was an act of faith, and the spiritual principle of giving out of scarcity came as easily to her as if she had invented it. Whenever we saw an old-fashioned pump in a farmyard, we knew what she would tell us: "If you drink the cup of water that's waiting there, you can slake your own thirst. But if you pour it into the pump and work the handle, you'll start enough water flowing to satisfy all our thirsts."

She likened the principle of priming the pump to God's law of abundance: We give, and He opens the windows of heaven and gives to us. It is a law of life, she explained to us children, and as certain to work as that the sun will rise tomorrow.

Mother had not been in Keyser long before she had a dream of helping the destitute of Radical Hill, a slum district where people lived in tin-roofed shacks along rutted roads strewn with debris. The "nice" citizens of the town gave the area a wide berth. Yet the children who lived there, often unwashed and with lice in their hair, sat alongside the "nice" children in the public schools.

Mother's first step was to enlist the help of some of the young people of our church to go with her to visit each home and take a survey of the district. Of some five hundred Radical Hill families, she found that only eighty were connected with any church.

At that juncture Mother offered her services to the county welfare board. To our surprise (but definitely not hers!), she was given a job to help improve conditions in any way she could. Day after day she would send us off to school in our hand-me-downs and artfully patched clothing, then go off to help what she called "the poor people."

The first thing Mother managed to do was to get the name of that area changed from Radical Hill to Potomac Heights—a new name for a new start. Then an old, abandoned hotel was remodeled—partitions torn out, repaired, painted; bathrooms and a kitchen put in. This was for meetings of all kinds, a Sunday school and a weekday nursery school. A health clinic, craft classes and Mother's own classes in childcare and Bible study were started. Soon the work was flourishing. Those who had given up hope began to take heart because someone cared.

Then one day Mother was told that county funds had run out and that her employment had to be terminated. For only a moment did she give in to discouragement. Then she approached the director of the welfare board.

"May I go on working?" she asked.

"But we can't pay."

"I understand," Mother said. "But why should I do for money what I would be willing to do for the love of God and humanity?"

The man stared at her. "What do you mean?"

"I mean," she said resolutely, "that the work must go on, salary or not. Shutting down now would be disastrous."

The director looked incredulous. Then, impressed by Mother's determination, his tone suddenly changed. Standing up, admiration and enthusiasm written on his face, he thrust out his hand. "All right, then, of course, go right on working. I'll do something. We'll *all* do something. Somehow we'll get the community behind us."

So day after day Mother trudged on foot to Potomac Heights, receiving not a nickel for her work. And the work not only prospered, it zoomed, as a large task force of enthusiastic teenagers rallied around Mother to help.

Years later I saw on television Kathryn Forbes' warm Norwegian-American reminiscences called *I Remember Mama*. Her family of five was exactly like ours—one son and two daughters. Like us, they, too, had lived from weekly payday to weekly payday.

There was another point of similarity. Kathryn Forbes' mama had a bank account. Each Saturday night as the stacks of coins were counted out for the landlord, for the grocer, for half-soling shoes and buying school notebooks, there was great relief when Mama finally smiled.

"Is good," she would say. "We do not have to go to the bank."

Mama's bank account was to be tapped only for the direst emergencies. By hard work and much cooperation, the family made it through year after year. Just knowing that Mama's bank account was there gave them a warm, secure feeling.

Twenty years later when daughter Kathryn Forbes sold her first story, she took the check proudly to Mama: "For you—to put in your bank account."

And at last the truth came out. There never had been a bank account. Mama had hit upon this device because, she explained, "Is not good for little ones to be afraid."

Suddenly in a blaze of revelation it occurred to me that my own mother also had a bank account that kept us, her children, from being afraid. Her bank account was real—as real as the mountain air we breathed and the nourishing bread she baked. Mother's family bank account was her faith in the Lord, her absolute trust that the promise of "Give and it shall be given unto you" was as eternal as the mountains around us.

Even by age twelve I had begun to realize that the secret of Mother's strength was related directly to her daily prayer-conversations with God. I watched her go off alone to talk with Him and wondered what it was like to have a real conversation with God. Could you hear His voice? Were His presence and love something you could actually feel? I had to find out.

At fourteen I was a thin, awkward-looking girl with too long a neck. I had unruly, naturally curly brown hair and large, blue eyes set in a pale face. I was a teenager with a head full of question marks, exclamation points and some ridiculous and implausible dreams. For how could one live with Leonora Wood and settle down to limited horizons?

"You are the beloved children of the King," she never tired of admonishing us. "Each of you is very special to Him, and He has important work for you to do in the world. It's up to you to find His dream for your life. And take warning, our King doesn't fool around with petty stuff. The sky is the limit!"

By the time I entered high school, I had focused on three major dreams. The first, the oldest, I hugged to myself: Someday I would write books.

I was fifteen when the other two dreams came into view. It happened that spring at the home of Mrs. William MacDonald, with whom I sometimes spent the night when her husband had to be away on law cases.

The MacDonalds' daughter, Janet, had gone to a college called Agnes Scott—glamorous and faraway in Decatur, Georgia, on the outskirts of Atlanta. "Mrs. Mac" talked about how special the college was, how much it had meant in molding Janet's life.

The MacDonald home seemed luxurious to me: real mahogany furniture, a tall grandfather clock whose musical chimes marked the quarter hour, current books, lovely volumes of history and travel lying about. They even received *The New York Times* every Sunday!

When I stayed with Mrs. Mac, it was her custom to serve us ice cream at bedtime—more ice cream than I could eat. Then she would tuck me in under an eiderdown in a bed with tall pineapple posts.

How well I remember one particular night when for me time stood still. She had started out of the room when at the door she stopped, half-turned and looked at me. "One of these days a wonderful man, just the right man for you, is going to come and carry you away. Just you wait!"

Her words, shockingly daring to me, yet standing straight and tall, marched across the room and found permanent lodging in my mind and heart. At that moment two dreams were planted inside me: to go to Agnes Scott College and to ready myself for that wonderful man who would come from far away to marry me.

I did not realize it at the time, but now that I had given my life to God, He was using that perfect time—impressionable adolescence—to reach down and plant in the fertile soil of my immature heart His big, pure, wonderful dreams. The fulfillment of them would be His work, not mine, but I was to learn that none of those gloriously impossible dreams could come true without the pain of self-realization and growth.

By the time I graduated from high school, the Depression was daily dealing our town devastating blows: businesses failing, banks closing, bankruptcies, suicides, almost everyone living on credit. With our family's hand-to-mouth existence, how could there possibly be any money for college?

Already I had been accepted at Agnes Scott. But though I had saved some money from debating prizes and had the promise of a work scholarship, we were still hundreds of dollars short of what was needed.

One evening Mother found me lying across my bed, face down, sobbing. She sat down beside me. "You and I are going to deal with this right now," she said.

Mother took me into the guest room and together we knelt beside the old-fashioned golden oak bed.

"Catherine, I know it's right for you to go to college," Mother said. "Let's ask God to tell us how to bring this dream to reality."

As we knelt together, I knew instinctively that this was an important moment, one to be recorded in heaven. We were about to meet God in a more intimate way than at bedtime prayers, or during grace before a meal, or in family prayers together in Dad's study, or even in the prayers in church. Mother was admitting me to the inner sanctum of her prayer closet.

In the silence, I quickly reviewed my relationship with this God with whom we were seeking an audience. At the age of nine I had given Him my life. My attendance at Sunday school and church had been regular ever since—little enough to do as the daughter of a preacher, I thought uneasily.

I had prayed many times since my encounter with Him years before, but how real had those prayers been? The truth struck me: Most had been for selfish purposes. I had given so little of myself to Him. I had not taken much part in Mother's work to transform Radical Hill. And with a sinking heart I remembered all the times when I had seen members of the church coming up the front walk, only to flee up the back stairs to my room where I would not have to give myself to others or share their problems.

Scene after scene flashed across my mind's eye of the times I had resented my brother and sister. When they had interfered with what I wanted to do, I had scolded them, avoided them, rejected them. As I thought of the many occasions when my parents had gone without something they needed so that we children could have new clothing, piano lessons, books or sports equipment, I felt more condemned than ever. And my going to college would call for yet more sacrifices from my parents.

I stole a look at Mother. She was praying soundlessly, her lips moving. Then, closing my eyes, silently I prayed the most honest prayer of my life to that point.

"Lord, I've been selfish. I've taken everything from You, from Your Church and from my parents, and given little of myself in return. Forgive me for this, Lord. Perhaps I don't deserve to go to a college like Agnes Scott."

A sob deep in my throat threatened to burst out. I knew what I now had to do. "So Lord, I turn this dream over to You. I give it up. It's in Your hands. You decide."

Now the tears did come!

Those quiet moments in the bedroom marked a new stage in my walk with God. I was learning that the price of a relationship with Him means dropping all our masks and pretense. We must come to Him with stark honesty, "as we are"—or not at all.

Several days later Dad and Mother decided that by faith I should go ahead and make preparations for Agnes Scott. They felt strongly that this was right and that the Lord would soon confirm it. I was not so sure. God had convicted me of my selfishness. Perhaps He wanted me to give up college and serve Him in some other way.

Days passed, then weeks. Then one day Mother opened a letter and gave a whoop of joy. "Here it is! Here's the answer to our prayers."

The letter contained an offer from a special project of the federal government for Mother to write the history of the county. With what I already had, her fee would be more than enough for my college expenses.

Once again, Mother's very real bank account had provided the necessary provision at a time of need. From those hours spent alone with Him each day had come her supreme confidence that He would provide out of His limitless supply. How often she had told us children, "And don't forget, He will never, never let us outgive Him."

Out of this solid wealth, this certainty, Mother could always afford to give to others, not just material things, but showering sparks of imagination, a gleam of hope, a thrust of courage—qualities that contained more substance than the coin of any realm and which opened the door for fulfillment in many a life she touched.

SECTION TWO

The Years with Peter

As it turned out, Agnes Scott College was the key not only to Catherine's education, but to meeting the "wonderful man" Mrs. Mac had foreseen entering her life.

Romance

I returned to Agnes Scott College the fall of my junior year, September 1934, to find a report circulating that the pastor of the Atlanta church I had been attending during the school years, Peter Marshall, was engaged to be married.

True or not, this reinforced the resolve I had made: I would be friendly but altogether casual with Peter. There was something ridiculous about a not-yet-twenty-year-old college student fancying herself in love with a 32-year-old bachelor-preacher who had captured so many other female hearts in the Atlanta area.

Peter Marshall was a tall, well-built Scot with the broad shoulders of a football player beneath his Geneva gown. His curly dark blond hair resisted his efforts to slick it down. His face was handsome in a rugged sort of way. There was in it a combination of gentleness and humor along with forcefulness and strength.

He seemed thoroughly at home in the pulpit. The impact of his message came through his voice—an extraordinarily resonant one, flexible, dramatic, with clear, precise diction. The indisputable fact was that, under the impact of this man's preaching, God became real to those who listened. When Peter led them in worship, God was no longer a remote, theological abstraction but a loving Father interested in each individual, who stooped to man's smallest need.

So men and women hungry for the love of God came back again and again, as I had done.

Why does he single me out with his eyes so much when he preaches? I asked myself.

A dozen other women probably think the same thing, my logical mind snapped back.

But then why all that special attention after church? Having his secretary, Ruby Coleman, intercept me to tell me Peter would drive me back to the campus in Decatur?

I had no answer to that. Better drop all such ruminations.

That October a young man from Emory began to date me. There was a strong physical attraction between us, and I began to wonder if I could be in love with Fred. But then one day I realized that there was neither spiritual nor intellectual rapport between us. I stopped dating Fred, tried to forget romance and concentrate on my studies.

But soon, inevitably, I was drawn back to Westminster Church and Peter because of an aching void in my life. This notation in my journal is revealing:

There are several reasons why I am attracted to Peter. For one thing, he has so much poetry in his soul. There is such a kinship between poetry and religion. They both try to see into the heart of things. One of the reasons I could never fall in love with Fred is that he has no appreciation for the beautiful.

Peter, however, has such a capacity for affection and tenderness, such a luscious sense of humor sprinkled with an earthy roguishness.

Why must the embodiment of all my dreams be twelve years older than I and as remote as the South Pole?

To my fellow students, I must have seemed on top of things. My grades were good, I was active as an intercollegiate debater, in poetry

club and other class activities. Yet underneath it all I was dissatisfied:

> Tonight I feel compelled to write until my hand is tired and
> exhausted. I am restless and unhappy these days because I am nei-
> ther right with myself nor with God. Why this dissatisfaction with
> myself? I am driven on and on by an overwhelming sense of some
> destiny, of some task to be done which I must do. I can never be
> peaceful and happy and enjoy life until I learn why I am here and
> where I am going.

Throughout that winter and into the spring my journal notes
were peppered with references to Peter Marshall.

> The more I hear him talk, the more I realize we have the same ideas
> and ideals—we like the same things. . . . How I wish I could tell
> him all the sleep he has made me lose. . . . Dreaming this way about
> Peter is the most foolish thing that has ever happened to me.

Reading through my journals of this period so many years later
makes me aware as never before how tender God was with me,
never intruding on my willful self-centeredness, but always there
when the heart-hungers inside me cried out. And how beautiful
was His timing in the slow—agonizingly slow, to me—way the
relationship between Peter and me developed until I, so much
younger, was mature enough to meet Peter where he was spiritually and intellectually.

The film version of *A Man Called Peter* indicated that the turning point in our relationship was May 3, 1935, the Prohibition rally
(turned into a youth rally in the movie) at which Peter and I and
several others spoke.

My journal shows that this rally was an interesting but only an
early step along the way. As a group of us drove to the schoolhouse

where the meeting was to take place, Peter pointedly squelched the rumor that he was engaged.

"Don't believe everything you hear, my dear girl. I certainly am not even about to be married."

He pronounced the word *mar-rried* with a very broad *a* and a rolling of the *r*'s.

When the meeting began with the singing of some old revival hymns, Peter quickly entered into the spirit of the evening, his fine baritone voice ringing out above all others. One by one then we were elaborately introduced, listened to patiently and given more applause than we deserved. Frankly, I can remember almost nothing about what we said.

On the return drive Peter and I were in the backseat. He tucked his arm through mine and held my hand all the way home. Before we said goodbye Peter asked me if I ever went bowling and said that he would take me out some night.

I was ecstatic. My dream of two long years' standing had at last been fulfilled—Peter was actually going to ask me for a date!

But a week went by, then another, and still Peter did not call. There were get-togethers at the church where he overflowed with warmth toward me. Each time he would go out of his way to drive me back to the college.

On May 12 he asked to return for me at 3:30 that afternoon, after which we walked and talked until eleven o'clock that night— our first real date. Lingeringly, tenderly, he bade me goodnight. His last words: "I'll be in touch with you this week."

But again the days dragged by. No call. What was I to think?

When summer vacation came, I went home to West Virginia more frustrated than the year before. Why did he always seem so interested when I was with him, but never follow up with a note or telephone call?

The ache in my heart continued through the summer and into the fall. I returned to college for my senior year determined to stay away from Westminster Church, convinced once and for all that there was no hope for the one thing my heart yearned for more than anything else. I must forget Peter Marshall.

Meanwhile, three years of college had greatly enriched and broadened the naïve, small-town girl from the West Virginia mountains. Whatever I lacked in ability I made up for in heartfelt desire and intensity and in hard, slugging work.

I must have averaged three hours a day in the college library where I dug into the classics, enjoyed novels, browsed through poetry and dove into history, always enchanted with personalities, lifestyle and human interest data on the men and women who had made history.

My reading ranged widely, from John Calvin's *Institutes* to William Hazlitt's and Thomas Carlyle's essays to the writings of James Madison to Dorothy Wordsworth's journal to Matthew Arnold's prose and poetry. I fell in love with Edna St. Vincent Millay and Robert Frost, who visited our campus via the lecture platform. Apart from studies, I poured my energies into debating, the hiking club and the poetry club. My resolve to stay away from Westminster Church lasted only until October 20 when I made this entry:

> Went to church at Westminster, but got there after 11 A.M. and had to sit in the vestibule and listen to Peter through the loudspeaker. I had planned not to speak to him afterwards, but suddenly changed my mind. He pumped my hand and commented that this was the first time I had been here this year. So he had noticed my absence! He promised to get in touch with me. I shan't hold my breath until he does.

The entries in my journals for the next four months continued the pattern. When he saw me Peter was all interest. He arranged to take me to meals at a friend's where we talked, sang, played games like Monopoly, Yacht, Parcheesi. Once I was back on campus, however, he seldom if ever called or sought me out.

It is clear to me now that Peter as a bachelor in his early 30s and a preacher of growing importance was reluctant to take the initiative in seeking out dates with a college girl many years younger than he. He knew that to others this would seem improper. And he was right. At the time I could not see this or have any feel for God's timing in the situation.

The crucial turning point in our relationship came a year to the day after the Prohibition rally that the moviemakers fixed on: Sunday, May 3, 1936. I had been asked to review a book at the Sunday afternoon fellowship hour at Peter's church. I chose one entitled *Prayer* by the Norwegian theologian Dr. O. Hallesby. This was an unusual book for any professor-theologian because its content was not theory; what Dr. Hallesby had to say seemed so obviously direct from his own experience.

Such an assignment would have been a challenge to me at any time and place. Since this was to be at Peter's church, and the pastor himself was likely to be in the audience, I did an inordinate amount of preparation. Intuition told me that this was the time and place for something important to happen between Peter and me—if it was ever meant to happen. The depths of Peter's inner being had been revealed to me through his preaching. But there had been no comparable chance for him to catch a glimpse of my inner spirit.

When I arrived at the church that Sunday afternoon, the fellowship hall was filled with people, including Peter Marshall. Just before I was to speak I was stricken, almost paralyzed by tension and nervousness. Did I have anything really worthwhile to say to these knowledgeable people?

"We tend to be superficial in our prayers," I began with quavering voice. "Most of us think of God as a kind of Santa Claus who waits to hear our requests. What He really wants to hear are the hungers of our heart and our confessions of deception and dishonesty."

As the meaning of my words penetrated my stage fright, confidence and strength surged through me. Dr. Hallesby had opened my eyes to my own smugness in certain areas, I admitted, and depicted how I had begun to change my approach to prayer. I confessed my hunger to know God better, to feel the presence of Jesus, to be able to talk to Jesus as a Friend.

Because the book had revealed it to me, I confessed how self-righteous I had been during my college years. Emotion poured through my words as I described how the book had revitalized my prayer life.

Though the audience was quiet and attentive, it was Peter's face that commanded my attention. He stared at me with such intentness that my stomach began churning. There was a moment when I almost felt that only the two of us were in the room.

After my talk Peter was subdued as he closed the meeting. He turned to me, took my hand and squeezed it tightly, a look in his blue-gray eyes I could not fathom. Then we went into the evening service where I made the mistake of sitting within three pews of the front.

My turbulent feelings and the emotion of the previous few hours were too much. The stone pillars and the Good Shepherd window behind the pulpit began to swim alarmingly. I was too sick to be embarrassed when Peter mentioned my name from the pulpit in connection with the talk I had just given. By the time he began his sermon, I knew it would be disastrous to stay.

As I rose to begin the longest walk in my life, the voice from the pulpit trailed off, and there was dead silence, broken only by the staccato clicking of my heels on the stone floor. I could feel Peter's eyes boring into my back every step of the way up the long aisle.

Not until I was well out into the foyer did the voice resume over the loudspeakers.

The college infirmary received me that night and attempted to diagnose this strange stomach ailment. The head nurse, properly starched and equipped with a strong nose for sniffing out lovesick maidens, had her suspicions.

In the early afternoon of the following day I was called to the infirmary telephone. The solicitous voice on the other end had a familiar Scottish accent.

"I'm talking from Miss Hopkins' office," the voice said, naming the school's headmistress. "I have secured her permission to come over and see you. May I?"

I gasped. No mere man—unless armed with a medical diploma—had ever, in all the college's history, been allowed inside the infirmary. Male visitors were simply taboo. After all, the young ladies were not properly clothed! How Peter had prevailed on Miss Hopkins I couldn't even imagine.

"I—really don't think you'd better," I said hastily. "I'm well enough to dress and come over. I'll meet you in the colonnade in ten minutes."

I should not have stopped him. Ever afterwards Peter accused me of having thwarted his only chance for fame with future generations of Agnes Scotters. If I had not interfered, Peter might someday have rated a bronze plaque on the infirmary wall as the first male visitor in this off-limits haven.

Almost every day after that my journal records items about the two of us.

> Peter was terribly solicitous about my illness. . . . I believe now he wants to be serious. . . . I think Peter is in love with me!! . . . Tonight we went to a play. Afterwards on the front porch he kissed me again and again. . . . Tonight we talked until three in the morning and he proposed. . . .

Marriage to Peter

Peter and I were married by my father in a simple church wedding in Keyser, West Virginia, on November 4, 1936. Later that same day my new husband and I traveled by train to Washington, D.C., and spent our honeymoon night at the Lee House Hotel. With considerable chagrin Peter had informed me several days before that he had agreed to meet the morning after the wedding with the pastoral committee of New York Avenue Presbyterian Church.

This prestigious old Washington church had literally grown up with the nation's capital. Located two blocks from the White House, it was where Abraham Lincoln had attended midweek and Sunday services. The President had been scheduled to become a communicant member on April 19, 1865. But five days before, at a few minutes before ten at night, he was assassinated.

It was not Peter's personal preference to move to the nation's capital. He loved Atlanta. Yet our word was that God had some larger plan in the offing. Yes, we were to go.

So at only 23 the young girl who had fled up the back stairs to avoid involvement with people now had to be hostess at a steady stream of social functions at the manse on Cathedral Avenue.

What was the background of this man I had married? Peter Marshall did not grow up wanting to be a minister. That was God's idea, not his. In fact, getting him to accept it took a lot of divine persuasion.

He was born in Coatbridge, Scotland, a city of 45,000 nicknamed "The Iron Burgh" because it was the center of the Scottish iron trade. Coatbridge was only nine miles east of Glasgow, the sea and the famous Clyde Shipyards; as a boy Peter had fallen under the spell of all the color and romance of British Navy tradition.

His father, whom Peter had loved with all the warmth of his affectionate nature, had died when Peter was only four. A few years later his mother remarried. Peter was filled, understandably, with emotional opposition, and nursed a secret, consuming desire to escape to sea.

But it didn't happen. One dark, foggy summer night Peter, a young man now, was walking down an unfamiliar lane when a Voice stopped him just before he would have plunged unwittingly into an abandoned stone quarry. There was never any doubt in Peter's mind about the source of that Voice. From then on he was convinced that God had some special reason for saving his life. His dream changed; his goal now was to become a pastor.

It was a cousin who had emigrated to the United States who encouraged Peter to go to America and gave him money for the trip. His cousin also had this word of advice: "Don't try for a desk job, Peter. Since you want to be a preacher, manual labor will be the best preparation. Most preachers don't know how the other half lives."

On April 5, 1927, Peter arrived in America with just enough money to last for two weeks. He began work as a manual laborer for a New Jersey utility company, getting up at 4 A.M. for ten hours of work with his hands. A job as molder in a foundry followed. Later Peter reminisced, "I thought I'd located the exact site of Dante's Inferno."

Friends steered Peter to Birmingham, Alabama, where he took a proofreader job with the *Birmingham News* and became a lay leader in the downtown First Presbyterian Church whose session sponsored him into Columbia Seminary. Peter's gifts of preaching and teaching developed quickly. His first pastorate was at Covington Presbyterian Church. Then came the call to Westminster Presbyterian Church in Atlanta, a church in deep trouble when Peter became pastor, yet under Peter was soon so revitalized that like a magnet it drew students like me from Agnes Scott.

Peter's ministry in Washington began on October 3, 1937. One observer noted: "At age 35 he seemed to be a sincere, guileless, transparent, naive boy compared to his predecessor, Dr. Joseph Sizoo, a most sophisticated divine."

Another pastor's comment: "At first Peter was a very conservative preacher, clinging rather too tenaciously and defensively to his conservatism. I watched Peter grow during those difficult years here, until he became one of the most thrilling evangelical preachers I have ever heard."

Peter's reputation as a "thrilling evangelical preacher" resulted before long in long lines of people waiting outside New York Avenue Church of a Sunday morning. Often four abreast, not all could get into the sanctuary. Loud-speakers had to be installed in the Lincoln Chapel and the downstairs lecture room to handle overflow crowds. When these rooms were filled, there was nothing left to do but turn would-be worshipers away.

These huge congregations comprised government workers, GIs, ordinary citizens, a constant stream of out-of-town visitors and a sprinkling of Washington's renowned. In our congregation, it was not unusual for a famous judge to worship beside a mail carrier or for a Senator to take the sacrament of holy Communion in fellowship with a government clerk.

Peter's work as a laborer had indeed put him in touch with the so-called common man. The democratic ideal was in his blood. At first, therefore, he was so afraid of paying any servile regard to the capital's notables that he was blinded to their real needs. He soon discovered, however, that the rich and famous have heartaches just like other folks. They cannot escape sickness, pain and bereavement. They and their families need succor and counsel just as the rest of us do. It soon became apparent that serving any of them, from the President of the United States down, was an integral part of ministry in the capital city.

In fact, less than three months after coming to Washington, Peter was asked by the Washington Federation of Churches to preach at the annual Christmas service to be attended by President Franklin D. Roosevelt and his family.

An immense crowd filled the building and overflowed into the streets. I was allotted a choice seat almost directly behind the President's family.

An editorial in *The Atlanta Journal* said:

The Rev. Peter Marshall . . . a preacher who was a favorite among Atlantans a short time ago, awoke last Sunday morning to find his name, and excerpts from his sermon, on the front page of practically every newspaper in the nation. . . .

Peter and I soon saw that God's way of dealing with us was to throw us into situations over our depth, then supply us with the necessary ability to swim.

Along with his growing impact on Washington's leaders and celebrities, Peter had an impact on the young. One area high school serving a cross-section of people had become a battleground for gang warfare. Discipline was quite out of hand and an ugly spirit permeated the school.

During the attempted talks of several guest speakers, peashooters and paper airplanes took over the auditorium. There were hisses and boos. Humming groups held forth first on one side, then on the other. Once a smoke bomb blew off one of the doors in the middle of a talk. More than one speaker had to simply give up and walk off the stage. All of this was so embarrassing to the principal that no assembly at all had been attempted for two months.

Then the principal heard of Peter Marshall and invited him to address the students. Whether or not Peter knew the school's history when he accepted the invitation, I don't know.

The youngsters heard that a preacher was coming and determined to fix him. One girl who wrote me of what happened said, "I fully expected Dr. Marshall to be ridiculed and booed off the stage."

At first the girl was fascinated by the preacher's smile and by his accent. He was talking about gardenias, of all things, her favorite corsage flower.

"You know how a gardenia's petals reveal any telltale fingermarks by turning brown," the preacher said. "Your lives are like that. Purity is like that. . . . Young people, don't give anything to the world to destroy. Don't be ashamed of high ideals, dreams and beautiful thoughts. . . ."

Suddenly the girl woke up to the fact that there was dead quiet in the auditorium. No peashooters or paper airplanes were in evidence. The eyes of all the teenagers around her were glued to the speaker.

"I can wish for you nothing better than that God will plant in your hearts a growing yearning to meet the Galilean, to know Him as your Friend. . . ."

As the preacher concluded, the room was swept by a tremendous ovation.

Fourteen years later the woman still remembered the theme of that talk and the gardenia illustration.

"We kids liked to hear Peter Marshall," she wrote thoughtfully, "because he spoke our language. He didn't talk over our heads. And he put the responsibility for what we made of our lives squarely on us."

Peter never "conducted" a service. Instead, he worshiped along with us. This was apparent when he read Scripture. As he read, we, his listeners, were impressed all over again with the timeless beauty of the biblical narratives. Peter's fine voice, his feeling for the rhythm of the King James Version, his almost perfect diction threw that beauty of language into sharp perspective.

To many moderns the Bible is a closed book; it seems dry and unintelligible. But when Peter read it for us, somehow it lived and breathed and throbbed with life. His feeling for the beauty and rhythm, as well as the meaning of the Scriptures, he had acquired as a boy when he read aloud from the Bible for hours at a time to his blind grandmother.

Then there were his pastoral prayers that seemed to make the presence of God almost palpable.

"As we wait in His house to keep this rendezvous with Jesus Christ," Peter might say at the outset, "our Lord, through the Holy Spirit, is waiting now to hear, to forgive, to strengthen, to cleanse, to bless. Whatever your burden of care, of anxiety, whatever your sorrow or worry, whatever the joy that bubbles within you, whatever impulse brought you here, you may use these moments of silent prayer to make your own prayer, and to seek your own peace with God—for He is here."

Our son, Peter John Marshall, or "Wee" Peter, as his father loved to call him, arrived at 8:53 on a snowy January morning in 1940.

His arrival interrupted a sermon. Thereafter he managed to inject himself into many a sermon.

The previous night my mother had arrived to take over the household during my stay in the hospital. Later some friends had dropped in for an evening of game-playing. This sort of impromptu fun in his own home with a few close friends made the kind of evening Peter enjoyed most, and which seemed to refresh him best in preparation for his heavy Sunday schedule. He always tried to reserve Saturday nights for some kind of relaxation.

Part of our regular Saturday night schedule was for Peter to read his Sunday morning sermon aloud to me. He was always apologetic about this, thinking it would surely spoil the sermon for me on Sunday. It never did. On this particular night he read the sermon the last thing before turning in—or so we thought.

In the very middle of it, strange things began happening to me. Remembering the doctor's briefing, I watched the clock on the nightstand and counted the intervals between pains, while listening with half a mind to the sermon.

Suddenly the situation seemed urgent. "I'm sorry, Peter, to have to interrupt you. I hate to do this to you on a Saturday night, but you'd better get me to the hospital right away."

At eight o'clock the next morning the doctor telephoned Peter. "You'll have to come to the hospital immediately if you want to be here when the baby is born."

Mother was watching Peter's face when the doctor told him we had a son. A look of amazement and incredulity, then undisguised delight crossed his features.

It was typical of Peter, however, that he went on down to the church, taught the young people's class and even went through the eleven o'clock service, all without telling a single soul his big news. Several people commented on the fact that he looked very tired, almost as if he had been up all night, as indeed he had.

It was not until a woman came up to him at the close of the service to inquire about me that finally he broke his self-imposed silence. He had simply been afraid that if he told the news to a single person before the service, he would get too excited to preach.

The entire congregation enjoyed this event and considered Peter John their baby, too. "Re-Pete" was immediately enrolled in the cradle roll of the Sunday school, and was flooded with such a supply of silver spoons, booties, sacques, blankets and carriage robes as could have outfitted ten babies.

My Jesus Encounter

The first sign of my illness came as a dizzy spell during a talk to church women. Three days of examinations and laboratory tests followed in a Baltimore hospital. Though the doctor's words were technical, his voice was gentle as if speaking to a child.

"The pictures show definite intrapulmonary markings and heavy linear shadows radiating out into both lungs. There are evidences of a light, soft spotting over both lungs. You are probably running some temperature in the afternoons. We recommend a period of absolute rest, perhaps in a sanatorium. You should not do any housework, or, in fact, work of any kind."

In spite of the diagnostician's studied effort to soften the blow he was forced to give me, I felt my heart pounding; the walls of the room and the doctor's voice seemed to be receding. Tuberculosis! It had always seemed to me the most loathsome of all diseases. I could not even bear to speak the despised word.

"Is . . . is there danger of giving the germs to my husband and child?" I stammered.

The doctor smiled, trying to force a little levity. "I don't think you are a very dangerous woman. We were unable to locate the bacilli. However, your doctor in Washington will undoubtedly want to try again."

"How long do you think it will take me to get well?"

He hesitated a long moment. "Oh, possibly three or four months." Then, seeing my stricken face: "Mrs. Marshall, don't feel so bad about it. People do recover from tuberculosis. There are worse diseases, you know—much, much worse."

I went to bed at the end of March 1943, staying at home because I had a "closed case" of tuberculosis, with no cough and the bacilli never found. Today it would probably be called histoplasmosis. For the first four months I had a nurse in addition to domestic help, while I tried to supervise the running of the household from my bed.

Eighteen months later I was still bedbound, and there had been no change in the x-rays. Five doctors, including the best lung specialists we could find, seemed unable to help me. Their only advice: "Wait and rest."

This was a time of great soul-searching. I began reading the New Testament, pondering Christ's healing miracles with my own great need in view. Up to this time I had given no particular thought to the question of whether or not Christ still performs miracles on people's bodies today. The advances made in medicine and surgery had seemed to me quite sufficient.

I was a child of the scientific Age. I knew that God set up this universe to be governed by unwavering scientific and mathematical laws. My generation believed in things we could "prove."

But . . . suppose the spiritual world, too, was governed by laws just as immutable as the law of physics. That would explain why some prayers were answered and some were not. Surely it was not just the caprice of God. The New Testament reveals that Jesus actually expected ordinary men and women in all ages to be able to do the same miracles He did. Wouldn't that point to the fact that those miracles worked for Jesus because He knew the inexorable spiritual laws of the universe, and intends us to learn them, too?

As I pondered these things and read my Bible, I found that Jesus never refused anyone who came to Him asking help. There was no record of His ever having said, "No, I won't heal you. This illness is good for your soul." Instead He was surprisingly concerned with the welfare of men's bodies, and the Bible assures us that not only is this very Jesus alive today, but that He is "the same, yesterday, today and forever." Why, then, could I not ask this Jesus to cure me?

I felt, however, unworthy to ask such a thing.

The practical ramifications of the fact that "God is love" began to dawn on me. I knew that anything unloving in me—any resentment, unforgiveness or impurity—shut out God, just as a muddy windowpane obscures the sunlight. Painfully, in an agony of mind and spirit, I began thinking back over my life, recalling all too vividly my transgressions and omissions.

Through many days I put down on paper all the things of which I was ashamed. Some of it I shared with my mother, some with Peter. To a number of people far away, I wrote letters asking their forgiveness for things they had probably long since forgotten, or never known about. It took me days to muster the courage to mail those letters. Then I claimed God's promise of forgiveness and cleansing.

Peter bore all this patiently, almost silently. He already knew what I still had to learn, that we human beings can never deserve any of God's good gifts, that when we have done the best we can, our best is still not good enough to merit anything from the Lord of all the earth. Peter knew that we can get nothing from God except, as he loved to say, "on the same old terms," always simply "by grace [the unmerited favor of God] through faith."

But he was also wise enough to know that there was a therapy in confession, and that I was traveling a spiritual road that I must travel alone, in my own way.

When this methodical task of confession was completed, I asked God to make me well. Confidently, with what I believed to be real faith, I awaited the verdict of the next x-rays. But they were just the same. The shadows were still there—all the soft spotting, the same intrapulmonary markings.

One day as I was leaving to spend a few bedfast weeks with my parents in their Virginia Beach home, Peter slipped a pamphlet casually into my hand. "I found this the other day in the church office. It seems to be about spiritual healing. I haven't had a chance to read it myself."

The pamphlet turned out to be momentous. In it was a nugget of a story about a former missionary who had been bedridden for eight years. During those long years she had persistently asked God why. She could not understand why she should be laid on the shelf when she was doing the Lord's work. There was rebellion in her heart at the lost opportunity to serve. The burden of her prayers was that God should make her well, in order that she might return to the mission field. But nothing happened.

Finally, worn out with the failure of those prayers and with a desperate sort of resignation within her, she prayed, "All right, Lord, I give in. If I am to be sick for the rest of my life, I bow to Thy will. I want Thee even more than I want health. It is for Thee to decide."

Thus leaving herself entirely in God's hands, she began to feel a peace she had known at no time during her illness. In two weeks she was out of bed, completely well.

Privately, with tears eloquent of the reality of what I was doing, I lay in bed in my parents' home and prayed, "Lord, I've done everything I've known how to do, and it hasn't been good enough. I'm desperately weary of the struggle of trying to persuade You to give me what I want. I'm beaten, whipped, through. If You want me to be an invalid for the rest of my life, all right. Here I am. Do anything You like with me and my life."

There was no trace of graciousness about the gift of my life and will, nothing victorious, nothing expectant. I had no faith left, as I understood faith. Nevertheless, a strange, deep peace settled into my heart.

In the early hours of the next morning something awakened me. The luminous hands of the clock on my nightstand told me it was 3 A.M. The room was in darkness, that total darkness known only in the country where there are no streetlights. My mind was active, chewing on the spiritual adventure of the day before. I, who had deliberately surrendered all hope of health, now discovered an active, newborn hope in my heart.

My imagination supplied dramatic possibilities. Jesus might tell me, for example, to appear downstairs for breakfast with the family the next morning. I could picture their surprise and mingled delight and alarm.

I had no sooner prayed, "Lord, what would You ask me to do?" when it happened. Past all credible belief, suddenly, unaccountably, Christ was there, in Person, standing by the right side of my bed.

I could see nothing but deep, velvety blackness, but the bedroom was filled with an intensity of power, as if the Dynamo of the Universe were there. Every nerve in my body tingled with it, as with a shock of electricity. I knew that Jesus was smiling at me tenderly, lovingly, whimsically—a trifle amused at my too-intense seriousness about myself.

"Go," He said, in direct reply to my question. "Go and tell your mother. That's easy enough, isn't it?"

I faltered. What would Mother think? It's the middle of the night. She would think I had suddenly gone crazy.

Christ said nothing more. He had told me what to do. It was clear to me that He would not compel me, and that if I did not obey, the chance might be gone forever. In a flash I understood the real freedom of choice God always allows His human creatures.

"I'll do it if it kills me," I said, climbing out of bed, sensing even as I did so the ludicrousness of my own words. Somehow I knew that Christ's eyes flashed humor as He stood aside quietly to let me pass.

I groped my way into the dark hall to the bedroom at the other end. Naturally my parents were startled. Mother sat bolt upright in bed. "What—what on earth?"

"It's all right. Don't be alarmed," I reassured them. "I just want to tell you that I'll be all right now. It seemed important to tell you tonight."

"What has happened?" Dad asked.

"I'm sorry to have wakened you. I'll tell you all about it in the morning. I promise. Everything's all right."

When I returned to my bedroom, although that vivid Presence was gone, I found myself more excited than I have ever been before or since, and more wide-awake. It was not until the first streaks of dawn appeared in the eastern sky that I slept again.

The question was: Did Christ mean that I had been healed instantaneously, or that recovery would come sometime in the future? I did not know. There was nothing to do but wait for the next x-rays.

The healing of my lungs, as it turned out, came slowly, no doubt because my faith grew slowly. But the next x-rays showed, for the first time, definite progress. And thereafter there was steady, solid healing, never with the least retrogression, until finally the doctors pronounced me completely well.

Life Is a Vapor

On Sunday, December 7, 1941, Peter was to preach to the regiment of midshipmen in the Naval Academy at Annapolis, Maryland. All the preceding week he had been haunted by a strange feeling that he should change his announced topic and preach a particular sermon. It was a feeling he could not shake off. On Sunday morning he confided it to Chaplain Thomas.

"If your feeling about it is that strong, follow it, by all means" was the chaplain's advice.

So Peter preached on the text, seemingly a strange text for young midshipmen: "For what is your life? It is even a vapor, that appeareth for a little time, and then vanisheth away" (James 4:14).

In the chapel before him was the December graduating class, young men who in a few days would receive their commissions and go on active duty in a peacetime Navy.

As we were driving back to Washington that afternoon, suddenly the program on the car radio was interrupted. The announcer's voice was grave: "Ladies and gentlemen. Stand by for an important announcement. This morning the United States Naval Base at Pearl Harbor was bombed in a surprise Japanese attack. . . ."

Instantly we knew we were living through one of history's dramatic moments, the "date which will live in infamy."

Within a few months some of the boys to whom Peter had just preached would go down to heroes' graves in strange waters. Soon all of them would be exposed to the risks and dangers of war; and Peter, under God's direction, had preached to them—young, vital, alive as they were that morning—about death and immortality.

Peter Marshall believed in immortality more surely than anyone I have ever known. As a very young preacher he had been curious about the details of the life we human beings are going to live "behind the curtain."

One evening at the manse we received a telephone call telling us that a dear friend, a woman in our congregation, had just died. She had been desperately ill for a long time, so her death was not unexpected.

Peter came away from the telephone slowly and sank down in his favorite chair. His mind seemed far away.

"Gertrude died about ten minutes ago," he said thoughtfully. "I wonder what thrilling experience she's having at this very moment."

Peter's own brush with death came in 1946 at the time of his first heart attack. After that experience, Peter saw precious human life only in relation to time and eternity, which is its true perspective.

Nothing reveals quite so clearly Peter Marshall's own clear-eyed humility about himself than a little incident that took place shortly thereafter. When he had resumed work, a minister friend from Hagerstown, Maryland, dropped in on him at the church office.

"Well, Peter," the friend asked, "I'm curious to know something. What did you learn during your illness?"

"Do you really want to know?" Peter answered promptly. "I learned that the Kingdom of God goes on without Peter Marshall."

The offer to become chaplain of the U.S. Senate in January 1947 was an irresistible challenge to Peter. Because of his rather severe heart attack, with months of convalescence needed, the prudent step would have been to refuse for health reasons. But prudence was not one of Peter's traits.

At first he was troubled that the official reporters of Senate debates wanted a typed copy of his prayer before it was delivered each day. Peter turned this minus into a plus, asking God to write each prayer through him.

Soon the press all over the United States began to note the brevity of these prayers, their pungency, their sharp relevance. An article in *The Kansas City Star* noted:

> Not without reason are the prayers of the Rev. Peter Marshall, Chaplain of the Senate of the United States, attracting national attention. . . . Even the Senators are now listening to the prayers that open the session. . . .

June 16 was a day of varied business in the Senate, including a brisk argument on a resolution to authorize the Committee on Civil Service to investigate the appointment of first-, second- or third-class postmasters. Dr. Marshall's prayer asked,

> Since we strain at gnats and swallow camels, give us a new standard of values and the ability to know a trifle when we see it and to deal with it as such.

When Secretary of State Marshall left Washington to attend the Council of Foreign Ministers, the Senate chaplain gave voice to the prayers of many when he asked,

> May Thy Spirit move them, that there may be concession without coercion and conciliation without compromise.

Commented *The Chicago Sun-Times* under the headline "A New Bite to Senate Prayers":

The least heeded of any of the millions of words uttered in the United States Senate had usually been those of the chaplain, who opens each session with prayer. But now some observers are beginning to urge Senators to get there early enough to hear these utterances, for the new chaplain, the Rev. Peter Marshall, pastor of the New York Avenue Presbyterian Church, avoids the usual platitudes and is handing out some tart advice to the lawmakers. . . .

When Dr. Marshall prayerfully addressed his God, he first took pains to throw the stuffed shirt into the laundry bag. "We confess, our Father," he prayed one day in the chamber of the United States Senate, "that we know we need Thee, yet our swelled heads and our stubborn wills keep us trying to do without Thee. Forgive us for making so many mountains out of molehills and for exaggerating both our own importance and the problems that confront us. . . ."

About 3:30 on Tuesday morning, January 25, 1949, Peter awakened with severe pains in his chest and arms. He had only to speak my name once to arouse me; for some reason I had been lying there awake for some time.

"Catherine, I'm in great pain. Will you call the doctor for me?"

I knew at once from Peter's tone of voice that this was a major crisis. As I sat up and reached for the bedside telephone, I could hear my own heart pounding.

As we waited downstairs for the ambulance, Peter looked up at me and said, "Catherine, don't try to come with me. We mustn't leave Wee Peter alone in this big house. You can come to the hospital in the morning."

Reluctantly I agreed.

After the ambulance came and Peter was on the way to the hospital, I went back upstairs and knelt by my bed. But before I could speak a word, there surged through me, over and around me as a great wave, an overwhelming experience of the love of God. It was as if the everlasting arms were literally enfolding me. It seemed unnecessary to ask God for anything. I simply gave Peter and myself into the care and keeping of that great love.

At the time, I thought this meant that Peter's heart would be healed here on earth. God knew, of course, what I did not know. There in the downstairs hall, just before the ambulance had left, I had seen Peter alive for the last time.

At 8:15 that morning Peter stepped over into the Larger Life. At 8:20 the doctor telephoned to tell me. Little Peter had been making final preparations for school. He was by the phone as I got the news, and burst into a flood of little-boy tears. I was too stunned to weep.

Later I sat for an hour by Peter's hospital bed. He had been dozing, the nurse told me, and had slipped away very peacefully.

I felt that I knew just what had happened before I got there. All at once Peter had seen his Lord, and later his own father, whom he had longed all his life to know. There had been moments of glad reunion. Then, suddenly, Peter had realized: He was dead!

"You know, this will be hard for Catherine," I could hear him saying. "What can we do for her?"

And Jesus had smiled at Peter. "She'll be all right. We can supply her with every resource she needs."

So they had waited for me there. That was why, when I opened the door and stepped quietly into the bare little hospital room, it was filled with the glory of God.

Yet the splendor was not to last. In that still hospital room, at a precise moment, the two vivid presences withdrew. Suddenly I saw death stripped bare, in all its ugliness. . . . Carbon dioxide escaping from the sagging jaw. The limp hands. The coldness and white, white pallor of the flesh.

Shivering, I rose to leave the room. Two paces from the door I was stopped as by an invisible hand. As I paused, a message was spoken with emphasis and clarity, not audibly, but with the peculiar authority I had come to recognize as the Lord's own voice: *Surely goodness and mercy shall follow you all the days of your life.*

It was His personal pledge to me and to a son who would now surely miss his father.

It was not until the following June that I suddenly remembered something, the last words I had ever spoken to Peter. Was it possible that God had prompted these words, seemingly so casual?

The scene was etched forever on my mind—Peter lying on the stretcher where the two orderlies had put him down for a moment while the ambulance waited just outside the front door. Peter had looked up at me and smiled through his pain, his eyes full of tenderness, and I had leaned close to him and said, "Darling, I'll see you in the morning."

I knew now that those words would go singing in my heart down through all the years: *See you, darling, see you in the Morning. . . .*

SECTION
THREE

The Years Alone

The ten years following Peter Marshall's death was a period of challenge for Catherine. Her gift of writing emerged and provided financial support for her and her son. She was tested painfully as a single parent. Indeed, all of Catherine's weaknesses and strengths came to a head during this period.

Paradoxically, perhaps, one of Catherine's greatest strengths was her willingness to be open and vulnerable about her shortcomings. God was to use this quality to reach and touch the lives of many strugglers.

To Be Comforted

t the death of a loved one, the first need of the bereaved person is for comfort—just plain comfort. In sorrow we are all like little children, hurt children who yearn to creep into a mother's arms and rest there; to have her stroke our foreheads and speak softly to us. But, of course, that is impossible; we are grown men and women.

Or is it?

"For thus saith the LORD. . . . As one whom his mother comforteth, so will I comfort you. . . ."

In my case I had been given that experience of comfort prior to my husband's death.

After the ambulance had gone, I went back upstairs and sank to my knees beside the bed. And there, over the turbulent emotions, crept a strange, all-pervading peace. Through me and around me flowed love as I had never before experienced it—as if Someone who loved me very much was wrapping me round and round with His love.

I thought at first it meant that everything was going to be all right. But when Peter died I knew that my experience of a few hours before had meant something far different. It had been granted so that when the blow fell, I might have the certainty that a loving Father had not deserted me.

After comfort, the next need of the bereaved is for the ability to distinguish between body and spirit. In this age of materialism most of us have had little practice at this.

One recently widowed friend expressed this perfectly. "My biggest need," she told me, "is to believe that Bill is not in that grave. If I could be sure of that, I could stand the personal hurt."

I understood her difficulty. The moment I had stepped into Peter's hospital room after his death, I had known that the man I loved was no longer in the body on the bed. That was a patent, indisputable fact. I had thought I would be able to hold on to that conviction. Yet less than two weeks later, I was having difficulty with it.

One morning about that time I was awakened early by the chirping of birds in the ivy outside my bedroom window. Somewhere in that twilight zone between sleeping and waking it seemed that Peter spoke to me.

"Catherine," he said clearly, "don't think of me as dead."

How could he possibly have known? I wondered. Since the brief committal service I had been unable to think of him except as dead. In my imagination I saw his body lying in the receiving vault (a temporary arrangement until a final decision about burial could be made).

Was this really Peter speaking to me, or was it some sort of subconscious suggestion? I did not know. I wanted to believe that my husband was still alive. But my descent to earth after the funeral had been so abrupt that doubts had come crowding in. At any rate, wherever the brief message came from, it was the precise word I needed at the moment.

In subsequent days I found myself pondering those words. If I was not to think of Peter as dead, how was I to think of him? If he were still alive, then where was he? What was he doing? With no answers to these questions, how could I visualize him or think of him as alive?

That brought me to a question my every emotion cried out to have answered: What is my relationship to my husband now?

In marriage I had found my identity, my answer to the question "Who am I?" As a woman, much of my orientation in life had been centered in my relationship to one man. When death cleaves the marriage partnership, the woman left alone feels that her whole basis for living has been washed away. She must begin all over again. "Who am I now?"

These words at Peter's funeral service kept coming back to me:

This morning . . . we are endeavoring to establish a new relationship. We have known Peter Marshall in the flesh. From now on we are to endeavor to know him in the spirit. . . . The fellowship with him will remain unbroken. . . . `

Those had been sincere if lofty words. Were they true? For me, the fellowship had certainly been broken.

"Till death do us part," Peter and I had vowed on our wedding day. The fact was that death had now suddenly and ruthlessly parted us. Across that chasm I was to build a bridge to Peter Marshall's spirit.

I could not imagine how to begin. Thus I found my prayers taking a new turn. In a childlike way I began pleading with God for some glimpse of Peter, for some knowledge of his new setting, of what he was doing.

The response came in a vivid dream. Now, years later, every detail is still clear. In the dream I was allowed to visit Peter in his new environment. First I searched for him in a large, rambling house with many rooms and airy porches. There were crowds of people about, but Peter was not among them.

Then I sought him in the yard. Finally, at some distance, I saw him.

I'd recognize that characteristic gesture, that certain toss of the head, anytime, I thought as I began running toward him. I found myself able to run with a freedom I had not known since childhood. My body was light; my feet were sure. As I drew nearer I saw that Peter was working in a rose garden. He saw me coming and stood leaning on his spade, waiting for me.

I rushed into his arms. Laughing, he pulled me close and rubbed his nose on mine.

"I knew it was you," I said breathlessly, "by the way you tossed your head. I've come home to you."

Then, resting there in his arms, I felt something strange. Mixed with the tenderness of Peter's love was a certain restraint. He was not holding me as a lover.

My impression was that Peter was bewildered at what had happened, still surprised at his own death. I wondered if the large, many-roomed house, the yard and the rose garden composed some small part of what the Scriptures call *heaven*. I had always thought that people in heaven would be extremely happy. Peter's attitude did not quite fit that pattern.

Then I awakened. The feeling of Peter's strong arms around me lingered, and my cheeks were wet with tears.

Days later I was still asking God to reveal the meaning of this strange dream. Certain elements seemed clear. Peter had not expected his life to end so suddenly on that gloomy Tuesday morning. He, like me, had confidently anticipated a different outcome to the problem of his damaged heart.

Five minutes after death he was essentially the same person he had been before death. There had been no dramatic change except that he had shed his physical body as one would take off an overcoat. But the spiritual body in which he found himself—if that's what one could call it—gave him the same appearance as before.

In "heaven" he was being left alone to work in the rose garden to give him time to recover from his bewilderment, to find himself again. It seemed an especially thoughtful and loving touch that, in the meantime, he had been given work of a kind he had especially enjoyed on earth.

But it was that touch of restraint toward me in Peter's attitude about which I thought most. I asked God to tell me what that meant.

When the reply came, it was to have considerable significance for my future. A long time was to pass before I would have the courage to share this bit of insight with other widows, especially when their grief was new. For the dead are so terribly silent. The one whose sorrow is fresh longs for nothing so much as the touch of a vanished hand, the sound of a beloved voice. One in whom the wound of grief is still unhealed yearns for the assurance that, if immortality means anything at all, it means that one's love will be untampered with, will be just as it was here on earth.

Yet will the relationship between husband and wife be the same? From Christ's own lips, as recorded in the Gospel of Matthew, we are given quite another portrait of this. He spoke in answer to a sardonic question put to him by a group of Sadducees, who did not believe in the resurrection of the body. They posed a case about a woman who in this life had had seven husbands, and then asked the pointedly ridiculous question, "Therefore in the resurrection, whose wife shall she be of the seven? for they all had her."

And Jesus answered in part:

In the resurrection they neither marry, nor are given in marriage, but are as the angels of God in heaven.

Matthew 22:30

Christ seemed to be saying, in other words, that after death the woman would not be "a wife" to any one of her former husbands. That is, one's relationship to the person one has loved on earth will be different.

Precisely what the new relationship was to be I did not then understand. I did not know what being like "the angels of God in heaven" would be like, and I was not at all sure I wanted to know. On the whole, I thought it a revolting idea.

In the days following my dream, it was as if God were saying to me, "Because I want you to get this matter straight from the beginning, I am trusting you now with part of this truth. Some of it you will not understand; some of it will be hard for you to take. But I shall never give you more than you can bear."

Single Parent

eter John had just turned nine when his father died. I can still see his stricken face when he heard the news and feel his trembling body as I knelt to take him in my arms. There were just the two of us now, mother and son.

Still, after the first state of shock, young Peter seemed to be bearing the loss of a father much better than I was taking the loss of a husband. He asked such boyish questions as "Who will help me finish my train set?" "Where will we live now?" "Will I have to change schools?" "Can I still join the Boy Scouts?"

The questions seemed so normal that at the time I did not realize the noxious brew of anxiety, loneliness, desolation and anger the questions were covering up. Few children can articulate the real issue underneath the anger: "If God loves me, then why did He take away my daddy?"

Peter John was included in the planning and in every part of his father's funeral. Repeated attempts were made to explain death and immortality to him. He seemed to understand. Here again, adults often assume a comprehension simply not there.

Too shy and fearful to bare his heart—I, too, had been like that in childhood—my son became quiet and withdrawn. Pictures of him during this period show a sad, strained face. I was not sufficiently aware of his inner desolation during these months and thus failed him at this point.

How should a bereaved mother or father handle such a situation? I know now that we should never give up easily our efforts at dialogue. At meals I would ask questions about Peter's activities at school and get one-word answers: "Fine." "O.K." "Good." Of course these were phony answers, an effort to head off deeper probing into painful areas.

As time went on during our limping dinner table attempts at conversation, I would get the mental picture of a boy crouching behind a stone wall, peering over now and again but afraid to come out.

I sought the advice of counselor after counselor, had session after session, but we could neither find the way to bring down that wall nor make Peter come out from behind it.

In summer, as the two of us drove the five hundred-plus miles to Cape Cod, I struggled to find subjects of interest to my son. After receiving monosyllabic responses, I would give up and retreat into my own thought world—to Peter's relief, I sensed.

Usually my son would then find a ballgame on the car radio. To me these were interminably boring affairs. "Ball one, strike one. . . ." "Ball two, strike two. . . ." Every now and then there would be a flurry of action, but the litany of balls and strikes and other statistical information seemed to be nine-tenths of the verbiage.

Who cares, I would ask myself, whether the pitcher first scratched his left ear, then his right thigh, then shifted his feet three times while he was winding up? How could such repetitious commentary possibly interest a young boy?

But in an effort to relate, I forced myself to go to baseball games, football games, hockey games with my son.

Baseball to me was excruciatingly slow and boring, with the players constantly chasing after a small white ball. Football seemed to fall into the category of bloody hand combat—men throwing themselves ferociously at one another, sometimes even knocking each other unconscious. The idea that millions of people could go into a frenzy of shrieking excitement about the progress of a melonsized brown ball down a field was more than I could comprehend.

Ice hockey was more enjoyable, the speed and grace of the skaters exhilarating to watch. But again, the vicious body contact made me wince.

My mistake was in not trying harder to get interested in these sports so that Peter and I could talk about them together. The key to this for me, I discovered belatedly, was the human-interest side of sports—learning the names of the players, their histories, something of their family life.

There were other ways open to me in helping my son grow up without a father. One was to bring him as much as I could into contact with other men in the family. My dad spent many hours with young Peter, trying to teach him to handle tools and do odd jobs around the house. My brother, Bob, could talk Peter's sports language and work on handicraft projects with him.

All of this was to the good, but there was never enough of it. It takes a great deal of masculine companionship to make up for missing a father's steady presence in the everydayness of life.

My experience indicates that our church fellowships fail to pick up a God-ordained responsibility in relation to widows. Many references in Scripture indicate that this ministry—spiritual, financial and help in child-rearing—is important to God. Apparently the New Testament church took seriously their ministry to widows and their children. For instance:

> Now in these days when the disciples were increasing in number, the Hellenists murmured against the Hebrews because their widows were neglected in the daily distribution.

Acts 6:1, RSV

Religion that is pure and undefiled before God and the Father is this: to visit orphans and widows in their affliction, and to keep oneself unstained from the world.

James 1:27, RSV

The need is urgent. Present estimates are that in the United States, over fifty percent of all children will live with only one parent—usually the mother—at some time before they are eighteen.

In my situation the best answers to the sense of helplessness and frustration came through my early morning quiet time, when in prayer I would seek God's guidance for my son. One entry in my journal read:

Do not be afraid for young Peter. No harm will come to him. He also is My child. I love him more than you do!

But it was hard to overcome my fears for Peter John as he moved into his teens. When I caught him smoking cigarettes at age fourteen, I was devastated. My anger erupted and he retreated into sullen silence. When I stormed heaven about my inadequacies as a mother, I wrote down this answer:

You have still not completely released Peter to Me. Don't strain too much after it, though. It will come gradually, if you let Me do it. Even as a plant grows under My care, so a child grows.

One day while cleaning Peter's room I found a stack of sex-saturated paperback novels. How was I to deal with this? My first inclination was to let my anger boil over and explode. The inner voice said there was a better way.

Quietly that evening I asked him if there was any real reason he felt it necessary to seek out this kind of reading. He shrugged. "All the kids at school are reading it."

This led into a discussion of peer pressure that he picked up and talked about quite freely. He admitted that being accepted by others was far too important to him, that he was inclined to be a follower of what the crowd did. At the end of our discussion, on his own volition, Peter threw the paperbacks into the trash.

But the problem of peer pressure at school began a new period of fear in me. Not focused fear; more a spiritual unrest that would come to me upon occasion, vague and undefinable, like a splinter in one's soul. One night I asked God what this feeling was all about and what I should do about it. This is the message I got:

> You are fearful for Peter because of deep-hidden guilt concerning him. Fear usually comes from guilt. You feel instinctively—and rightly so—that where you fail to supply strong enough discipline, then I, Peter's heavenly Father, will have to permit those disciplines to be supplied by hard and difficult circumstances.

In prayer I seemed to receive these instructions:

1. TV and movies: You are to keep a careful check on what he sees. Plan ahead. Be so well-informed about films and TV programs that you will earn Peter's respect in this regard.
2. Tidiness and taking care of his own clothes: Insist that he take responsibility here.
3. Money, allowance, etc.: You have not been handling this properly. You must take time to come back to Me to think these matters through.

For a period of months following this there was a big improvement in Peter's and my relationship. Children thrive under structure, and I was being given daily guidance on how to use consistent discipline.

Then early one morning the telephone rang. "This is Detective C—of the Eighth Precinct, Juvenile Squad. Your son, Peter John Marshall, and three other boys got into trouble last Saturday night. They are being accused of taking school property, two axes and a fire extinguisher, and breaking the headlights of two schoolbuses."

I began trembling as he talked. When he told me that I was to appear with Peter John at the Eighth Precinct station at 3:30 that afternoon, my throat was almost too dry to respond.

No members of my family were nearby, so I called several church friends for prayer support. I asked Peter to stay home from school so that we could talk through what had happened. He was defensive and communicated only the bare details. He and some friends had been messing around the school and a few back alleys nearby. They hadn't meant to destroy any property. "Honest!"

Later as I prayed alone, I saw that I could be in danger of being too pridefully concerned about what the publicity might do to my reputation as a Christian. So many people had put Peter Marshall's family on a pedestal. Would such publicity hurt Christ's cause?

Peter and I were at the Eighth Precinct station from 3:30 until 6:30. As we waited nervously for the two men from the juvenile board to arrive, I noticed inconsequential details: the dirt in the corners of the room; the sad, shocked face of the father of one of the other boys, his eyes like those of a hurt animal; the luminous brown eyes of the man representing the school, whose name, ironically enough, was also Peter. His black hair peppered with gray, he was wearing tennis shoes on a winter's day.

One of the boys, the son of the man whose eyes revealed so much, put his head down on the table and cried very softly. Since a very little boy, I learned later, he had wanted to get into West Point. If this went on his record, he would never get there.

Peter's face was tense. Not in a long time had I heard him snap to and say *sir*. His blond complexion seemed to have a permanent blush. He kept chewing on his fingernails long after there was no bit of surplus nail to chew. When the decision was finally made to let the boys off lightly because they had no previous arrests, he was relieved but deeply sobered.

I was impressed with the way the District of Columbia handled these first offenders. Each boy, with his parents, had to appear before a judge. When Peter and I appeared before a kindly magistrate for our talk, to my surprise the judge raised the issue I had considered too prideful.

"Peter, your father stood for something in the greater Washington community. You have a proud heritage. Don't tarnish it."

In the aftermath of the episode, I saw that the wall between young Peter and me was in part my doing. I had failed to admit Peter to the depths of my spirit. Our whole relationship had been pitched too much on the level of daily schedules, all the superficialities of life between a mother and her sixteen-year-old son.

Was it too late to change this? I would try. The inner voice instructed me to open the deep places of my own life and feelings to Peter and share with him. How much he would understand, I could not know. My business was to obey; God was to supply the communication.

A Christian counselor advised me that Peter needed male authority figures in his life; that, therefore, a Christian boys' school was indicated for his senior year in high school.

As I prayed for God's guidance on this, the Lord responded:

You have done all you can just now. The time has come to relinquish your son. Others will take over the role of parents in his life. You must accept this as natural and trust Me.

My spirit was heavy as we packed the car that September day for the drive to Massachusetts. Peter had obtained his driver's

license and insisted on taking the wheel. Now over six feet tall, he
so towered over me that I felt almost intimidated by his sheer size.

As we drove there was little conversation between us. As usual,
he was listening to a baseball game on the radio.

When the time came to leave our rooms in the inn the next day,
I tried to keep my heart from showing—not because I was afraid
of the heart, but because I didn't want to embarrass Peter John.

"This is a significant day for us both. Would you be willing for
us to have a prayer together and ask God's blessing on it?"

Peter nodded a little impatiently, so I made the prayer brief. The
moment hung in space, passed. But I had the unmistakable feeling as we prayed that we were not two but three, with "Big Peter"
a part in this intercession around the throne of God, united across
barriers that were no barriers.

I was a little disappointed in his room at school—circa 1890,
golden oak woodwork, the floor well worn by generations of boys'
feet, battered furniture, two small windows almost covered with a
summer's growth of ivy.

But Peter did not seem to mind. He had just met his roommate,
Bruce, and liked him—as blond as he, also a senior. The room
would be their digs, their very own. What did nineteenth-century
woodwork and worn floors matter?

I stood on tiptoe to hug my tall son and walked out, down the
worn, uneven steps.

Another era was over. I had parted with my husband. In a very
real sense I had just parted with my son. This was the beginning
of his life on his own.

As I drove away I was thinking: So to what do I return now? An
empty house? Greater loneliness than ever?

A sudden rainstorm came up, the car's jerky windshield wipers
keeping pace with my jumbled thoughts. Ten minutes later the rain
ceased as quickly as it had come. I was driving into the setting sun,

and the sun turned the droplets of rain on the windshield into glittering globules of light.

Then, to my astonishment, a rainbow appeared, every gorgeous color of the spectrum in its wide, perfect arc.

The rainbow of promise. I could forget my dread of returning to an empty house. He would be there.

Into the World

hen it was time to deal with Peter's estate, in many ways I was still a little girl. I had adored and leaned on my husband. Like many a sheltered woman who has married young, I had never once figured out an income tax blank, had a car inspected, consulted a lawyer or tried to read an insurance policy. Railroad timetables and plane schedules were enigmas to me. My household checking account rarely balanced. I had never invested any money; I had been driving a car for only three months when Peter died. I would never even have considered braving a car trip alone.

Now I was faced with all these practical matters, plus many, many more.

There was some insurance, but not enough. I had no idea where Peter John and I would live after we left the manse. I was not trained to earn a living. I had married when my college diploma was warm from the dean's hand, before I had even earned a teacher's certificate. The adjustment that faced me, therefore, posed a challenge in every way.

My confrontation with the future took place a week or so after the funeral. Three men, all of them Peter's friends, arrived one evening to give me the grim facts. They were kind, eager to be helpful, but determined that I be realistic about my bleak financial situation. One of them, a knowledgeable insurance agent, had everything worked out neatly on a graph.

"I recommend that you spread Dr. Marshall's insurance over a reasonably long period of time. After all, it will be eight years before Peter John goes to college."

"How much income will we have each month?" I asked.

"One hundred and seventy-one dollars a month for the first eight years. Then the monthly income will take a drop."

"You must be clear-eyed about this, Catherine," chimed in the other businessman. "That won't be enough to maintain your car. You should probably sell it."

"And you're scarcely strong enough yet to hold down a job," the other friend added. "It's only been two years since you regained your health. By the way, what could you do job-wise?"

I began to have a suffocating feeling. "I-I don't quite know. I married right out of college—have only a bachelor of arts degree. I couldn't be a secretary, I don't know shorthand."

The three men were genuinely fond of me. Yet they considered me a poor prospect indeed for a breadwinning widow. I could see it in their eyes, feel it in the way they were approaching the subject of finances.

"I don't think you realize how desperate your situation is," one insisted. "One hundred and seventy-one dollars a month in Washington won't even cover the bare necessities."

"The Cape Cod cottage is a tangible asset," another added. "I think you should sell it quickly."

The three men left that night distressed because I did not seem fearful enough. They suspected that they had failed to convince me I was facing a crisis.

They were right. It was not so much my refusal to accept their gloomy forecasts; rather, that even as a protective shield had been thrown over my emotions at the time of Peter's death, now I felt that same shield covering my faith regarding the future. It was not my doing; someone else was sheltering me. Their fear-darts, however well-meaning, had simply hit the protective covering and bounced off.

Yet I had not argued with these solicitous friends because facts and figures had substantiated all they had said. There the facts were, all down on paper in neat columns and graphs. How could figures lie? Yet somehow I felt that they did lie. Something was missing.

Alone in my room later, I stared out the window into the moonlight shining on swaying treetops. One brilliant star winked like a solitaire. Suddenly, standing there at the window, I knew what the missing factor was. My three friends who saw my many inadequacies, who had meant to be so kind, had reckoned without God.

I remembered how often Peter had faced this same attitude with his church officers. He would come home from a trustees' meeting sad and grim. "Cath'rine, no matter what's presented for their approval, their litany is always the same: 'But Dr. Marshall, where is the money coming from?' Where's their faith in God?"

But either God was there—*I am that I am*, a fact more real than any figures or graphs—or He was not. If He was there, then reckoning without Him was certainly not being "realistic." In fact, it could be the most hazardous miscalculation of all.

God had met me in Peter's hospital room the morning of his death. I had felt His presence. And the words He had spoken so clearly to me as I left the room were emblazoned on my consciousness: *Surely goodness and mercy shall follow you all the days of your life.* It was His personal pledge to me. In the days ahead—and indeed, during all the years to follow—I would cling to that promise.

So now I was facing one of those crises, a crossroads of life. I had to walk on into that new life, but which road should I take?

One decision I could make immediately: I would refuse to be destitute. The thrust of Mother's teaching in this regard had gone deep. Why should any child of the King consent to poverty?

So I claimed for Peter John and for me that great promise that stirs the imagination and sends creativity whirring into action. . . .

And we know that all things work together for good to them that love God, to them who are the called according to his purpose.

Romans 8:28

How often Peter, in quoting this promise from the pulpit, had pointed out that God never meant for this "good" to be limited to spiritual blessing; that He knows perfectly well our need for housing and clothes and food.

But now the Spirit was spotlighting in this promise—His *rhema* for me at this moment—"to them who are the called according to His purpose."

I felt a tingling at the top of my spine. Dared I entertain hope that He could actually be calling me for a purpose of His own; that there was some special work for me to do?

A sense of adventure beckoned. It would be exciting to see what God wanted me to do with my new life. I was sure that when His design for me was revealed in its entirety, it would include much more than provision for economic needs.

Meanwhile, there were other things I was learning that I would share in the years ahead with those who had lost a loved one, whether through death or divorce. For one thing, no major decisions should be made in the weeks immediately following the crisis. Sufficient time must be allowed for recovery from a state of shock.

I was fortunate in not having to make an immediate determination about where my son and I were going to live. We were able to stay in the manse for almost ten months while the church searched for a new pastor. During those months familiar, beloved and once-shared possessions helped to soothe my sore spirit: Peter's wildly turbulent seascapes on the walls of our home, the well-worn games in the game closet. Being able to walk our cocker spaniel, Jeff, along the same familiar few blocks was, rather than added hurt, balm to my spirit.

Next, I found that the mechanics connected with separation are actually helpful, hard though they seem at first. In the beginning these practical activities come as an intrusion into grief. The wounded person looks out on the world marveling that other people on the streets and in the shops are going on about their business as if nothing has happened. How is it possible, one wonders at such a time, to force oneself to sort out dresser and desk drawers; to put one's mind to business and insurance details; to cope with the dozens of telephone calls and personal messages, and deal with the loving concern of friends and family?

The truth is that the empty heart needs work for the hands to do. I learned that there is a certain therapy in these necessary mechanics, plus a strange, sweet easing of pain.

An entry in my journal at this time charted an avenue of action:

I must use part of my quiet time to hear what the Lord has for me to do. He has indicated that He does have a plan for my life. Could it be that my dream of being a writer is part of this plan? I must be open to everything that could lead to this: letters, invitations, counsel of friends.

Several days later a friend wrote, "I, along with thousands, earnestly hope that you will see to it that Peter's sermons will be published." Soon these requests for a book making some of Peter's sermons and prayers available were coming at me from all sides.

Since I had no contacts in the publishing field, my response was this prayer: "Lord, if this is Your plan, then You open the door for it. That way I'll know."

Within six weeks I had received letters from three publishers asking the same question: Would I be interested in compiling and editing a book of Peter Marshall's sermons and prayers? It seemed that God's word was *Go*.

After conferring with several knowledgeable friends, of the three I chose the Fleming H. Revell Company in New York. A contract was worked out whereby I would edit a minimum of twelve of my husband's sermons for a book to be published in the late fall of 1949. A small advance was provided that helped me with living expenses during the next six months.

Peter had left some six hundred complete sermon manuscripts filed in three worn, black-and-white cardboard boxes. The proposed book could include at the most only fifteen to twenty. The problem was, on what basis should I go about trying to choose from the six hundred?

While the editors at Fleming Revell had caught a whiff of excitement about Peter's preaching, I know now that more deliberate reflection on their part, plus reactions from tough-minded salesmen, had quickly tempered their enthusiasm. "Fond widow editing preacher's sermons for publication" did not exactly herald a bestseller.

A casual or hurried job on my part could have defeated the project or produced a volume with a modest sale at best. But as the editing job progressed, I began to experience the deep satisfaction and inner contentment known only to those who have found just the right vocational spot.

It was not that my adjustment to bereavement was complete. In fact, it had scarcely begun. But in spite of the empty void inside me, it was as if I had finally come home to my natural habitat.

The work of editing, the virility of the sermon material itself, Peter's extraordinary handling of the English language, his intuitive use of the precise word, his humor, his certainty that people would find these messages food for their hungry spirits, the flashing facets of Peter's personality that leapt from the typewritten pages, the feel of paper and pencil in my hands—every bit of it was pure joy. And gradually I began to see that many things done in the years gone by had been preparation for this task.

The first printing of 10,000 copies of *Mr. Jones, Meet the Master* sold out before official publication day. Additional printings sold out as soon as they came off the press. When told the book was on *The New York Times* bestseller list, I was not as impressed as I should have been. Soon I was involved with a biography, *A Man Called Peter*, that would be on the bestseller list for fifty consecutive weeks and then be made into a successful movie.

God's goodness and mercy certainly were following me.

Loneliness

he years immediately after young Peter went away to school (first to Mount Hermon, then to Yale) were the most difficult of my widowhood.

The idea of living alone did not frighten me. In fact, like most writers I prefer being alone for long stretches of the day. But there is a big difference between aloneness and loneliness.

Loneliness is the aching need inside one to share one's life with another. There are wholesome relationships for single people outside of marriage where this void can be satisfied. My question was, What kind of life did God want for me?

During the first years after Peter's death I was convinced that it would be impossible for me ever to marry again, that this would violate something very precious that my husband and I had had together. But as the years passed, I began praying about this matter, telling God that I did not even know what it was right to ask for, that I would leave entirely up to Him the decision as to whether I should ever remarry.

But this was a cop-out, a sloppy way of praying. Surely I needed to know myself better than that, what my own deep desires were. Knowing these, I could then at least present them to Him for approval or disapproval.

My growing loneliness was brought into sharp focus the night of a mother-daughter banquet for which I had agreed to make an informal after-dinner talk. Before my part in the program, a young baritone rose to sing a group of semi-classical songs. The last in the group was "Drink to Me Only with Thine Eyes."

I had heard the words from Ben Jonson's poem sung many times. They held no special memories for me, nor had I ever felt in the least sentimental about this song. . . .

> Drink to me only with thine eyes,
>   And I will pledge with mine;
> Or leave a kiss within the cup,
>   And I'll not ask for wine.
> The thirst that from the soul doth rise
>   Doth ask a drink divine. . . .

Toward the end of the song, suddenly without warning I felt myself tighten. I was aware that my hands, hidden under the edge of the tablecloth, were clutching the evening bag in my lap until my fingers ached.

This won't do, I thought. I looked about for something less emotional to focus on. My eyes roamed over the scene before me—the mothers in their finery with their daughters beside them at the round tables, all listening intently to the tall young singer. I noticed a red-headed teenager's hairdo. Deliberately I studied it, trying to decide how some beautician had created the sleek, turned-under effect.

By the time the last notes of the song had died away, the tension in my hands had relaxed, the fullness in my throat had disappeared. I was able to get to my feet and even put some humor into my talk.

But this experience had pointed up a depth of loneliness in me of which I had been only subliminally aware. Years after Peter's death, my journey through the valley was still a running battle with self-pity. Several of the couples on our street would take a stroll in the early evening. Seeing them sometimes, I would think, *Were Peter still with me, he and I would be the youngest couple in the neighborhood.* Or at the theatre I would see a gray-haired man reach for his wife's hand, and wince with a pang of envy.

There is a price to be paid in reaching out again for a relationship. The first tribute exacted is a modicum of honesty with ourselves. Are we in some perverse way enjoying the pity-parties? How badly do we want to make connection with other people? For, let's admit it, there are pluses in having only oneself to think of.

In the light of honest answers to questions like these, I decided the negatives of a solitary life outweighed the dubious benefits. The first step was to perform a freshening-up on myself. Having to make public appearances forced me to review my clothes situation. I found a specialist who, after studying my current wardrobe, my figure and my features, advised me skillfully on clothes-shopping.

Then came some quiet reappraisal of certain restrictions my parents had placed on me in my growing-up years. Our home had been so full of love that the taboos they had put on activities like ballroom dancing and card games had mattered little to me—then. But now as a widow in sophisticated Washington, I was embarrassed when someone asked me to dance, or I had to decline an invitation to play bridge.

The answer was to develop these social assets—and I did. I enrolled for a series of lessons in ballroom dancing. Then three women friends and I set aside an evening a week to master bridge. We spread out teaching manuals on a second table beside us and learned the game together by playing it.

Seven years after Peter's death a battle was going on inside me. While resigned in my mind to widowhood, emotionally I was preparing myself for a new kind of life. This entry appears in my journal at about this time:

> God does want me to be happy. God does want Peter John to be well-adjusted and happy. God has made me the way I am, has made me for happiness and love; I do not believe that He means or wants me to stay by myself for the rest of my life.

Odd, how as soon as I opened the inner door, outer doors began swinging open, too. Men began seeking me out for dates, a procession of men. Widowers—one a college president, one an insurance agent. Older bachelors—a wealthy California citrus-grower, a Washington professor, a Texas investment broker.

Then there was Howard, a tall, slim, distinguished-looking businessman and widower. I liked him immediately. He invited me out for lunch, then dinner, then for a weekend at his large family estate in South Carolina where his sister was the hostess. I was impressed, and Howard's two sons seemed to like me.

Howard was appointed to a government position in Washington and moved into an office in the Pentagon. As we saw each other more often, I became aware of some unsettling qualities in him.

He tended to avoid any discussions about Christianity. I sensed that any faith he had was a sort of inherited social grace with nothing personal about it. He seemed overly fond of the superficialities of life—eating, drinking, clothes, cars and so on. He was restless and ill-at-ease whenever other people paid attention to me in regard to my books. Yet his charm, dignity and statesmanlike approach to issues, and his warm, affectionate nature, appealed to me. Then I didn't see him for several months.

That June a letter came from Howard—a short note, actually. He was to be married again. The woman was the daughter of a general, a widow with three small children.

When the letter came I thought I had already relinquished the whole matter. Apparently not so. There was a surprising emotional backwash. I found it almost impossible to get back to my work. The fact that I was in demand as an author and speaker seemed meaningless. I was a 42-year-old widow whom life was passing by.

I met Jim at church. He was from Wyoming, a plastics manufacturer, married with two young children, but he had to be in Washington frequently on business matters.

Jim was a virile-looking, warm-hearted man with a good sense of humor and a fine mind. Though he had dabbled some in Wyoming politics, he was an outdoor man who reveled in hunting and sports.

I was delighted when he invited Peter John for a two-day hunting trip or spent long hours with him in target practice. The two males seemed to enjoy each other immensely.

Then Jim began dropping by our home, and since he was there to see Peter, it seemed natural to invite him to dinner.

As time went on, Jim began asking questions about my life and activities, and I found myself responding quite openly and honestly about how lonely the life of a so-called Christian celebrity could be. He in turn began sharing with me some difficulties in his marriage. In the beginning, Jim's marital problems had not sounded serious; now they seemed to worsen the more he talked about them.

This should have rung alarm bells for me since I well knew that a single, unattached person of the opposite sex should not have been Jim's choice for a marriage counselor. Instead I would listen sympathetically, lulled into a false sense of security by Jim's ability to laugh at himself. That seemed to indicate at least a degree of healthy objectivity.

I will help him see how important it is for him to work out these differences with his wife, I told myself. And I did talk to him almost sternly about how important it was to get back to Wyoming and his family as soon as possible.

Then one evening after Peter had gone to his room, Jim blurted out, "Catherine, I've fallen in love with you."

A kaleidoscope of feelings swept over me: surprise, dismay, concern, fear and, yes, longing. But I knew it had to be squelched—and quickly.

"I'm startled, Jim. And—well, grateful. But it can't be right."

"I think it could be right, Catherine. But not until I'm a free man. I intend to get a divorce."

I protested and he argued. When he left that evening, I could tell he was very determined. I knew what I had to do the next morning: set the alarm, get up at 6:30 and come penitently before my Lord.

With some trepidation I did this, then waited. I felt such kindness and love pouring from Him that my tears came in a flood. I knew I had to be honest with my feelings, ruthlessly so. I poured out the residue of pain about Howard, then took pen in hand to try to analyze how I felt about Jim:

The moments we have been together have had a special flavor, a special character. Maybe that's what often happens when one really lives in the present. But the companionship has the quality of something one may not keep. It's like walking through a garden and catching the whiff of a fragrance one cannot quite capture or identify because one doesn't belong in that particular garden and cannot linger there.

Jim's friendship has done something for me. I have felt more alive during these days than in a long time. It's as if his touch on my life has awakened my emotions, the potential warmth of me, out of a long, long sleep.

But Jim will go back to his family. He must. I must be "hands-off" in my emotional attitude toward him.

Then I wrote Jim a letter that would spell *finis* to the whole thing, stating clearly that God would never honor any relationship between Jim and me that came at the expense of his wife and children.

When I mailed the letter, it was as if I had shed a twenty-pound weight from my shoulders. The next morning I felt a surge of creative vitality I had not experienced in months. Confession and restitution had freed my spirit, and out poured a torrent of words on paper:

For the past year I have felt defeated and frustrated. And this certainly is not as God wishes it. Here are some of the ways I have allowed my loneliness to defeat me:

1. The salt, the savor has gone out of life. Nothing, not even the very great success of *A Man Called Peter*, thrills me much now. "Success" has turned to ashes in my mouth.

2. There has been, over the past several years, a growing coldness in my heart toward other people rather than an increasing love and warmth. Visiting the sick has been a chore—no joy in it.

3. There has come an increasing preoccupation with self. Or perhaps the preoccupation with self is the real cause of the defeats.

4. I have sought satisfaction in material things and have not found anything here that lasts.

5. I have become more irritable in the daily grind of everyday life. Slow drivers, inept salesgirls, parking lot attendants provoke me much more easily than they used to.

6. I have known that God wants me to get up an hour earlier each morning for prayer and Bible reading, yet have not been consistent about this.

7. I have failed almost totally in small disciplines of appetite—small self-denials that, at the time, I knew were right.

8. I have often failed to have the inner strength to discipline or say no to Peter John, when I knew I should have.

9. Along with all these failures, I have often had a feeling of supe-
riority to other human beings, which makes no sense at all.

In my early morning quiet time in my bedroom I even went back
to review the Howard relationship in my journals. I saw that what
I had written seldom contained any revelations from God about
whether He felt we had been right for each other. Most of my notations had amounted to wishful thinking. Too impressed with the
man's stature, his appearance, his wealth, I had decided that this
was the one.

He was not right for me, and God would have told me, had I
come to Him with will and heart wide open to His counsel. Months
later, viewing the relationship with God's help, I could easily see
how mismatched we had been both spiritually and emotionally.

No wonder, then, that the course of events with Jim had become
so tangled.

Jim was not at all satisfied with my letter. Weeks later he flew
east to Washington, determined to continue our relationship.

But the morning times had strengthened me and returned clear-
eyedness to me. Moreover, I was learning something about how to
cope with the temptations that come to the lonely: Admit you are
not able to resist on your own strength. Then step aside and let
Jesus handle the situation.

When I did this, inner direction came: Call your pastor and meet
with him. When I got the pastor, Gordon Cosby, on the phone, I
hesitated only a minute. Then I told him the whole story.

"Bring Jim down here and we'll pray about it, just the three of
us," he replied.

What a tremendous answer to prayer! Jim agreed to go. So we
made an appointment to meet at the Church of the Saviour.

"It isn't necessary for me to preach a sermon to you," Gordon
told Jim and me. "You've come here because each of you wants to

do what God wants you to do. I honor you both for this. Jesus always has the answer to every one of our needs."

He leaned back in his chair, smiling and relaxed. "How grateful we Christians should be! Without Jesus' agony on that cross, there would be no cleansing for the likes of any of us, no miracle of changing what's wrong on the inside of us to what's right. The blood shed on that cross literally saves our lives.

"That's what the sacrament of Communion should mean to us. I suggest we bring all this to the foot of Jesus' cross through Communion. How about it, Jim? Are you ready to lay there your desires in this matter, what you thought was your will?"

Jim nodded, his eyes moist.

Now Gordon looked at me. "Catherine?"

"Yes, I'd like that."

The bread and wine were there waiting on a little altar-table in Gordon's office. Never had the words been so meaningful: "This is His body broken for you. . . . This is the blood of the new covenant, shed for many for the remission of sins. Drink ye all of it."

We felt the presence of Jesus in that quiet room. At the conclusion of the little service, as we knelt, Gordon blessed us both.

"Jim and Catherine, you are good friends and want to stay that way—friends. God has endowed you both with special talents and has a plan for both of your lives. Jim has responsibilities to his God, his family and his business. God has given Catherine a son to rear and a ministry through her writing. Both need to be protected. Go your separate ways, freely forgiven, restored, refreshed, into new usefulness and creativity."

Then Gordon lifted us to our feet and hugged us both.

Several months later I heard that Jim was back with his wife and children.

SECTION FOUR

Second Marriage

As I look back on this event, I am overwhelmed at the supernatural way God brought Catherine and me together. On the basis of pure logic we were a mismatch. Catherine in 1959 was a nationally known author whose Christian stature intimidated eligible males. I was the little-known editor of an inspirational magazine and a single parent trying to rear three small children.

Why would Catherine at age 44, her own son approaching his twentieth birthday, want to take on children ages ten, six and three, and give up her Washington dream house to move to suburban New York?

As for me, I was hoping at age forty to build a new life with an exciting younger woman. I was certainly not looking for a spiritual celebrity, four and a half years my senior, whose romantic first marriage had been depicted in a best-selling book.

Yet there are times when God asks us to throw logic out. Both Catherine and I separately had asked God to be a matchmaker.

Letting Go

strange thing happened after Gordon Cosby's private Communion service for me and Jim. I stopped thinking about remarriage. Not that the desire for it was wiped out, just that it became much less important to me. My perspective had changed. This was the Lord's doing, of course, and came about because I was able to give the whole matter over to Him to handle.

One morning I wrote this in my journal:

I am to "seek first the Kingdom of God" in regard to remarriage. Should this be God's will for me, then in any given man I am to seek first those inner qualities of mind and heart that belong to God's Kingdom.

But what about me? What inner qualities should I have to qualify as a wife again?

The next day this is what I wrote:

Going back to the question I asked yesterday, I would list femininity, warmth of personality, vitality, interest in other people, the desire to give. A big order!

105

But I am being told this morning that since it is definitely God's will that I have these qualities, I am not to plead for them, but to believe that the prayer is already answered, that God is giving them to me in His own way and in His own time.

Shortly thereafter the president of a Midwestern college telephoned and asked to see me during his forthcoming trip to Washington. I had stayed at his home several years before while giving the commencement speech. Upon hearing that his wife had died, I had written him a note of sympathy.

He telephoned me upon his arrival in Washington and invited me out to dinner. By now I knew men well enough to realize that they usually ask you out for lunch if it concerns business, for dinner if it is more personal.

The college president arrived in a rented Cadillac and held my hand an extra moment when we met at the door. He was a small man, perhaps an inch or two taller than I, about 55, balding, a compulsive talker. During dinner at a fine restaurant I learned everything about his college: the $2 million debt, the growing enrollment, the championship baseball team, the new library, the problems with some of the faculty members.

But the rush of words covered up a rather surprising nervousness for a man in his position. He was obviously interested in me as a person and intended to express it before the evening was over.

He did just that, sitting in my living room later that evening. He proposed marriage. There was no attempt at any romantic buildup; it would be a marriage of convenience and mutual interest. He would supply me a home and security, in return for which I would be the first lady of the college campus.

I was touched and honored by his offer. But as graciously as I knew how, I refused. For me there could be no marriage without romance.

During that same year I declined two more proposals of marriage. What was happening? There could be only one answer. Relinquishment of my intense desire for remarriage, seeking God first instead of a husband, had relaxed me in a way that was now attracting men to me. I could not analyze how I was different except that I could now empathize more with the other person and be much less concerned with myself. And the Kingdom-of-God-first yardstick was enabling me to hear the Lord's word advising me about each person.

A telephone call came one day from Leonard LeSourd, the executive editor of *Guideposts* magazine, asking for a luncheon date to talk about an idea for a future article. It had no special significance for me. I had written before for *Guideposts* and had met Len briefly one evening when I spoke to the young adult group of the Marble Collegiate Church in New York City.

Over lunch in a Georgetown restaurant our talk ranged over many subjects. In an easygoing, personal way, Len asked many questions about me—probing, I thought, for a new subject on which to base an article. We found one, finished lunch and he drove me home.

As he stopped the car in front of my house, out of the blue came an intriguing statement: "In my twelve years at *Guideposts* I've learned a lot about the Christian faith. One aspect of it seems both bewildering and challenging."

"What is that?"

"The Holy Spirit. No one talks much about it, especially preachers. There's a mystery here—power, too. Sometime I want to cover it in the magazine."

"The Holy Spirit is a He, Len," I returned quietly.

He looked at me curiously. "You know Him, then?"

"Not as much as I'd like."

The conversation ended and Len helped me out of the car and to the door. Not once during the two hours we were together did it occur to me that there was anything but a professional motive behind his invitation to lunch.

But there was nothing of the professional editor about the letter I received from Len several months later in the summer of 1959.

"I would like to know you better," he wrote. "How do you react to this idea? We'll choose a day, and then you write on your calendar three letters: *F-U-N*. I'll pick you up in the morning in my car and we'll just take off to the beach or the mountains or whatever."

The letter seemed deliberately couched to say, "If you're interested in pursuing this relationship, let's have a go at it. If not, then tell me so right now."

I liked that approach. We set a day in early August. Len telephoned the night before from a Washington motel to say that he would call for me at 10:30 the next morning. He was delighted when I suggested fixing a picnic lunch.

The next morning turned out to be a beautiful summer day, not too hot. When I met Len at my front door, I found myself slipping easily into the adventurous mood he had suggested. I asked no questions about where we were going; he offered no hints. As he helped me pack the lunch into a picnic basket, I could sense his curiosity about my living situation.

"Peter John and I have lived here for several years," I volunteered, "that is, when Peter's home from Yale. This has been a good home for us, but I'm building a new house in Bethesda that will give me a better working situation."

"What's wrong with this?"

"Not enough privacy. Peter's friends are in and out a lot in the summer. I enjoy them, but there are so many other interruptions here, too, and not enough space for my secretary. Anyway, I've always wanted to build my own dream house. It's already about half-built."

"I see." Len was reflective. "Since Peter is at Yale nine months of the year, your dream house could end up being quite lonely for you."

"Yes, it could."

Len put the picnic lunch into the trunk of his car and we climbed into the front seat.

"What do you prefer," he asked casually, "ocean or mountains?"

"I would choose the mountains."

"Which direction?"

I aimed him west toward Skyline Drive. As we drove along, I studied this fortyish editor sitting beside me. He was of medium height; dark hair beginning to gray; lithe, athletic figure. His gray-blue eyes were direct, warm, the lids often crinkling with humor. He was a good conversationalist, probing but relaxed. I relaxed, too. It was going to be a good day.

While driving out Route 193 toward Route 7, we came to a sign: Great Falls Park.

"What's this?" Len asked.

"A scenic spot on the Potomac for picnics and walking on the rocks."

"Let's try it."

We parked, got out and walked along the water. Since it was rocky terrain, Len reached for my hand and continued to hold it. We had lemonade at the refreshment center and then continued our drive west.

By the time we were on Skyline Drive and heading south, it was time to look for a picnic spot. Len chose a grassy knoll under a large shade tree. He took a blanket from the trunk of his car and spread it out for us to sit on. Then, as I began removing the food from the picnic basket, he returned to his car trunk for another item. A ukulele!

Out of the corner of my eye as I watched Len tuning it up, I hoped that I was not about to receive a country music concert. I have nothing against country rhythms. They're fun sometimes. But on the whole, I much prefer classical music.

"I was dancing . . . with my darling . . . to the Tennessee waltz. . . ." Len's voice had a strong nasal quality. I winced a little in spite of my effort to keep an expressionless face.

After a few bars, Len put the ukulele aside and laughed self-consciously.

"You're not a country music fan, are you, Catherine? I taught myself to play—poorly, I'm afraid. And I have no singing voice. Anyhow, I'd rather talk than sing."

I sighed with relief, making a mental note that Len was perceptive or I was transparent—or perhaps a little of both.

It was hard to believe that two people could talk continually for eleven hours, yet feel they had scarcely made a start on subjects of mutual interest. But when Len said goodbye that night, I had no real indication he could be serious about me.

True, I sensed that he was surprised at certain discoveries, especially that I was not the overly sanctimonious, lofty creature some people had painted me. We also knew now that we were both seekers, strugglers, groping toward real growth as Christians. Both of us were reporters, always interested in how to capture on paper scenes, drama, personalities, new discoveries about people in relation to God. We had an open, honest communication at a deep level.

Len's home situation, however, put me on guard. For several years he had been trying to rear three small children alone; he was obviously interested in finding a wife who would be willing to share this load. It was hard to see myself in this role.

He Didn't Mean to Say It

 wasn't prepared for Len's persistence, the frequent telephone calls that followed our excursion to the mountains. When Len invited me to come for a weekend to his little town of Carmel, New York, to meet his children, to my surprise I found myself accepting. *The least I can do,* I told myself, *is be open-minded enough to take a look at this.*

On Friday afternoon Len met me at New York's La Guardia Airport. During the drive out to Carmel, he told me that I would meet only his two sons, Chester, six, and Jeffrey, three, that weekend. Ten-year-old Linda was at camp. Mrs. Goutremont, the elderly housekeeper, would serve as our chaperon.

The *Guideposts* property in Carmel included the magazine's business office (formerly a girl's school) and a sprawling, eight-room white clapboard house, once the home of the school president, where Len and his children were living.

A picnic table had been set up on the spacious lawn under a maple tree. Diminutive Jeffrey met me with a wide smile, impish blue eyes and a hug. Chester's big, sad brown eyes stared at me suspiciously; then he held out a tentative hand. During the less-than-gourmet supper of greasy, cold fried chicken, coleslaw, potato chips and watermelon, Chester's suspicion of me seemed to increase. Suddenly his hand knocked over a paper cup filled with milk. Quickly I moved to one side, barely avoiding a lapful.

When Len snapped a sharp rebuke at his son, Chester flounced from the table. With the order to come and sit back down, the small, brown-eyed boy fell on the ground in a wild tantrum of crying and kicking.

With a quick move, Len swept his son up in his arms, threw him over his shoulder like a sack of potatoes and carried him into the house. In a few minutes the annoyed father was back, alone.

"Chester will stay in his room until he's ready to apologize," he explained. "He seems to resent outsiders until he gets to know them, especially all women."

Jeffrey, meanwhile, had snuggled up close to me, obviously hungry for love.

"Well, I've made one conquest, anyway," I said.

"Two," replied Len with a grin.

After dinner a neighboring couple joined us for several rubbers of bridge, and I struggled to cope with three skilled players. *I'm about as adept at bridge as Len is with his ukulele,* I thought to myself.

The neighbors left, the children were asleep, Mrs. Goutremont had retired to her room. Len suggested we go outside for a walk about the grounds. It was a still, moonlit night. Suddenly his flow of talk stopped as he abruptly leaned over and kissed me gently. Then he chuckled rather self-consciously.

"We're right under Mrs. Goutremont's window, and I'll bet she's looking down at us."

I darted a quick look up at the window. It was dark. "How can you tell?"

"I can't. But she's very, very curious about us."

"Why?"

He did not answer, but led me instead to the other side of the house by the porch. Two lawn chairs were positioned there side by side and we sat down.

"I'm sorry about the episode with Chester," he began.

"It worked out fine. Your son came downstairs while you were in the kitchen and apologized. I think we're friends now."

Len sighed. "That's good. Chester looks to me for almost total security. Anyone who visits here seems to threaten him."

He talked about his two sons and daughter with pride. "They're such good kids. Smart, too. Being without a mother the past few years has been rough. Mrs. Goutremont is the sixth housekeeper we've had."

As Len talked about his children, I saw that he had a father's heart, and I liked what I saw. He was a caring man, affectionate, comfortable to be with, mature. He approached problems calmly, I decided, thought situations through carefully, acted deliberately.

After coming to these flattering conclusions about Len, he promptly blew apart my reasoning. As he was talking about his dreams for the future, suddenly I heard him say, "And I see the two of us together."

"How do you see us?" I asked, surprised.

Even in the moonlight I could see that Len looked startled, too.

"I hadn't meant to go this route." He paused, struggling. "I find myself wanting to say things that will probably seem very impulsive to you. Somehow I have to—I do see the two of us together, Catherine. There's something supernatural involved in all this that I'm not sure I understand."

He stopped again and shook his head with an almost dazed expression. "I was so miserable a few months ago. I told God I didn't see how I was going to make it alone and cried out to Him for help. Immediately after that prayer, your name, Catherine, dropped into my mind. It had to be God's doing."

"Why would you conclude that?" I queried. "I mean, why, necessarily?"

"Because on my own I would never have thought you were—well, my type."

"All you knew about me came through my book about Peter Marshall?"

Len nodded. "What man wants to play second fiddle to a famous Scottish preacher? Surely you must realize that *A Man Called Peter* made yours one of the great love stories of our time."

He paused, struggling again for the right words. "Frankly, I had concluded you were too ethereal and spiritual. But the Lord seemed to be telling me that this was pure assumption, that I'd never really know until I investigated. So I did. That first luncheon was really an effort to probe under that professional veneer of yours. I didn't get very far that day. It was that brief conversation we had about the Holy Spirit just before we parted that kept me from giving up on us."

He reached out for my hand to cradle it in his. "All my preconceptions were exploded that day we spent together on Skyline Drive. When I drove back to New York the next day, I kept thanking the Lord all the way home. I'm convinced He brought us together and that we are right for each other."

There was a long pause.

"But I certainly hadn't intended to tip my hand so soon," he went on. "I try to approach things carefully, not blurt out my intentions like this."

I said nothing for a moment. My mind was racing furiously. This amounts to a proposal of marriage. By making himself so vulnerable, Len was risking deep hurt.

Finally I found my voice. "Len, you astonish me. This is only the second date we've had. How can you be so sure so soon about us? Don't you realize that with what you've just said, you've walked out on the end of a limb? The limb could so easily be chopped off. Why would you deliberately put yourself in such a position?"

He smiled ruefully. "I don't understand it either. Maybe it's a deep desire for full honesty with you."

"And I honor that and respond to it. But Len, it's too soon for me to know. You're going too fast for me."

Only later did I realize: By following the dictates of his heart rather than the usual, sophisticated, game-playing approach, Len had unwittingly found the most direct route to my love.

A Weekend in Maine

few days after my return to Washington, Len was back on the phone. He wanted me to come with him to Christmas Cove, Maine, for Labor Day weekend to meet his parents. Almost wondering what would come out, I opened my mouth to reply and heard myself saying, "Yes, I could do that."

Again I flew to New York's La Guardia Airport, where Len was waiting. During the six-hour drive to Maine, Len briefed me on his parents. His father had been a Methodist minister for seven years before he had turned to education. Now he was dean of the School of Communications at Boston University. His mother, while rearing Len and his sister, Patricia, had been very active in women's clubs, Kappa Phi, church organizations.

For some time Len's parents had been conducting a yearly tour abroad and summering in Maine. From Europe his mother would bring home interesting items to stock the "Santa Claus Shop," which she had opened years before. It was a big hit with summer visitors in the Christmas Cove area.

"Mother is impressed that I am bringing you to Maine. She will want you to meet a lot of people," Len said uneasily. "I told her that we wanted to be alone to talk."

Len would be an unusual male, I thought, if he could turn off a socially conscious mother.

We arrived at the gray-shingled LeSourd cottage on the inlet at South Bristol, Maine. The invigorating salt air brought back nostalgic memories of "Waverly," our Cape Cod cottage. Len's parents greeted me warmly. The confrontation between him and his mother, however, took place almost immediately.

"I know you said you didn't want any parties, Leonard," she began soon after we had unpacked the car. "But Mrs. Stuart insisted on having us all for a lobster dinner tomorrow night. Leonard, there simply was no way I could refuse."

"Sorry you did that, Mother," Len replied quietly. "You'll have to tell Mrs. Stuart we had already made other plans. Tomorrow night Catherine and I are going over to Boothbay."

"But, Leonard, you can go to Boothbay Sunday night."

Len shook his head. "We're going to Boothbay tomorrow night, Mother. I'll explain to Mrs. Stuart, if you like. And please—no more surprises."

Mrs. LeSourd protested a little more, to no avail. Then she swallowed her disappointment and made no further attempts to tie us down socially.

Len's firmness was a relief. The last thing I wanted was a mother-dominated male. His plan was for me to meet his parents, then for the two of us to be alone, to relax in the sun and talk. We started the next morning, sitting on the rocks at Pemaquid Point. At three o'clock in the afternoon we suddenly realized that we had forgotten about lunch and had been in the sun too long. My legs were lobster-red from sunburn.

For the next three days the almost-nonstop exchange went on in cooler places. Though Len appeared to be by nature an easygoing, relaxed person, he could also be determined.

"We're middle-aged adults, Catherine, who have reached a point of maturity where we can make decisions more quickly," he pressed on. "I feel that the Lord has brought us together; He's given me a love for you that overwhelms me, and I am ready and eager to marry you as soon as possible."

"Len, you may have your word from God, but He hasn't spoken to me yet," was my answer. "I think I'm in love with you, but I'm not yet ready to make a decision about marriage. Be patient with me."

Back in Washington after Labor Day weekend, my emotions were in a turmoil. I was facing the ultimate question: Was I going to give the rest of my life solely to a writing career—or did God's plan for me also include remarriage?

If I married Len I would have to move to the New York area near his work. That would mean putting my unfinished dream house on the market. I would have to leave Washington, all my friends, my family and more than twenty years of memories.

One morning that still, small voice in my inner spirit asked me some searching questions:

You are right to be counting the cost and taking a good look at the major readjustments necessary for another marriage.

Are there not certain areas of your life where some rigidity is creeping in? Did you not realize that My way would be to send you a man not just to satisfy your own needs of love and romance, but because he has gigantic needs himself?

Pondering this, I realized that in a first marriage, in the beginning, romance usually suffuses and dominates everything. It is only later, deep into the relationship, that commitment to one another and the responsibilities that go along with this become equally important—if the marriage is to succeed.

But in second marriages, when we are older, commitment is writ large even at the beginning.

The question was whether I was ready for that much commitment, not just to a husband, but to three children, too. Part of me was excited and stirred; the other part wanted to flee. Now I began to pray almost desperately for help and guidance.

When Len came down to Washington to meet my family and friends, Peter greeted him suspiciously at first. But I could soon tell that Len's amazing knowledge of sports was making an impression.

Len and I had dinner with my sister, Em, her husband, Harlow, and their two daughters, Lynn and Winifred. We drove to Evergreen Farm in Virginia to meet my parents. There we also met my brother, Bob, his wife, Mary, and their three children, Bobby, Mary Margaret and Johnny. It was a difficult time for Len to be put under such intense scrutiny. I liked the way he handled himself: no attempt to impress, no straining for acceptance.

There were several more trips back and forth . . . to meet Linda, Len's ten-year-old daughter, and to talk to Norman and Ruth Peale, old friends of mine, older friends of the LeSourd family. Len had been at *Guideposts*, which the Peales had founded, for more than thirteen years. Norman and Ruth confirmed all that I had heard already about him: talented editor, devoted father, spiritual seeker.

The time arrived and I knew it. D-Day—"Decision Day."

I was flying back to Washington from New York. As I sat in the hot, stuffy plane waiting for takeoff, flocks of birds darted and wheeled beyond the edge of the runway. *Just like my darting, confused thoughts*, I mused.

Buckling my seatbelt, I realized something: I had thought I wanted love again. But now that love was staring me in the face, I was afraid. Why did I so want to flee? What was my heart trying to tell me? Could it be because this romance was not tailor-made to my dream specifications? Len was asking me to love not only him, but to begin all over again with child-rearing. At my age!

"Lord, You always give it to me straight," I breathed. "What am I to do?"

I thought with longing of the new house being built for me in Washington, almost finished now. Adjoining my bedroom, cut off from the rest of the house, was a step-down room—a sanctuary where I would write. Still, I would live in that house alone except for those brief holiday times when Peter John was home from Yale.

Two roads stretched ahead, and I was at the place where they parted. In that house being built I might produce many articles and books. There I would have a cushioned, sheltered life—yes, and probably a lonely one.

And if I chose the other road, I would plunge directly back into a turbulent life. It meant being a mother to Jeffrey, that mischievous imp; to Chester, with those enormous brown eyes and a passion for baseball; to Linda, approaching adolescence—and I had had no experience in rearing a daughter! I would battle to find enough time for my writing. Someone else would enjoy that beautiful, step-down room off the bedroom.

My thoughts turned again to Him.

"Lord," my plea continued, "aren't You overdoing it? A while back I told You that I was ready to reenter the mainstream of life, but does it have to be quite this much life?"

And then I remembered a sermon Peter Marshall had preached with the intriguing title "Praying Is Dangerous Business." With a clarity I would not have thought possible, several sentences came back to me:

It is dangerous business to pray for something unless you really and truly mean it. You see, God might call your bluff and take you up on it!

Again, God may require something of the one who prays. The answer to a particular prayer may involve some real effort . . . maybe even some sacrifice. God's method in answering almost any prayer is the march-into-the-Red-Sea-and-it-divides technique. You've got to have faith for that sort of venture, and courage, too.

My prayer about remarriage had turned out to be one of those dangerous prayers. My bluff was indeed being called.

I took a deep breath, for there was a luminosity about this moment that I recognized. I had met it before. It had nothing to do with the other-worldly type of inspiration that many people associate with getting a message from God. It was no off-in-a-rosy-cloud vision. Actually, it was more like being slapped in the face with a wet washcloth. Or like being brought to earth with a thud and bidden sharply to stand on one's feet and behave with maturity.

Suddenly the choice God was presenting to me was clear. To say yes meant adjustment, involvement. Yet I saw that if I chose the other road, I would be turning away from the challenge of life. That way would be comfortable, but it would take me further and further from contact with people. It could also mean the slow, softening deterioration of the real person inside, of the spirit God had been molding and shaping and chiseling, often so painfully.

The plane was moving now, gathering speed rapidly. We were lifting off the runway, climbing at a steep angle. The sun glazed off the silvery wings and was reflected back in pinpoints of brilliant light.

At that instant I knew I would say yes, to life.

We were married on November 14, 1959, in the Presbyterian Church in Leesburg, Virginia, with my son, Peter, giving me away. Never have the bonds of matrimony been tied more completely by clergy: my father, a Presbyterian pastor; Len's father, a Methodist minister; and Dr. Norman Vincent Peale, a pastor to both of us—

all three officiating at the ceremony, using the memorable wedding service Peter Marshall had always used, part of which he had written himself.

Linda was starry-eyed as she edged up to Peter John, her new six-foot-five brother. Chester had by now accepted me. Jeffrey, Len had decided, was too young to attend, but was eagerly waiting to see his "new mommy" again.

Early that evening after the reception at Evergreen Farm, Len and I would be flying to Los Angeles, then on to Hawaii for our honeymoon.

On our way from the church back to the farm, Len and I learned that Chester had missed seeing the ceremony. Seated beside his Grandmother LeSourd, at a moment when her attention was on the wedding service, he had slid his lithe body off the pew to the floor and disappeared mysteriously from his grandmother's grasp. Chester had spent the remainder of the service crawling under the pews from the front of the church to the back, slithering his way between the legs of the wedding guests, mopping up the floor with his best pants.

At the time we laughed over the ludicrous antics of a small boy.

It should have been fair warning about what lay ahead.

Merging Two Broken Homes

pon Len's and my return from our honey-moon, I found it deeply satisfying once again to assume the role of all-out homemaker. We found a home in Chappaqua, New York, forty miles north of New York City, and began blending our two families. First there was the task of com-bining our possessions, deciding what to take to the new house, what to eliminate, what gaps were left to fill. The decorating job of bringing together this amalgamation was challenging and fun.

The yard dared me to make it beautiful. An outcropping of New York granite in the front yard cried out for a rock garden. A stone wall across the entire front of the property demanded a perennial border. Soon I was poring over nursery catalogs and garden books.

The children watched all this with fascination, Linda enchanted with her own room and the chance to help decide colors and other details, the boys elated over their immediate discovery of playmates next door and of so much space outdoors in which to roam.

But it takes more than a house, no matter how attractive, and possessions, and even a wonderful yard, to make a home. For what is a home but people, the individuals in it and the interaction among them?

The scene of our first dinner together as a new family is forever etched in my memory. We were gathered around the dinner table, two adults and three children; Peter was away at school.

I had lovingly prepared food I thought the children would enjoy—meatloaf, scalloped potatoes, broccoli, a green salad. Len's face was alive with happiness as he blessed the food.

But then as Chester's big brown eyes regarded the food on his plate, he grimaced, suddenly bolted from the table and fled upstairs, slamming the bedroom door behind him.

"Let him go, Catherine," Len said.

Then, seeing my stricken face, he explained ruefully, "I'm afraid my children aren't used to much variety in food. Mostly I've just fed them hamburgers, hot dogs or fried chicken from a takeout place."

Len went upstairs to try to persuade Chester to come back to the table. He found the little boy in bed, covers over his head. When he tearfully refused to come back downstairs, my new husband told his son sternly to undress and go to bed. There would be no supper for him. I was devastated at the thought of Chester going to sleep hungry. The dinner was spoiled for all of us.

And the disastrous evening was not over. Linda's resistance toward her new stepmother surfaced that first night when she refused to wear slippers on the cold hardwood floors, insisting she had always gone barefoot around the house. I understood only too well what it must have been like to be the only female in the family. Now suddenly she was vying with me for Len's time and affection.

The two boys had asked to room together, yet immediately began tussling like bear cubs. When they started scrapping yet again after the lights were out, Len summarily removed Jeff to another room. The little fellow sobbed himself to sleep.

That night as I was sitting propped up in bed reading, my attention kept wandering from the child psychology book to the problems at hand.

"Sibling rivalry," the learned author tagged it. "Parents, remain calm and unperturbed," his advice ran. "It happens in every family. Just remember, this, too, will pass."

Oh, sure, went my rebellious ruminations. *It will pass by the time the parents are basket cases.*

I could see it so clearly: the bespectacled child psychologist before his typewriter in his cubicle of an office, the door bolted against "siblings" of all ages, cheerfully clacking out his words of wisdom for us beleaguered parents in the thick of it.

It was later that same night, after Len and I, exhausted, had fallen asleep, that the shrill ringing of the telephone awoke us. It was Peter.

"Mom, I got picked up for speeding on the Merritt Parkway. I'm at the police station."

We agreed to post bond for Peter's release.

Yet all these troubles were but surface symptoms, the tip of the iceberg of difficulties. Surfacing day after day were problems relating to our extended family—Len's parents and mine, along with other relatives, together with the children's emotional trauma from that succession of housekeepers over the past two years. Peter, too, was in many ways still suffering from the loss and shock of his father's death ten years before.

How do you put broken families back together again? How can a group of individuals of diverse backgrounds, life experiences and ages ever become a family at all? I did not have the answers, but I knew Someone who did.

So I began slipping out of the bedroom at dawn while Len and the children were asleep for a quiet time of talking-things-over prayers, Bible reading and writing down thoughts in the ever-present journal. For example:

> Our very first step in solving family problems is resolutely to view our particular difficulties as God's schoolroom for the truths He longs to teach us and the immense riches of His glory He wants to pour into our lives—if only we will let Him. He's going to have to be our Teacher all the way. What's required of us is the open-mindedness of the eager learner, plus taking the time day by day to submit practical questions to Him.

During those early morning times there dawned the realization of something I had not wanted to face: Len was one of those men who felt that his wife was more "spiritual" than he, that she somehow had more Christian know-how. Len liked to point out that I was more articulate in prayer. He was assuming, therefore, that I would take charge of spiritual matters in our home while he handled disciplining the children, finances and so forth.

I already knew from my mail how many, many women there are who find it difficult even to talk with their husbands about anything religious, much less look to them for leadership in this area. How could I make Len see that "spirituality" was as much his responsibility as mine?

Lord, what do I do about this one? I hurled heavenward.

Somehow the answer was given me that nagging a man about this would not work. My directive was to go on morning by morning with my quiet time, saying nothing about it but otherwise refusing to accept the spiritual responsibility for the home. The assurance was given me that then God would work it out.

Meanwhile, how desperately I needed that early time with Him! I had been transplanted from metropolitan Washington to typical suburbia, U.S.A. Chappaqua was and still is a sprawling Westchester County community nicknamed "the bedroom of New York

City." Every weekday Len and most of the other Chappaqua men caught early morning trains to the city, arriving back in the evening at a weary 6:45 or later. During these long days, the women had to carry all family responsibilities, including seemingly endless chauffeuring of children.

A typical morning for me was this one: A loud yelp from the boys' bedroom took me there on the run. Chester was rubbing his leg. "Jeff bit me!" Sure enough, there were teeth marks on Chester's leg.

"You're going to be punished for this," I told Jeff sternly.

"But Chester kicked me first. Want to see where?"

I really didn't, but Jeff showed me anyway.

At that moment Linda appeared in the hallway in her night clothes, her feet bare.

"Linda, the floor is cold. Put on your slippers."

"Can't, Mom. Can't get my feet in. The washing machine shrank them."

Obviously it was to be "one of those mornings." I went to the kitchen to start breakfast and fix Chester's school lunch. But I had not done my housework properly the night before: It was necessary to empty his lunch box before I could fill it. I extracted two packages of bubble gum, three rocks, a pack of well-thumbed baseball cards and a teacher's note that he had forgotten to deliver.

The doorbell rang with a special delivery letter. The telephone rang. Chester dropped jam on his freshly pressed school pants and had to change them. Peter, who was home between semesters at Yale, called out that he had a dental appointment in New York and couldn't find any clean undershorts. Linda and Chester dashed for the bus, banging the door behind them. Through the window, I saw that they had made it. I turned around to pour myself a second cup of coffee, and there on the kitchen counter was Chester's lunch. So-o-o, yet another errand.

I sank into the nearest chair, sorely needing that cup of coffee. As I sipped it, trying to get back some calmness and perspective, in my mind I was addressing the Almighty. *Lord, what is this about, anyway? When You put people together in families, just what did You really have in mind?*

Despite myself, I saw the humor in all this. *Lord Jesus, are You sure this family bit is not one of Your sneakier tricks? I mean, for hammering and chiseling and molding us into the characters You intend us to be?*

Then I remembered that during His time on earth, He Himself had to get along with at least six other children in a humble Nazareth household. What a comfort to know that He has experienced what families are up against, sympathizes and stands waiting and available with the wisdom and help we need.

Spiritual Head

s the days went by, Len was becoming curious about my early arising.

"What are you doing each morning?" he asked one day.

"Seeking God's answers for my day. I know He has them, but I have to ask Him, give Him the chance to give me His perspective and His practical helps."

"That would be good for me, too," was Len's reaction. "After all, we're in this together. Let's set the alarm thirty minutes earlier so that we can pray together."

Thus an experiment began that was to change our lives. The next day at a local hardware store I found an electric timer to plug into a small, four-cup coffeepot. That night I prepared the coffee tray at bedtime and carried it to the bedroom. The following morning we were wakened by the pleasant aroma of coffee rather than the shrill ringing of an alarm clock.

We drank our coffee, and I started to read at a spot in Philippians. But Len wanted to get on with the prayer.

"You start, Catherine," he said sleepily.

"But how are we going to pray about this problem of Linda's lack of motivation to study?" I asked.

A discussion began. It got so intense that time ran out before we got to actual prayer.

After a few mornings of this, Len agreed that we needed more time. Our wake-up hour went from 6:30 back to 6:00 A.M. Discipline in the morning meant going to bed earlier. It became a matter of priorities. The morning time together soon changed from an experiment to a shared adventure in prayer.

By this time Len, always methodical, had purchased himself a five-by-seven, brown loose-leaf notebook. He began jotting down the prayer requests, listing them by date. When the answers came, those, too, were recorded, also by date, together with how God had chosen to fill that particular need. Rapidly the notebook was becoming a real prayer log.

Not only that, but as husband and wife we had found a great way of communication. Bedtime, we had already learned, was a dangerous time to present controversial matters to one another. When we were fatigued from the wear and pressures of the day, disagreements could easily erupt. Yet when we tackled these same topics the next morning in an atmosphere of prayer, simply asking God for His wisdom about them, controversy dissolved, with communication flowing easily between us.

Of the hundreds of prayer requests in Len's brown notebook during this period, these were the most repeated:

1. That household help be found so that Catherine can continue the writing of her novel *Christy*.
2. That Peter will forget trying to be a playboy at Yale and find God's purpose for his life.
3. That Linda will stop rebelling against authority at home and at school.
4. That Chester will learn to control his temper and accept his new home situation.
5. That we can find the way to get Jeff out of diapers at night.

Morning by morning the requests from outside our home also piled up and up: a neighbor dying of cancer, a close friend involved in adultery, an associate with a drinking problem, parents we knew asking prayers for runaway children, and on and on. We were learning that specific prayer requests yield specific answers, all of them set down in the brown notebook.

I had tried to get help with Jeff's diaper problem from a pediatrician in nearby Mount Kisco. All that netted was: "Mrs. LeSourd"—and the doctor's voice was tinged with sarcasm—"forget it! He'll get over it before he goes to college."

What was the point of reminding this professional about the wasted time, the added daily washload of three to six diapers and sheets? Yet nothing we tried solved this puzzler.

That summer when we went to visit my parents at Evergreen Farm in Virginia, I felt an inner nudge to seek the homely advice of the local country practitioner.

After he had heard me out, the doctor, his eyes compassionate, said, "I meet the bed-wetting problem often and I sympathize. But Catherine, you've made it too easy for Jeffrey. Nothing's wrong except that he's simply too lazy to get up and go to the bathroom, too well-padded with too many soft diapers.

"So here's the solution I suggest: Waterproof the bed well. Take all diapers off. Steel yourself to let Jeff wallow in wet misery for a few nights.

"But temper that with praise and reward. Put a monthly chart marked off into days on the wall by his bed. Each morning Jeff makes it dry through the night, paste a big gold star on the chart and praise him lavishly."

It worked. And we thanked God and the country doctor for his humor and common sense.

But unless we had been recording and dating both the prayer requests and the answers, we might have assumed these to be "coincidences" or things that would have happened anyway. The prayer log was a marvelous stimulus to faith.

Len and I were certainly being taught about prayer as we submitted the practicalities of daily life to God.

For instance, not all prayers were answered the way we anticipated. We found that prayer is not handing God a want-list and having beautiful answers float down on rosy clouds. Also, His timing is certainly not ours; most answers came more slowly than we wished, and piecemeal. And what God had to say to us in our early morning times was even more important than what we presented to Him.

Out of His direction came some household rules:

1. Meals at regular hours and at least the evening meal eaten together as a family unit whenever possible. Dinner thus to be the focal point of each day. Each child soon learned to say a grace, was encouraged to articulate personal thoughts and needs. At the end of the meal Len or I read something from the Bible and then closed with prayer, again with each child participating, if only one sentence.
2. Regular bedtime, later on weekends.
3. No television for children on school nights. TV and movies on weekends carefully screened.
4. Linda's endless telephone conversations with friends to be limited to one stretch of time, 3:30 to 6 each afternoon. No twosome dates until she is 16.
5. Time reserved for the children on weekends for family outings and/or home games. (We kept a bulging closet of games.)
6. On Sundays go as a family to church.
7. Len and I to share checking on children's homework. Full interest and participation in the Parent-Teacher Association and school events.

8. Listen carefully to children's complaints about school matters, but stress that the teacher's and principal's authority always to be upheld.
9. Discipline always to be part of our life together; punishment to fit the crime; spankings (administered by Len) by no means ruled out.

The implementation of all this was never easy. In the seventh grade, Linda was bright and freckle-faced with all the instincts of a tragic actress. Like her peers, she was trying to grow up too soon. Len and I became accustomed to the cry "You just don't understand!"

Naturally during those early years the majority of our notations in the prayer log focused on our children. In rearing them, we were gradually learning that God was more interested in our cultivating the patience to wait for His answers than in our rushing ahead of Him with schemes we had devised.

Patience? What could be better calculated to teach patience than trying to drum manners and tidiness into the children? Before dinner on three nights out of five: "Boys, you call those hands clean?" "Jeff, elbows off the table." "Chester, it's no good trying to hide the carrots under the lettuce leaf." From Len: "Linda, are you trying to use your hair for dental floss? Take your hair out of your mouth."

So much practice in forgiveness! There was the matter of Jeffrey repeatedly leaving ink cartridges in his pants pocket and ruining an entire tub of laundry. Each time I put away the family wash, every white garment had the navy-blue measles. Forgiveness. Forgiveness!

Then there was Chester's forgetfulness. He could not wear his P.F. Flyers because he had left them at the public tennis courts; his sweater was abandoned at Donn's house; it was impossible to do his assignment because he had left his book at school.

Late one afternoon I glanced out one of the front windows and did a double-take at Linda kneeling in the newly planted rock garden. My mind refused to believe what my eyes were seeing. Carefully, methodically, she was dragging, first on one side, then the other, newly purchased white sneakers through the garden dirt. My indignant protest brought only a withering "Mom, everyone wears dirty sneakers. I can't go to school in new white ones."

And there was Jeffrey's strange fascination with, of all things, shoelaces. One morning in nursery school the teacher asked him to stand up and recite. Jeff tried to struggle to his feet; he really did. But how could a guy straighten up when he had tied the laces of his Keds securely to his belt?

Then there was the afternoon I put him down for a nap. In no time disconsolate crying was issuing from the bedroom. I found Jeff trapped under the bed, his shoelaces woven in and out of the bedsprings, knotted over and over.

Yet through it all we learned that even though children resist discipline, all of them crave the security of firm structure and are confused and rudderless without it. Years later our children would be admitting that secretly they had been relieved at the way we had stood our ground with them.

Linda, as an older girl, would often comment, "I feel sorry for poor So-and-So. She can do anything she wants to. I think her parents just don't care."

As time went on, an especially significant answer to prayer was unfolding before me—my plea that Len would assume his proper role as the spiritual head of our home.

His first insight was the realization that the two boys were going to pattern almost everything after him. This was obvious with something like athletics. Len had begun teaching his sons to swing a baseball bat as soon as they could lift it. He pored over the newspaper sports pages each morning. As soon as Chester and Jeff could read, they, too, were studying the sports pages.

If the Christian faith was to become important to them, he realized, it would happen through their father. Otherwise the two boys would conclude that religion was for the womenfolk and ignore it.

With this revelation, Len did an about-face on turning spiritual matters over to me. He became the one to call the family together for prayer around the table. As the boys witnessed their father praying spontaneously and were called on to follow, they were soon responding, praying aloud with no self-consciousness.

One evening we went to dinner at a crowded restaurant. I had just picked up my fork when Chester remarked quietly, "In school today our teacher was talking about saying grace before meals. He said that we should not skip doing this even when we're eating out."

There was a pause during which Len and I looked at one another.

Len nodded in agreement. "Your teacher was absolutely right, Chester. We should have done that all along."

Around the table we inclined our heads slightly. In a low-key voice Len thanked God for the food. Jeff's chatter started as soon as the soft *Amen* was out of his father's mouth.

We thought we had been exceptionally unobtrusive in the crowded dining room. But when the meal was over a nice-looking young man approached Len, leaned over, spoke several sentences for his ear alone, smiled and left.

"What was that all about?" I asked curiously.

Len was looking bemused. "The man wanted me to know that he thought it was great for a family not to be ashamed to pray in public. I feel I've been given credit for something I don't deserve."

So part of the beautiful answer to this prayer, I sat there thinking, is that Len himself does not realize how far he's come. As he

became the spiritual head of the household, I was given the freedom to play the supporting role, as I had in my marriage to Peter.
In no way did I consider this a secondary role. Len and I continued as a team, checking and sometimes correcting each other. But
the team captain was my husband.

SECTION FIVE

Schoolteacher

During our courtship Catherine had told me a little about the novel she was writing based on her mother's experience as a nineteen-year-old schoolteacher in the Great Smokey Mountains of Tennessee. Although her mother's name was Leonora Wood, Catherine had titled the main character and the novel *Christy*.

"I've never written much fiction," Catherine confessed. "Have you?"

"Not really," I admitted. "But I know something of the techniques."

A few weeks after our marriage Catherine handed me the first 52 pages of the *Christy* manuscript. I read it with a sinking feeling. It contained good descriptions, the mountain people were colorful, but no action. The characters were not

137

confronting each other. Catherine's research was painfully evident in the dialogue, which was hard to decipher.

Our writer-editor relationship was to be tested early, I concluded. Should I be honest? Or tell her what she wanted to hear?

Drawing a deep breath, I pointed out the pluses in her work, but also what it lacked. Catherine didn't like criticism (who does?), but she was a professional. After an intense dialogue, she agreed that drastic changes were needed.

A perfectionist, she rewrote the first chapter of *Christy* eighteen times. Later she said, "Thank you for being honest. We could never work together if you weren't."

Christy, a first-person novel, was a learning experience for Catherine. (It took her nine years from the day she began her research in 1958 until publication day in 1967.) A learning time, too, for me and Elizabeth Sherrill, her editors. *Christy* became an immediate bestseller and has gone on to sell over 8,000,000 copies worldwide.

Smells

very Monday morning handed me problems in schoolteaching for which no teacher's training course could ever have prepared me. First of all, strangely enough, were the smells. What was I to do about the body odors of children who were disinclined to take any baths during the cold months; who, if they owned any underwear, usually had it sewn on for the winter?

Whenever my pupils and I could stand the cold, we would conduct school with as many windows up as possible. That helped. But on some days the wintry blasts sweeping down from the mountains would whistle through the Cove, shaking the frame building as if it had been a rat in the teeth of some giant terrier, quivering the timbers, shivering us, making it impossible to open the windows.

Of a morning while I was dressing, I came to recognize these bad days by the truculent whistling of the wind: We would have to huddle close to the stove that day. So I would prepare by carrying up my sleeve a handkerchief saturated with perfume. Then when one of my more difficult pupils had to be near me to recite, I could always pull the handkerchief out and dab at my nose. I hoped that none of the children guessed my strategy.

Over and over I rued that too-sensitive nose of mine. Many an evening in my bedroom as I was preparing the next day's lessons, some incident would rise to haunt me: how I had backed away from Larmie Holt when I should have hovered close to check his work. There had been that certain look in the child's eyes, puzzled, a little hurt. Larmie had not understood. How could he!

Then I would chew my pencil and walk the floor pondering my dilemma. I wondered how others trapped in similar situations had managed. All those foreign missionaries, hundreds of them, must have had it far worse than I. Yet I had never heard any returned missionary speak of grappling with poor sanitation and uncleanliness. Perhaps they considered it too delicate a subject to discuss.

Then, in desperation, I would feel like crying out, "O God, it might be funny, but it isn't, really it isn't. Ple-ease—change my nose, or help me get the children cleaned up in a hurry."

This led directly to the idea of including a hygiene or health lesson in each day's curriculum. I sent to Asheville for several hygiene textbooks. These gave me lots of material.

One day we would talk about the skin, how the body got rid of waste through the pores and the necessity of washing perspiration and sloughed-off cells off the skin. But then we had to get down to practical points about *how* to bathe, since most of my pupils had only a granite tub or pan to use in front of the open fire, and even that was not easy with a large family in a one- or two-room cabin.

Another day the lesson would be about pure drinking water, the dangers of typhoid and hookworm and how to keep a spring clean. It was then I discovered how often the children would go to the bathroom in a mountain stream, and I realized that I had to forget prudishness and speak candidly.

In addition, as I saw how closely the children watched "Teacher," how much they wanted to be like me and in how many ways they were copying me, I tried to be more meticulous about grooming than I had ever been, wearing freshly starched and ironed shirtwaists, always keeping my hair clean and shining.

I hoped that some of this effort would rub off on my pupils—and it did. Soon Lizette Holcombe, Bessie Coburn, Ruby Mae and Clara Spencer were asking me if they could take a bath or wash and iron clothes in the mission house. Since Miss Ida did not take too kindly to this, my room had to be the scene for most of this activity. And when the girls would comment wistfully, "Teacher, you smell so good," I furthered my crusade by keeping a can of violet-scented talc on hand just for them.

Then, as time went on, I made an amazing discovery: The odors ("funks," as my children said, using a sturdy Shakespearean word) were no longer so much of a problem for me. It was not that my hygiene lessons had yet made that much difference, nor that I had grown accustomed to the smells, because in other situations my crazy nose bothered me as much as always.

It was rather that as I came to know the children and think of them as persons rather than names in my grade book, I forgot my reactions and began to love them. I suppose the principle was that the higher affection will always expel the lower whenever we give the higher affection sway. For me, it was letting love for the mountain children come in the front door while my preoccupation with bad smells crept out the rathole.

A problem of a different sort was the plight of those pupils who were far behind their age group in everything. It was not fair that a big boy like Lundy Taylor should have to recite in the primer class with six-year-olds just because he had never before been in school.

But I felt equally sorry about a child like Mountie O'Teale whose real problem was the O'Teale family home. When Mountie tried to speak, she showed a serious speech defect—halted gruntings and croakings like an animal—more like a three- or four-year-old than a ten-year-old.

Also, Mountie wore hand-me-down clothes and her hair was rarely combed. And the little girl never smiled or laughed or showed any emotion whatever. She seemed so dead inside that I could not be sure there was any possibility of helping her.

Then one afternoon I caught Creed Allen and her own brother Smith teasing her. On the playground they bent a sycamore sapling into a bow, lured her by, then released the branch to hit her in the face. It hurt, and when she started crying, they chanted in unison,

> Mush-mouthed Millie,
> Can't even speak,
> Jabber jabber jaybird
> Marbles in the beak.

"Look at her blubber, bawlin' her eyes out. Dare you t' blab to Teacher," I heard them stage-whisper to taunt her. "Only Teacher couldn't understand you if'n you did blab. Cotton-mouth!"

Since I was trying not to interfere too often on the playground, I waited to see what would happen. No, Mountie did not tell on the boys, but I looked at her and saw misery staring out of her eyes. So she *was* able to feel, feel deeply. Suddenly I glimpsed real intelligence buried behind the wall she had put up to ward off more hurt. There was just a chance that Mountie might turn out to be the white lamb of the O'Teale family. But what to do for her? How to begin?

It may be that my wondering and pondering, and the fact that now I really wanted to help Mountie, constituted a sort of prayer. Prayer (that is, the kind that asks for idea-help with some particular problem life hands you) was still new to me.

However that may be, later on that day, as I was standing before my front bedroom window letting my eyes drink in "my view," the clear thought came to me: Watch for an opportunity to do something special for Mountie O'Teale, something that will please her.

The chance came the next day. For the first time, I noticed that the shabby coat the little girl always wore to school had no buttons. So during recess I dashed over to the mission house, selected some large buttons from Miss Ida's button box, along with needle and thread. As I ate my lunch, I sewed on the buttons, then carefully hung Mountie's coat back on the peg at the back of the room where I had found it.

After school was dismissed, while I was straightening my desk, suddenly I heard a giggle at the back of the room. I looked up and saw that it was Mountie.

"Mountie, what's funny?"

She came bouncing up to my desk, pointing to the buttons, stood there, gleeful and excited. "Look at my buttons! Look at my buttons!"

"Mountie, what did you say?"

"Teacher, look! Look at my buttons! See my pretty buttons!"

I could scarcely believe what I was hearing. In spite of the chortling, the giggles up and down the scale, the child was speaking plainly for the first time. It was like watching something open up inside her. I felt triumphant for her and left school so excited that I wanted to tell everyone about it.

That night as I pondered this breakthrough, the thought came that Mountie's speech defect just might have an emotional base. Perhaps what she needed most of all was to be sure that she was a real person, that someone loved her for herself.

For two days I wondered how best to demonstrate that to her. Finally I decided to give her a gift—that bright red scarf my mother had knitted for me. This had to be presented privately after school the next day so that the other girls would not be envious. The scarf was meant to tell Mountie that she was a very special person to me.

It conveyed the message, all right. This time she not only laughed delightedly but hugged and hugged me, did an impromptu dance up and down the schoolroom, waving the scarf. Then we practiced over and over, "See my buttons." "I like the scarf." "Pretty scarf."

"Oh, pretty red scarf." And the child's heart and mind opened up some more.

With every bit of encouragement Mountie received, with each time I could tell her she was doing better, she would try even harder. Teacher cared about her. Teacher loved her. Did she not have the buttons and the scarf to prove it?

Now that the little girl's mind was released, it could function. Mountie O'Teale's reading ability grew astonishingly fast. Later on that year, I gave all my pupils reading tests. I could scarcely believe my own grades when the results showed that in her age group, Mountie had come out highest of all.

Of course, the speech defect was by no means over; the emotional blocks went too deep. But astonishing progress was being made. And this little girl was teaching me a lot about what an adventure schoolteaching is—and, more, that what these children needed most was love instead of lives governed by fear and hate. The adults, hanging onto hatred in the name of virtue, were reaping a bitter harvest in their children.

Part of the harvest was a morbid preoccupation with the negatives of life: sickness, death and dying. An obsession with death was typical of most of the children. This came out in their play.

"Let's Play Funeral" was a favorite game at recess. To me, it seemed bizarre and mawkish play. All that saved it was the spontaneous creativity of the children and the fact that, unerringly, they caught the incongruities and absurdities of their elders.

One child would be elected to be "dead" and would lay himself out on the ground, eyes closed, hands dutifully crossed over his chest. Another would be chosen to be the "preacher"; all the rest, "mourners." I remember one day when Sam Houston Holcombe was the "corpse" and Creed Allen, always the clown of the group, was elected "preacher." Creed, already at ten an accomplished mimic, was turning in an outstanding performance. I stood watching, half-hidden in the shadow of the doorway.

Creed (bellowing in stentorian tones): "You-all had better stop your meanness and I'll tell you for why. Praise the Lord! If you'uns don't stop being so derned ornery, you ain't never goin' to git to see Brother Holcombe on them streets paved with rubies and suchlike, to give him the time of day, 'cause you'uns are goin' to be laid out on the coolin' board and then roasted in hellfire."

The congregation shivered with delight, as if they were hearing a deliciously scary ghost story. The corpse opened one eye to see how his mourners were taking this blast; he sighed contentedly at their palpitations; wriggled right leg where a fly was tickling; adjusted grubby hands more comfortably across chest.

Creed then grasped his right ear with his right hand and spat. Only there wasn't enough to make the stream impressive. So preacher paused, working his mouth vigorously, trying to collect more spit. Another pucker and heave. Ah, better!

Sermon now resumed: "Friends and neighbors, we air lookin' on Brother Holcombe's face for the last time. [Impressive pause.] Praise the Lord! We ain't never goin' see him again in this life. [Another pause.] Praise the Lord!"

Small preacher was now really getting warmed up. He remembered something he must have heard at the last real funeral. Hefty spit first, more pulling of ear. "You air enjoyin' life now, folks. Me, I used to git pleasured and enjoy life, too. But now that I've got religion, I don't enjoy life no more."

At this point I retreated behind the door lest I betray my presence by laughing aloud.

"And now let us all sing our departed brother's favorite song:

> I'm as free a little bird as I can be,
> I'll build a nest in a weeping willow tree. . . ."

And then later: "Now all of you'uns gather 'round and see how nateral Brother Holcombe looks."

Now it was the mourners' chance for action, mostly the girls. Much screeching, groaning and moaning followed; they pantomimed throwing themselves, sobbing, on the coffin and talking to the dead person.

"Ah, Lordy, he be a sweet bouquet in heaven," someone shouted.

Suddenly from somewhere in the middle of the huddle, the corpse's booming voice was heard: "Stop it, yer ticklin' me. Ground's too hard anyway. Lemme go. I ain't no sweet bouquet in heaven yit. I'm a-gittin' out of here."

The Hunger for Touch

fter I had been teaching for a while, I began to realize how hungry my pupils were for love expressed in physical contact. They were forever reaching for me, touching me, squeezing me—like Little Burl, on my first day of teaching, coming up again and again to my desk to crowd his little body close to mine and trace the embroidery on my shirtwaist with a stubby forefinger.

At first I had not realized the significance of this yearning for touch, even as I had not known how far into childhood the need for physical contact is carried. But then I stumbled onto the link between the need for touch and a child's ability to learn. Three of my beginners, Jake and Larmie Holt and Mary O'Teale, were having a great deal of trouble learning to read. When I would take them one by one on my lap and give them a lesson, they learned twice as fast. Loving them up seemed to remove blocks, just as it had with Mountie.

Naturally, with 67 pupils in all grades to teach, it was hard to find time for such individual attention. Nor did it seem right to give most of my time to the dull, slow children rather than to the bright ones. Part of this I solved by appointing Junior Teachers to help me. These were my oldest and best pupils like Bob Allen, John

Spencer, Lizette and John Holcombe. They in turn profited from the experience of teaching the younger ones.

In no time at all, being appointed a Junior Teacher became the most coveted honor in school. So much so that I had to design a special badge for these children to wear: a piece of heavy cloth cut in the shape of a shield, each one trimmed differently with bits of fancy braids or beading or shiny buttons or sequins off the dresses in the mission barrels.

Recess provided me with another way of trying to appease this hunger for touch with several children at once. Whenever I would go out on the playground, my littlest ones would swarm to me, each wanting to hold onto a finger.

Gradually the "Finger Game" evolved. Ten children could play, five on each side of me, each holding onto one finger. But in order not to get tangled in one another's legs, fall down and break one of Teacher's fingers in the process, we had to march close together with me at the center of the flying wedge, each child with one hand on the child in front, in a lock-step with perfect rhythm and coordination. If one of the ten got out of step, then all of us fell in a heap. But whether we marched perfectly or whether we tumbled, always there would be gales of laughter.

The Finger Game proved to be perfect for teaching a first lesson in working together in order to live together happily. I was at that time still too new to the Cove to realize how desperately the lesson was needed by the parents of the children, too. For cooperation beyond the immediate family unit came hard to the highlanders.

It was at that point that they showed rather more of their highland Scottish heritage than the typical American frontier pattern. For I had always supposed that in frontier days a high degree of neighborliness and cooperation had been necessary for survival: the "workings" for building cabins or barns, for clearing land and harvesting crops; the drawing together into stockades for protection against Indian attacks; the relay system in pushing westward.

But in the mountains, though there were still a few workings, many factors, including the terrain itself, the isolated coves and the difficulty of travel, bred a self-contained individualism. Set down in its own hollow, each household had to depend on itself—and did. The Cove people were suspicious about joining any group effort or organization. Sometimes I wondered if they yet considered themselves to have joined the United States of America.

Trying to get work done for the school or mission was often like trying to move mountains by shoving against the mountain with one's shoulder. As I struggled to like, much less love, some of the worst of these individualists who wanted no part of accepting anyone's ideas or leadership, I comforted myself with the thought that "Oh well, it's certainly my privilege not to like everyone."

It was Little Burl, of all people, who helped me understand that, rather, it was my privilege to try to like everyone—at least to make an effort to see the good in each individual.

One morning we had interrupted our spelling lesson to watch the birds at our school feeding station. At my suggestion, Mr. Spencer had built this for us and placed it atop a pole close to one of the schoolroom windows. As spring approached, a greater and greater variety of birds were appearing. My pupils were fascinated. This morning we had seen several juncos and some titmice. Now a pair of cardinals, the male with the most brilliant red feathers I had ever seen on a bird, were stuffing themselves on the crumbs and sunflower seeds.

Looking at that glorious red plumage, I exclaimed, "Isn't it great how many different kinds of birds there are, each one so special! God must have cared about them or He wouldn't have made them so beautiful."

Then I couldn't help adding, "He loves everything He's made—every bird, every animal, every flower, every man and woman, every single one of you—loves you extra specially."

Little Burl was not working on spelling at all, but sitting at his desk staring up at the ceiling, his cowlick standing straight up, his funny little face puckered into a look of intense concentration. Something I had said had made an impression on him; I hoped he would let me in on his secret thought.

I had reached down to get fresh papers out of my desk drawer when I felt arms around my neck hugging me fiercely. It was Little Burl. He put his bare feet on top of my larger ones, locked his two hands behind my neck, stretched his head up to look me full in the eyes.

"Teacher, Teacher, hain't it true, Teacher, that if God loves ever'body, then we'uns got to love ever'body, too?"

I looked at the six-year-old in astonishment. "Yes, Little Burl, it is true." Forever and forever and forever.

So once I shut down my privilege of disliking anyone I chose and holding myself aloof if I could manage it, greater understanding and growing compassion came to me, more love for the children and, as time passed, for the older people, too. And suddenly I woke to the fact that smells in the schoolroom no longer seemed a problem.

Troublemaker

It was never clear which of the boys had put marbles in the stove, then scattered them on the floor hoping a barefoot student would step on them and get a hot foot. I suspected Lundy Taylor who, older and bigger than all the other children, was bored by school and constantly creating disturbances.

Then there was the time I went over to the stove to poke up the fire. I had no sooner opened the iron grating and thrust the poker in than a series of explosions like a gun going off spit sparks and flames into my face and onto my hair and dress. With an involuntary cry I backed away, slapping at the sparks.

Ruby Mae, who was sitting in the nearest seat, rushed to me, frantically raking burning pieces of something out of my hair. When we had finally gotten all the tiny conflagrations stamped out, I saw that there were several scorched places and burned holes in my dress, and the way one place on my neck was stinging, I knew it must be burned.

I stood there with flushed face and disheveled hair looking at my schoolroom, so flustered that for a moment I could not trust myself to speak. Finally with a shaking voice I asked, "What was it that exploded?"

There was a long silence. Some of the children would not look at me. Finally Joshua Bean Beck spoke up. "Hit be buckeyes,

151

ma'am. Buckeyes in the ashes. They git hot and then pop and fly all t' pieces when the air hits 'em."

I was opening my mouth for the next obvious question but Joshua Bean was ahead of me. "No, ma'am, Teacher. I wouldn't do that to ye. Not me, Teacher."

I heard a torrent of angry words start to pour out of my own mouth. I bit my lip, choked back the words. In an effort to get control of myself I whirled to the blackboard to get on with the writing of the spelling words that the buckeye trick had interrupted.

But I had written only a few words when a steady noise at the back of the room penetrated my tortured thoughts. I whirled just in time to see Lundy stalking down the aisle, poking a stick into Mountie O'Teale's back, loudly "He-heeing" as he went.

It was deliberate defiance. The sneer on his face and the shifty look in his eyes made me suspect that he was the one responsible for the buckeyes. Yet of course I could not be sure.

"Lundy," I said with an immense effort to speak calmly, "stop that and get back to your seat."

The huge boy stood there gawking at me, stick in his hand, his mouth slack, his eyes empty. Then fire leapt to his eyes.

"No gal-woman's goin' tell me what to do," he snarled. "I'll stop when I'm good and ready."

Momentarily I was startled, then fury took over. The storm inside gave me a courage I would not ordinarily have had. I walked rapidly down the aisle toward the sneering face. The fact that the boy towered at least a head above me mattered not at all now.

"You'll stop when I tell you to," I said, almost shrieking, "and I'm telling you right now."

Then I reached up and grabbed his shock of hair with all the strength I had, dragged him down and shook him as I shoved him into the nearest seat.

The yank of the hair took Lundy by surprise. His watery blue eyes blinked back tears. But then the next moment he was standing up, his fist doubled as if to fight me back. Most of the children were on their feet now. I could feel John Spencer close to me trying to force his body between Lundy and me.

"Lundy-stay-right-there-in-your-seat!" A stern masculine voice spoke from the doorway. It was David Grantland who had arrived for the mathematics lessons. "One more word out of you, and I'm the one you'll fight," he added.

The boy slunk down immediately. Then I could feel David's eyes riveted to my face. Now that the immediate crisis was over, suddenly I was shaking all over.

The next instant David was by my side propelling me to the front of the room.

"Sit down," he whispered. "I'll take over for awhile now. We'll settle with Lundy later."

That week Lundy Taylor did not come back to school. By the second week gossip began to reach me that Lundy's father, Bird's-Eye Taylor, had taken my jerking his son by the hair as an affront to the Taylor clan and was busy plotting revenge for the new "brought-on" teacher. Though I did not believe this, still, the object of discipline was not to alienate pupils from the school. So as one day followed another and Lundy did not appear, I knew that I was going to have to wade into this misunderstanding—and I dreaded it.

One morning my redheaded shadow, Ruby Mae, was waiting for me. "Teacher, ye're in for trouble with Bird's-Eye. More trouble than ever ye saw in all your born days."

It was a beautiful sunshiny day, much too nice to talk about problems. "What kind of trouble?" I asked unconcernedly.

Ruby Mae hugged herself with both arms and shivered. "Don't know what kind. But he's the awfulest man. Don't take nothin' off nobody."

"But I've never even seen Mr. Taylor."

"Ye seen his son right enough, the way ye yanked Lundy's hair most right out'n his head."

"Lundy deserved it. Probably if we only knew, his father is relieved that somebody could finally discipline Lundy."

Ruby Mae looked at me as if I were a freak. "Y'mean ye ain't scairt?"

"No, I'm not scared."

"But Teacher, his hair or his son's hair, don't make a particle of difference to Bird's-Eye. Talk is that he's sore as a skinned owl at you and is planning his re-venge."

"And my talk is that I think you're getting a big whiz-bang out of exaggerating the whole thing."

Ruby Mae was nonplused at my frankness. Then she said slowly, "But ye see, Teacher, what happened in school ain't lost a bitty-bit in the tellin'."

"I'm sure it hasn't. That's the trouble. And you be careful that you don't—"

"No'm, I won't. But I'm a-feared Mr. Taylor has heerd that ye did things that ye didn't do."

"Oh, I'm beginning to see."

"Yes'm. And he has his head set to believe what ain't true."

"Then that decides it. I'm going to have to go see him and tell him what is true."

Real consternation now constricted Ruby Mae's freckled face. "Oh, no'm, you mustn't do that! Not on yer life, ye mustn't. Teacher, you couldn't stand that man off. He be fractious. He's been known to spill mortal gorm. And them as he don't want t'kill, he may take a notion to rock."

"Rock? You mean he throws stones at them?"

"Yes'm, and if the rock jest happens t' hit a mortal spot, then hit be the rock's fault."

Her face showed that she did not think this funny.

"Ruby Mae, you're a chatterbox for sure. You talk and talk and I haven't the least idea what to take seriously."

She grinned at me. "It's true, Teacher. My mouth don't open jest for feedin' baby birds. But pleas'm, don't ever go to nobody's cabin 'round here without stoppin' at the edge of the yard and hollerin'. Ye should take that serious."

"That a custom in the cove?"

"Well'm, not a custom, exactly. It's jest that if'n ye don't holler, ye mought git shot at."

I could forget all of Ruby Mae's jabber, but if I was going to keep my promise to give school my all, then I could not forget the Lundy matter. Apparently there was no way to resolve it except by seeking out Mr. Taylor.

A Visit to Bird's-Eye

he Bird's-Eye Taylor cabin was the most isolated and freakishly placed one I had seen so far. It had been built between twin shelves of rock planes forming the top of a small mountain and it looked more like a fortress than a home. So steep was the final ascent that I tethered my horse to a tree two hundred feet or so below the cabin to climb the rest of the way on foot. But I paused first to "Hallo" as Ruby Mae had advised.

There was no porch to this cabin perched like an eagle's nest on the rocks. From where I stood, it looked as if one stepped out the front door into space.

No sooner was the call out of my mouth than the doorway was filled with a man's figure, shotgun in hand. It was too quick; he had been watching me all the way up the mountain.

"I want to talk to you, Mr. Taylor," I called. "May I come up?"

"Come up, then," but it was said grudgingly.

The path was steep, hard-packed and slippery. As I came closer I saw that there was a level spot something over a yard wide in front of the door. Bird's-Eye Taylor was not as large a man as I had imagined. Of a different build from his son, he was not quite medium height and slight, though slim and erect. He was dressed in a dirty plaid flannel shirt above a pair of shabby trousers held up by galluses.

"I'm Christy Huddleston, the new teacher, Mr. Taylor." I tried to sound as if there was nothing unusual about this visit.

"What d' ye want with us?" The tone was churlish. The eyes looking into mine were watery blue, hard eyes. A slit of a mouth was set in the grizzled face that had not known a razor in days. He was wearing a felt hat with the brim turned down all around, holes in the top held together with a large safety pin.

"Just wanted to meet you, Mr. Taylor. And talk to you about Lundy. We've been missing him at school. We wondered why."

"Ye know why."

"May I come in?"

"Ain't no place fer a woman. Jest Lundy and me here."

"I know. I understand. But I'd like to talk to you."

He seemed surprised at my persistence in the face of his deliberate coldness, but finally moved to one side. "Come in and set then." For the first time I saw Lundy standing behind his father.

The interior of the building was tiny and seemed more like a cave than a cabin. There was a fieldstone chimney at the back with black pots on cranes, no cookstove in sight. I had the impression that somewhere in the walls there might be an entrance to a cave under the rock ledges. The room was furnished with only bare essentials and had not been cleaned for a long time.

With one foot, Mr. Taylor pushed a straight chair across the floor lazily in my direction, then sat down on another beside the one table.

"Hello, Lundy." I tried to put as much warmth as possible into my voice. The hulk of a boy so much larger than his father had still not moved from Mr. Taylor's side. "When are you coming back to school?"

"Dunno."

The slits of eyes were ogling me so that I felt as if he were undressing me. For the first time I was afraid and realized how foolish I had been to place myself in such a defenseless position. What was worse, no one at the mission knew where I was.

"Mought as well tell ye," Mr. Taylor said, "don't confidence women teachers none."

How was I to answer that?

I started in lamely, "Mr. Taylor, I know you must want Lundy to have some schooling so he can get on in life. I'm not the best teacher in the world. But I think I can teach Lundy something."

He ignored my speech, rubbing his hand over his stubbled chin. "Want t' whop my young'uns my own self. Don't want no gal-woman a-doin' it."

"Mr. Taylor, I didn't whip Lundy."

"Didn't hide him?"

"No, I didn't. Lundy is bigger than I am. How do you think I could whip him?"

Lundy was sidling toward the door. His father's hand shot out to whack at him but the boy ducked. "Consarned fool. Ye lied to t' me."

"Ah, Pap, I jest—"

"I'm a-goin' t' ketch a-hold of ye and smoke yer britches till the fire catches."

But Lundy was already out the door.

"Don't be too hard on him, Mr. Taylor. Lundy was testing me out, that's all. I have had a little trouble with him talking and wandering around the room, changing seats and playing mean tricks on younger pupils. Finally I had to talk sternly to him. And I did jerk him by the hair."

For the first time there was something close to a thaw on Bird's-Eye Taylor's face. He did not seem to think yanking Lundy's hair such a bad idea.

"Lundy will be all right. I hope you'll send him back."

"Oh, law! Dunno if schoolin's any use to Lundy. He may be twit-ter-witted. His maw was."

Cautiously I asked, "How do you mean, Mr. Taylor?"

"His maw was fitified and addlepated. Acrost the line in North Carolina that was. Pulled out from thar. That's why I'm a-raisin' Lundy."

"I see. Well then, seems to me you need help. That's what the mission's here for—to help."

"Ye can't squeeze milk out'n a flint rock."

"No, but don't give up on Lundy. He can learn."

"Maybe. Maybe not. Look-a-here, churches and their goin's-on ain't fer us. Always been a sinner myself. Ain't never been no hypo-crite, though. Never lied to the Lord. Ain't no sech can enter the king-dom of heaven. Course I know that ain't the edzact words."

"But I'm a sinner, too. Everybody is. As I understand it, that's what church is all about—to save sinners."

"Don't want savin'. Always been a sinner. Always will be. I dis-gust churches."

There seemed little point in pursuing this. "Mr. Taylor, I'd bet-ter be going. You'll send Lundy back to school, then?"

"I'll study on it."

"And drop by the mission house yourself sometime. We'd like to be friends."

He did not respond to that, but then said slowly, "I ain't got no rocks to throw at nobody."

What a queer comment, I thought. Then I remembered what Ruby Mae had said about Bird's-Eye Taylor "rocking" his adversaries at times.

"Well, goodbye," I called over my shoulder, and I hurried down the slope as quickly as I dared. I had the feeling that somewhere nearby Lundy was spying on me from behind a bush or tree trunk, but I did not wait to find out.

More than a week went by. Then one day at school I looked up from my desk and there, to my astonishment, stood Lundy looking at me. "Could I clean the blackboard for ye, Teacher?"

He seemed like a new Lundy, not so sullen or obstructive. It was plain that his attitude toward me had changed. He looked at me differently; he came up to my desk as often as he dared; he hung around after dismissal time, talking and ogling.

I sensed the new Lundy would create a new problem for me.

Fairlight

There was a warm touch of spring in the air as I climbed the ridge to the Spencer cabin. The evergreens were tipped with vivid green, and the willows overhanging the streams were a whisper of green lace. Here and there in the fields of the valley, spicewood bushes waved yellow plumes.

It was a site that must have been chosen carefully by someone a long time ago. I felt almost on top of the world. Here with the silent gaze of the mountains upon me, trivialities and pettiness and meanness faded and dropped out of sight. Entering the Spencer cabin was like sticking one's nose into one of those souvenir pillows filled with balsam needles or cedar chips.

Mrs. Fairlight Spencer had arranged galax leaves in two old pewter bowls, the leaves mostly bronze and winey-red from the winter, here and there new green; and in a chipped cup she had put trillium and violets.

"The very first," she told me, and reached out slender fingers unself-consciously to caress the flowers. "The least'uns of the springtime."

The grace of the gesture and the long, tapering fingers (even though they were red and rough with chipped and broken nails) caught my attention. I stood there thinking that these should be the hands of a lady handling an ivory fan or smoothing her skirts

161

of velvet or satin. They were the hands of an aristocrat, and here they were on a mountain woman, buried at the back of beyond.

She was eager to show me everything, including an unusual quilt stretched on a quilting frame near the hearth. While examining the quilt, I saw it was not the commonplace hit-and-miss patchwork, but a moon-and-star motif. When I asked Mrs. Spencer about it, she pointed to a small window set high in the wall to the right of the fireplace.

"See that lookout? I get a heap of joy from that. When I'm lonesome-like, it perts me up to look up there and see the sun-ball or the moon and stars. So thrice one night I drawed me an idea—three picture-pretties of the new moon and a star."

I looked at her in astonishment. "Mrs. Spencer, you mean you drew a picture of the new moon at three different positions and then copied that onto your quilt?"

She nodded. "Weren't much work. Seems right nice to have the starry heavens on my counterpin."

Then her expression changed. "Look-a-here—you've never handled a school afore. That's a heap of young'uns for one gal-woman. Is there anything I can do to help, like clean up the school yard? I'm a good hand to work. Or wash some of your go-to-meetin' clothes? It's my turn to favor you now."

The words were spoken with a gentle dignity, as if a gift were being bestowed on me, as was indeed the case. Here was a mountain woman with a husband and five children to care for, living in such poverty that if she had any shoes, she was saving them to be worn outside the house, yet thinking of me. Even as I started to answer, I realized something else: There was more to this gracious offer than met the eye. Fairlight Spencer was not just volunteering to do some washing and ironing for me; she was also holding out to me the gift of her friendship.

"Mrs. Spencer, that's the nicest offer anyone has made me since I left home. You're right. Sixty-seven children are a handful and I do need help."

I paused, groping for words that had no condescension in them. "I'll accept your wonderful offer, if you'll let me be your friend. You see, Mrs. Spencer, I'm a long way from home. Sometimes I get lonesome for another woman to talk to. And maybe there'll be something I can do for you, too."

The face that in repose could look so spartan and pioneer was now wreathed in smiles. "Aye, you can holp, Miz Christy." Suddenly she was shy again, her voice sinking almost to a whisper. "I cain't read nor write. Would —you learn me how? I'd like that!"

The eagerness in her voice added such pathos that at that moment I wanted to teach this woman to read more than I'd ever wanted to do anything before. "I'd love doing that, Mrs. Spencer. Could you come down to the mission house, maybe Saturday?"

"For shore and sartin, I'll be there," she said joyously. "Oh, and would you—handle my front name, 'Fairlight'?"

On Saturday morning Fairlight arrived at the mission before we had finished breakfast. She was wearing a freshly laundered blue-checked gingham dress with a wide white collar and, this time, shoes. I took Fairlight over to the empty schoolhouse, where we started our lesson on two desks pulled side by side before an open window.

I had a box of materials ready and Fairlight was all eagerness to see what was in the box. From magazines I had cut out some pictures of landscapes to use for background scenery; some figures of men, women and children pasted onto cardboard bases so that they could be stood upright (as I used to do with my paper dolls when I was a very little girl); a copy of the alphabet printed in large, clear letters from my first-grade class; a Bible; a fresh ruled pad and some pencils.

Since teaching an adult to read was a new experience for me, I was not sure how to begin. It would not do, I felt, to downgrade the dignity of a human being like Fairlight Spencer by using the primer books for six- and seven-year-olds: "The rat ran from the cat." "Here the boy sat."

Then, too, I believed that Fairlight would learn more readily than the children, and I wanted to give her even in this first lesson the concept of words as ideas. And since I knew from having seen some of her quilt patterns and flower arrangements that she was a creative person, surely she would learn fastest if I could find an imaginative way to teach her. My problem was how to achieve this.

I picked up the Bible. "There are lots and lots of words in this book."

"How soon will I be able to read it, Miz Christy?"

"In no time! And I'll tell you why. Every single word in this book and all the words together use only 26 English letters—these here. So after you've learned just 26 and know how to put the letters together to form different words, then you can read. Easy!"

Her eyes shone. "I'd like that the best in the world." Already she was concentrating on that alphabet.

After we had read it aloud twice, she became so intent on learning it that she almost forgot I was there. So I sat back watching her, feeling instinctively that I should let her set the pace, even do most of the talking, if she would.

At last she sighed and looked at me. "Think I've got it—A, B, C, D," and on she went, making only one mistake.

Next we propped up a backdrop picture of a landscape drenched in sunlight. "Now, Fairlight, you pick out one of the paper people from this pile." So she selected a dapper-looking man and stood him up before the landscape.

We learned *man* and my eager pupil practiced saying it and form-ing the letters. Soon we went on to *tree, light, sun, grass, sky.*

It was at this point that Fairlight stumbled onto her own kind of phonetics—the relation between the way the word looked and how it sounded. She was as thrilled as if she had found a jewel in the dust. She rolled the word *sky* over and over her tongue, spelled it again and again. This went on until we had our first ten words.

Then I opened the Bible to the first chapter of Genesis. "Now, Fairlight, look at this. The words on this page are just ideas march-ing. Like this one: 'And God said, Let there be light—'"

"*L-i-g-h-t.* There it is! I see it." Her slender forefinger was on the word. "Oh, I love the light! Don't you? I hate the darkness."

Let there be light. . . . I sat there thinking that I had never seen light dawn so quickly for anyone as for this woman. What an alive mind she had! She scarcely needed instruction, only a chance to let the light come.

I was seeing more and more of Fairlight Spencer. Our friend-ship was a natural outgrowth of my teaching her.

What the record time is for learning to read, I do not know, but the prize probably belongs to Fairlight. Three long sessions accom-plished it. She "practiced" all the time, read everything imagin-able—the old newspapers pasted on the walls of the Spencer cabin, the pieces of a tattered dictionary, the family Bible, even the labels on jars and bottles. Within a few weeks, so far as reading was con-cerned, she had caught up with most of the pupils in my school and was borrowing books two or three at a time.

I wondered if Fairlight's family might not suffer; after all, they could not eat books. I need not have feared. The young Spencers' stomachs were too healthy and clamorous to stand for any neglect.

But Fairlight did invent ingenious ways to do her housework and read at the same time: a book propped on the windowsill while she was washing dishes; a book open on a chair at her side while she was churning or spinning or shelling shucky beans or stringing green beans.

In the beginning I had thought of teaching her to read as just another do-good project. (I admit it, to my shame.) But Fairlight soon changed that with the debt in her favor. Her return to me was, all unknowing, such priceless insights into her heart and spirit that in a few short weeks I had begun to love this mountain woman.

For example, she taught me something important about the use of time and how to enjoy life. With a husband and five children to cook, clean, wash, even make clothes for, and with no modern conveniences at all, not even piped-in water, Fairlight might have felt burdened and sorry for herself—but she did not. Often she found time to pause in her dishwashing to let her eyes and her spirit drink in the beauty of a sunset. She would interrupt her work to call the children and revel with them in the grandeur of thunderheads piling up over the mountain peaks, heat lightning flashing behind the clouds like fireworks.

"It lifts the heart," she would say, and that was explanation enough for any interruption.

There was always time for a story in front of the fire with the children snuggled against her; always leisure for the family to gather on the porch "to sing the moon up."

Fairlight told me how on the first fine spring day, she considered it only right and proper to drop her housework. "The house, it's already been a-settin' here for a hundred years. It'll be right here tomorrow. It's today I must be livin'"—and she would make her way to one particular spot she knew. There she would kneel, and with her long, slender fingers brush aside the dead, sodden leaves and gaze wonderingly on the first blossoms of the trailing arbutus. Knowing her as I did, I could picture her fairly crooning over the flowers.

She and I agreed that never had we known such delight at an end of winter, perhaps because it had been a drab one. Yet I was discovering that spring did not come suddenly in the mountains but on tiptoe, stealthily, with retreats and skirmishes, what Fairlight called "sarvice winter" and sometimes "redbud winter."

Still, the mountainsides were burgeoning at last and I was eager to explore them. Since Fairlight knew just where to take me, she and I were often in the woods, sometimes just the two of us, sometimes like a pair of female Pied Pipers with the Spencer children and some of my other pupils trailing along. They would race ahead of us swinging on the limbs of trees or on wild grapevines, "plumb crazy," as Fairlight would say, "cuttin' shines. Never did see such a doo-raw." Obviously my pupils considered all of Teacher's excursions "jollifications."

We were out so often that I began to question Fairlight about whether a proposed lesson or walk would interfere with her work. I can only remember twice when there were household tasks she could not interrupt lest something be spoilt. Her reply was more likely to be, "It's a fair day. Shorely we'uns can pass the time with one another." Then, more shyly, "Never have been with you enough, Miz Christy, to see my satisfaction yet."

The highlanders were often accused of being lazy and shiftless. As I got to know them better, my conclusion was: relaxed, yes; shiftless, a few of them; greedy, scarcely ever. Fairlight's "It's today I must be livin'" summed up their philosophy well, a philosophy that aggressive people would spurn.

Yet which is right? Human life is short. Each of us has a limited number of years. So are we going to go through those so-few years with little time for our family and friends and unseeing eyes for the beauties around us, concentrating on accumulating money and things when we have to leave them all behind anyway? I began to wonder if the mountain values were not more civilized than civilization's. At least I found the absence of greed and pushiness as refreshing as a long, cool drink of sparkling mountain spring water.

Now I realized why these mountain people were shy with strangers. They had never learned the citified arts of hiding feelings or of smiling when the heart is cold. Friendship was dangerous to them because they had built up no protection against it. Once they let you in it must be into the deep places of the heart, as Fairlight had with me. Though I had known her only four months, already I was far closer to her than to members of my own family or girlfriends I had always known.

Through Fairlight's eyes I came to know a quality of friendship that bore little resemblance to the casualness of our relationships back home. The mountain type of friendship was a tie of substance between people with a sort of gallant fealty about it. It had to do with a time in the past when there was no more final bond than a man's pledged word; when every connection of blood or oath was firm and strong, forged in the past, stretching into the future.

SECTION SIX

Guideposts Writer

When Catherine and I were married in 1959, she was the Women's Editor of *Christian Herald* magazine and I was the Executive Editor of *Guideposts*. I had been with *Guideposts* since 1946, working my way up from reporter to the top editorial position. In 1946 *Guideposts* had a few thousand subscribers; in 1960 we passed the one million mark.

There was an enchantment, an excitement, a joyous creativity about the *Guideposts* editorial meetings. One reason: the mix of people—young and old, liberal and conservative, black and white, Catholic, Protestant and Jew. Different viewpoints came together with one central focus: How can every page of *Guideposts* be helpful to the reader?

"What is the takeaway of this piece?" This oft-repeated question at meetings helped the writer decide exactly what he wanted the reader to receive from a particular article.

Some meetings we brainstormed ideas for a new feature or a new series, a *Guideposts* book, a *Guideposts* Christmas card, a *Guideposts* film, on one occasion a *Guideposts* exhibit at the New York World's Fair.

For a while Catherine continued on as *Christian Herald's* Women's Editor, then was drawn irresistibly to *Guideposts* editorial sessions, developing lifelong friendships with editors John and Elizabeth Sherrill, Starr Jones, Van Varner, Glenn Kittler, Arthur Gordon, Sidney Fields, Dina Donohue, Fred Bauer and Art Director Sal Lazzarotti.

When Catherine became a roving editor for *Guideposts* in 1960, she developed her journalistic gifts in tracking down stories in many parts of the world. Here is a selection from the nearly fifty articles she wrote for the magazine.

The Protecting Power

(*Guideposts*, November 1966)

t is obvious that fear is growing each year among women in our country. Every week we read about some new violence to our sex. We are told what to do: keep away from dark streets, carry a squirtgun filled with ammonia in our purse, put special locks in our house or apartment and so on.

Some of these are wise precautions. Yet there are times when all the safeguards man can devise cannot stand between us and the raw evil loose in this world. At these times we need a surer protection—what is perhaps the only real protection we can have.

Let me tell you how this helped a friend of mine who lives near us in Florida.

On a bright, sunshiny morning last June, Jean Klinger started out in her car for Delray Beach to take her final Montessori teacher's examination. As she turned her car from Military Trail down Fourth Street, she noted the time on her watch. It was 8:50. Good: She would be at school by nine.

Fourth Street near Military Trail is a lonely stretch of road until it runs into the residential area. There are few houses; the terrain is dotted with farms and sand flats.

Just ahead of Jean Klinger was a light-colored pickup truck. It slowed down, then pulled over to the side of the road. An arm out the car window signaled to Mrs. Klinger to pull over, too. She did so instinctively, wondering if something was wrong with her car.

A big, burly man wearing a sport shirt open at the neck strode up to her window. "Lady, can you tell me how to get to Dixie Highway?"

Mrs. Klinger was unsuspecting. After all, it was broad daylight. "I'm so sorry. I don't live in Delray. I'm just on my way to school here. Afraid I can't give you directions."

The man was looking at her intently. He glanced about him, then suddenly jerked open the car door and pressed a hard metal object into Jean's back. As she sat there, paralyzed, he shoved her to one side and climbed in beside her.

Jean screamed and, reaching over, pressed hard on the horn. But there was not a car or pedestrian around, no one to hear.

"Don't try that again or I'll kill you," the man growled, pressing the metal object harder into her back. Fear, panic, terror washed in waves over her. . . .

Jean admits she has always had many fears. Sensitive, intense, vivacious, she feels deeply. Long ago she determined to face up to her fears and search for ways to eradicate them. Her search led her to God and asking for His help in freeing her from these shackles. She even dared to ask that in certain circumstances He would help her be willing to do the thing she feared.

At her church Bible class she confided to her instructor that she had not yet learned how to deal with her fears. The instructor gave her a copy of a prayer that became part of the fabric of Jean Klinger's life.

> The light of God surrounds me.
> The love of God enfolds me.
> The power of God protects me.

> The presence of God watches over me.
> Wherever I am, God is.

Upon arising that June morning, she had, as every morning, prayed that prayer of affirmation. Now at the crisis moment, sitting beside the threatening man in the car, when panic and terror almost overcame her, she was forced back on this prayer resource. Jean cannot remember the exact words she used, but she knows the essence of them.

"How can you force yourself on me this way?" she cried. "You are a child of God. You do not want to hurt anyone. God's love is in you. God wants you to be a good man. He cares about you. And I am His child, too. And completely under His protection. His love and protection surround me. . . ."

As she spoke the words, she felt warmed. There seemed to be a kind of aura around her, like a soft light. Then into her mind there came the clear picture of the face of the janitor at her church school, one of the kindest, most gentle men she had ever known, beloved by everyone who knew him. It was as if God were saying to her, "You told the man sitting beside you that he is a child of Mine. True, but now to help you really see that, superimpose the janitor's face and image on this man."

Jean followed directions and, sure enough, after that she could actually sense God's love enfold her abductor.

The result was immediate. The lust seemed to leave the man. He removed the object from Jean's back. Jean saw that it was merely a key case.

The man started Jean's car, drove on in silence for a while, little trickles of perspiration running down his face. He seemed more and more confused. Then he drew over to the side of the road and stopped.

"Get out," he ordered. Quickly Jean opened the door and jumped out. The man drove off, the car careening down the road.

Later Jean Klinger found her car undamaged at the spot where she had first been stopped. The man and his pickup truck had disappeared.

When I met with Jean, she stated to me that she was glad to share her experience because she believes it may point to the most important protection of all for women.

And I agree with her.

"I am the light of the world," Jesus told us. Usually we have thought this to be some kind of Oriental imagery. I wonder! The experience of an increasing number of women would indicate that in His contemporary presence, in His name and His person, there is literal light, protection, power—largely unrealized, untapped, unresearched.

Jesus goes on to make another common sense observation: "For every one that doeth evil hateth the light, neither cometh to the light, lest his deeds should be reproved." To me it is significant that Jean Klinger felt an aura of light around her and that her attacker either could not or would not penetrate it. By repeating the prayer of protection so regularly, she had bathed herself in this light; it was there the moment she called out for help.

It has probably never occurred to most lifelong Christians that in the light of Jesus Christ there is such help and protection. We tend toward materialism, let us admit it, so we believe in the efficacy of material protection: guns, locks, police, sirens.

While all these means are valuable, obviously they are not enough, for never have assaults on women been so high. There are times when, like Jean Klinger, we may have no protection left other than spiritual. "Let us therefore cast off the works of darkness, and let us put on the armor of light."

The Man Who Couldn't Stand Leisure

(*Guideposts*, September 1969)

uring the five years I have been living and writing in Florida, I have become very much aware of the retired couples living about us. At first, retirement seems as good to these people as the advertisements promised. The skies are sunny; the restaurants are fun; there is time for sleeping late, much talk, bridge, tennis, golf, boating.

But then what? Soon a certain lethargy creeps up on them. In its wake, nagging questions arise: Does anyone need us anymore? Is happiness more than leisure and a sunny climate? Isn't there something useful we can do?

Those questions are pertinent to more than eighteen million retired Americans, as well as millions more who are planning for this event.[1]

Paul Pepys is one man, a widower, who is using the last part of life creatively. Paul had had a brilliant career in business—vice-president of one corporation, president of another. He had always

1. As of August 1992 there were more than $25\frac{1}{2}$ million retired Americans.

been terribly active, flying here and there across the world. But at age 60 he began to wonder what there was to look forward to in retirement. His health declined. Then what he feared most came upon him four years too early: involuntary retirement.

"A kind of paralysis set in," Paul recalls today. "It seemed that no one needed me anymore. I began sleeping nineteen hours a day. When awake I could barely drag myself around."

After losing 43 pounds in a few months, he was admitted to a hospital. No serious ailment was found. In desperation, Paul's sister gave him a Bible and several inspirational books to read. It was in the Gospels that Paul saw his first shaft of light. Jesus' words "Follow me" came back to him again and again. What, then, was to be his first step in following?

When the minister of a local church called on him, Paul felt prompted to ask, "Do you have some small job I could do as a contribution of my time—anything, really?"

The pastor thought for a moment. "Yes, we need someone to set up a file system for our church visitation program. Could you begin Monday?"

Paul said he could. He startled his doctor by saying he had to leave the hospital and start work in five days. Reluctantly the doctor agreed to release him, but advised Paul to take it easy.

The advice was unnecessary. Paul discovered that he could hardly stand, much less walk. Somehow he found strength to get up, dress and check out of the hospital.

On Monday at 9 A.M. this former president of a large industrial company was seated at a small table in the church office before a huge stack of 3 x 5 cards. So dizzy he had to cup his chin in his hand to keep his head steady, he forced himself to concentrate on the job at hand. After an hour he went home exhausted.

"Lord," he prayed that night, "please get me going again tomorrow morning."

He was back the next morning and the next. Each day he extended his time one half-hour. At the end of the first week, Paul had made so little progress he apologized to the minister.

"Don't worry about it," he was told. "You're doing fine."

The second week went better. Ideas were beginning to come. One day Paul approached the minister. "I see that a notation is made when a minister calls on a member of the congregation, but there is no record of any laymen making calls on members except during the canvass for the church budget."

The minister hesitated. "You think we should ask laymen to make calls the year 'round? Hmmm. Wonder if they would?"

"I can't speak for other laymen, but I'd be glad to make some calls."

And so Paul had himself another job. This particular church had a large membership. On the calls he made, Paul saw lonely people who needed to know that someone cared. Wasn't the first step to let them know that Jesus cared? And wasn't that the Church's chief business, after all? And how could you do that without personal contact?

Clearly the ministers could not possibly do all that. So Paul sold both the ministers and the layleaders on the idea that all church members had to be responsible for visitation. Yet that idea had no chance of functioning efficiently without careful planning. Paul assumed the task. Those close to Paul could see health and strength and wholeness returning to his life.

One day Paul noticed that the young associate minister missed a call because his ten-year-old car had broken down. Paul went home that night and made a careful study of his financial situation for the first time in three years. The next morning he talked to an old friend who ran a local automobile agency.

That afternoon the associate minister burst excitedly into the church office.

"The most amazing thing," he said to Paul and the clerical staff. "I've got a new car. It's a gift—from some church member who insists he remain anonymous." His eyes filled with tears.

So touched was Paul by the minister's gratitude that he shut himself in his office at home that evening to do some deep thinking and praying.

"The Someone who had called me out of my hospital bed was there giving me the vision of a whole new kind of giving," said Paul, recalling that night. "I'd come close to losing my life. Now Christ was saying, 'I want you to give your life away in My name.' With abandon and in secret I was to give four things: my time, my money, my knowledge and my love."

Meanwhile, Paul began making calls in poorer neighborhoods. One man was out of work.

"Could I see your resume?" Paul asked.

The man just looked at him blankly.

"If you'll come down to the church this afternoon," Paul said, "I'll help you prepare one."

Paul's counseling on employment problems resulted in an employment clinic held two evenings a month in the church basement. Men and women, members and nonmembers looking for jobs in the community were invited to come have their resumes sharpened and to talk with specialists in various fields, most of whom Paul recruited from among the church's laymen.

Four years passed. Paul awakens now at 5 A.M. eager to get going. After juice and coffee, he reads from the Bible and meditates for an hour to prepare himself inwardly for the day ahead. Next comes a brisk walk, plus work in his garden, then a shower.

By 8 A.M. he is at his downtown office. After dictating letters for an hour, Paul is back in his car to attend a real estate meeting in connection with his new investments. Then to the church for a luncheon meeting on a special program. In the afternoon he drives across town to spend several hours with a ten-year-old boy, his special charge as a member of the Big Brother Movement. If there is time, he will play two sets of tennis.

By 8 P.M. he is due at the university where he takes a two-hour extension course in chamber music one night a week. Paul plays the violin in a 75-piece amateur symphony orchestra several nights a month and fills in as organist for a small church whenever needed.

Paul's finances have improved to the point where he anonymously gives away several cars a year to hardship cases and new suits to as many as ten people. He has given a home to a destitute widow and made the down payment on a house for a man who does not have the faintest idea who the donor is, though Paul sees the man about once a week.

Paul's insistence on secrecy remains; he has learned that power flows in literal fulfillment of Christ's promise.[2] Paul made the same condition of secrecy in letting me tell his story, requesting that his name and certain details be changed so that no one would recognize him.

And so the man who once slept nineteen hours a day has, in four years, had his life completely turned around to an active nineteen-hour working day.

"The key to a worthwhile life for the retired person," says Paul, "is not the usual advice 'to get interested in something.' Rather, for me it has been to 'get interested in Someone—Jesus Christ.' How can I ever forget the way He came into that hospital room and told me to get out of bed and start living for other people? I've accomplished more and had more fun in the last four years than in all the rest of my life put together."

2. "Be careful not to do your 'acts of righteousness' before men, to be seen by them. If you do, you will have no reward from your Father in heaven. So when you give to the needy, do not announce it with trumpets, as the hypocrites do in the synagogues and on the streets, to be honored by men. I tell you the truth, they have received their reward in full. But when you give to the needy, do not let your left hand know what your right hand is doing, so that your giving may be in secret. Then your Father, who sees what is done in secret, will reward you" (Matthew 6:1–4, NIV).

God's Work Is Where You Are

(*Guideposts*, January 1968)

very time I hear someone complain that he has "no time" for God, I think about our friend Ellie Armstrong. Ellie is in full-time religious work—running a motel.

It is a small but neat motel on U.S. Route 6 in the rolling hills of western Pennsylvania. Ellie was behind the desk when my husband, Len, and I stopped there one night recently. She is in her early 30s and the eyes framed by her dark hair are very blue. It is her eyes that invite you to linger and chat awhile after you have signed the register.

The place, she said, had been named Port Motel after the nearby town of Port Allegany, long before she borrowed the money to buy it three years ago.

"But isn't it the very name you would choose if you were starting a motel new?" she asked. "A name Jesus used about Himself!"

"He did?"

"Of course. 'I am the door'—the portal. 'By me if any man enter in, he shall be saved, and . . . have life, and . . . have it more abundantly' (John 10:9–10). Isn't that the point with everyone we meet, to lead them to that door? And a motel—well, it means a chance to meet new people all the time!"

The blue eyes returned our startled looks with surprise of their own.

"That's why I wanted a motel, you know," she said, as though wondering why else one would be in business. "To meet people who might not have heard about Him."

Like, for example, the unsuspecting pharmaceutical salesman who had stopped for a good night's sleep a few months back. As he registered at the desk, Ellie noticed a large growth on his left eye, almost forcing the lid shut.

"You don't have to have that growth on your eye," she told him.

The salesman stared at her. "What do you mean?"

"I mean Jesus can take it off. He doesn't want you to have it. He'll take it from you."

"Look, lady, I don't believe in magic. I don't even believe in God."

"But," she said gently, "that doesn't stop Him from believing in you."

And with that Ellie gave him the key to Room 3, which she has labeled "the miracle room for unbelievers."

"The miracle room?" I broke in.

Well, Ellie said, in a way all the rooms are miracle rooms. Each of the fourteen motel units had been dedicated to God for a specific purpose: a room for healing, a special room for honeymooners, one for alcoholics, another for the mending of broken relationships, the conviction room, the happiness room and so on.

No outward sign set the rooms apart, she said, just a ceremony held on April 20, 1965, when she had formally offered the motel to God. Ministers and friends came to take part in the service. First came a dedication prayer; then the group walked from room to room claiming each for its special purpose.

"We even anointed the doors and the beds with oil, the way it says in Exodus: 'And thou shalt take the anointing oil, and anoint . . . all that is therein, and shalt hallow it' (Exodus 40:9)."

"Oh, I know it sounds a little crazy," she added hastily, catching what must have been slightly quizzical looks from us. "And of course we don't know what God is going to do with the different people who stay. We just asked Him to be present in each room, to meet each guest."

As in the case of the pharmaceutical salesman. That night some members of Ellie's church were meeting for prayer in her living room. She invited the salesman to join them, but he declined. And so they prayed for him in his absence.

He left the next morning before anyone else was up. A few days later he was back. Even before he got to the desk Ellie could see that both eyes were perfectly normal—no growth.

"Shook me up," he blurted out. "I was driving down the road that morning when I happened to look in the rearview mirror, and that thing was gone! Simply wasn't there! Lady, I told you I don't believe in God, but maybe, if you introduced me. . . ."

If the salesman was surprised, Ellie was not. Answered prayer is a common experience here. In fact, keeping the motel open at all requires daily answers. To cut down expenses Ellie, her sister and her mother not only do all the maid work but also the painting, repairs and upkeep.

Even so, there are many debts, for in order to purchase the motel Ellie had to borrow not only the mortgage money but the down payment as well.

"I asked God never to let me miss a payment, even by a day, to any of those people who had believed in the idea of the motel. And He never has."

He has, however, tested Ellie often and taught her much through this life of constant financial dependence. There was the time one midwinter when a $300 mortgage payment was due in a few days. She had but fifty dollars. For five consecutive nights not a single car stopped at the motel. And so, as she had done so often when money was lacking, Ellie began to pray. At last an inner voice seemed to tell her, *Send the fifty dollars to Dave Wilkerson in New York for his work with young drug addicts.*

Ellie was startled, as any of us would have been. Surely this was not the time to give away money! Then she remembered that Jesus had said, "Give, and it shall be given unto you" (Luke 6:38). It took courage, but she mailed off the fifty dollars that afternoon to Mr. Wilkerson.

That same night nine cars came in, one right after the other. The rest of the week the motel was filled to capacity. The mortgage money was paid on time.

Len and I sat silent a moment, digesting this idea.

"And all those customers," Len said at last. "How did you know which rooms to put them in?"

For some, like the salesman, it would be obvious, but most motorists stopping overnight simply pick up their room keys and say goodnight. How often, we asked her, do people stay to talk about their troubles?

Ellie's blue eyes smiled at us. "More often than you'd think. And when they don't, then I simply ask God about them."

One evening God seemed to tell her to put a certain man in the room where alcoholics had often been helped, although there was nothing in his appearance to suggest this problem. Only the next morning did she learn what happened.

The guest was indeed a recovering alcoholic who had not had a drink for two years. But this night he was despondent because he had just lost his sister to cancer. Life was meaningless, he had decided. He tossed his suitcase onto the bed and was turning to leave the room, intending to get drunk, when he saw a book on the nightstand, *The Cross and the Switchblade* by Dave Wilkerson. He picked it up, curious. Three hours later he finished reading it.

"I knelt down by the bed," he confided to Ellie the next morning, "and once again rededicated my life to God."

The man has been returning regularly for what he calls "refilling."

The literature in each room is part of the ministry, and it goes far beyond the usual Gideon Bible. In our room, besides several books, I spotted the latest *Upper Room* and *Guideposts* and a pamphlet, *The Incomparable Christ.*

But even more important than what travelers read, Ellie is finding, is what they say when they know that someone is listening. She meets many lonely people crushed by problems or isolated in prisons of self, and she is often up half the night hearing their griefs. Indeed, the night we were there she sat up until two, talking and praying with a young couple who had just left their baby in a home for the retarded.

But there Ellie was next morning, bright and early, a stack of clean towels in one hand, a can of scouring powder in the other.

"Isn't it too bad," I said, "that someone else can't do these routine jobs, when God has given you so much work to do for Him?"

"For Him?" Ellie looked puzzled. "Oh, but this is the best time I spend with Him! This is when I go into each room and thank Him for His presence there."

As she sweeps, she said, she asks God to sweep away the fears, angers or doubts that have been left behind. Washing windows, she prays that His light may shine into the room. And making beds. . . .

"I've always had a bad back and making so many beds each day used to be a problem. Then I discovered that if I made beds kneeling, I wouldn't have to stoop over, and now it's the best prayer time I have!"

Stop doing God's work to wash and sweep and clean? Ellie cannot. For as she sees it, floors and beds and motel windows are as much His as church pews and stained glass. In fact, there is no work that cannot be done for Him.

The Healing of Maude Blanford

(*Guideposts*, April 1972)

t was such a great healing story that I flew down to Louisville, Kentucky, to get the details from Maude Blanford herself.

The woman across the dining table from me had no trace of gray in her reddish hair, though she was past middle age, a grandmotherly type, comfortable to be with.

"My left leg had been hurting me," Mrs. Blanford began. "I thought it was because I was on my feet so much. Finally I went to the doctor. He found several tumor masses on my left side."

A specialist, Dr. O. J. Hayes, pronounced them malignant and prescribed radiation treatment. The treatment was followed by surgery.

After the operation, when Mrs. Blanford pleaded for the truth, the doctor admitted, "It is cancer and it's gone too far to remove. One kidney is almost nonfunctioning. The pelvic bone is affected— that's why the pain in your leg. I am so sorry."

Maude Blanford was sent home to die. Over a six-month period, while consuming $1,000 worth of pain-relieving drugs, she took stock of her spiritual resources and found them meager indeed. She had no church affiliation, no knowledge of the Bible, only the vaguest, most shadowy concept of Jesus.

The first week in January she suffered a cerebral hemorrhage and was rushed back to the hospital. For twelve days she lay unconscious; her husband was warned that if she survived the crisis it would probably be as a vegetable.

But Maude Blanford, oblivious to the world around her, was awake in a very different world. In her deep coma, a vivid image came to her. She saw a house with no top on it. The partitions between the rooms were there, the furniture in place, but there was no roof. She remembers thinking, *Oh, we must put a roof on the house! If it rains, all the furniture will be spoiled.*

When she came out of the coma, Mrs. Blanford's mind was very much intact, but bewildered. What could the roofless house have meant? As she puzzled over it, a Presence seemed to answer her.

"This Spirit seemed to show me," explained Mrs. Blanford, "that the house represented my body, but that without Jesus as my covering, my body had no protection."

I leaned forward, excited by an insight: Wasn't this what I had always been taught about the Holy Spirit—that His role was to show us Jesus and our need of Him?

"At that time," Mrs. Blanford went on, "I didn't know how to get the roof on my house."

From January until July, her condition worsened. Heart action and breathing became so difficult that she was reduced from normal speech to weak whispers. Even with the drugs, the suffering became unbearable. By July she knew she no longer had the strength to make the trip for radiation treatment. "On July first I told the nurse I wouldn't be coming back."

But that day, as her son-in-law helped her into the car outside the medical building, she broke down and wept.

"At that moment I didn't want anything except for God to take me quickly, as I was. I said, 'God, I don't know who You are. I don't know anything about You. I don't even know how to pray. Just, Lord, have Your own way with me.'"

Though she did not realize it, Maude Blanford had just prayed one of the most powerful of all prayers—the prayer of relinquishment. By getting her own mind and will out of the way, she had opened the door to the Holy Spirit, as had happened during her period of unconsciousness in the hospital.

She did not have long to wait for evidence of His presence. Monday, July 4, dawned beautiful but hot. That afternoon Joe Blanford set up a cot for his wife outdoors under the trees. As the ill woman rested, hoping for the relief of a bit of breeze, into her mind poured some beautiful sentences:

> Is not this the fast that I have chosen? to loose the bands of wickedness, to undo the heavy burdens, and to let the oppressed go free, and that ye break every yoke? . . . Then shall thy light break forth as the morning, and thine health shall spring forth speedily. . . . Here I am.

I stared at Maude Blanford over the rim of my coffee cup. "But I thought you didn't know the Bible."

"I didn't! I'd never read a word of it. Only I knew this didn't sound like ordinary English. I thought, *Is that in the Bible?* And right away the words came: *Isaiah 58.* Well, my husband got a Bible for me. I had to hunt and hunt to find the part called Isaiah. But then when I found those verses just exactly as I had heard them—except for the last three words, 'Here I am'—well, I knew God Himself had really spoken to me!"

Over the next weeks Maude Blanford read the Bible constantly, often until two or three in the morning, seeing the Person of Jesus take shape before her eyes. It was an amazing experience, without human assistance of any kind —no Bible teacher, no commentary, no study guide, simply reading the Bible with the Holy Spirit.

Along with her hunger to meet Jesus in the Word, the Holy Spirit gave her an intense desire to be out-of-doors, close to His world.

"Joe," she told her astonished husband one day, "I want to go fishing."

This made no sense to him. The terrain to the lake was rough. She would have to be carried down and then back up a steep hill.

But then some kindly neighbors offered to help him take her, so her husband acquiesced. She could not fish, of course, but she could observe: a breeze rippling the water, the wheeling birds and the distant hills. And as she looked, a response grew in her, a response that is another of the Holy Spirit's workings in the human heart: *praise*. All that day she praised Jesus for the world He had made. That night she slept like a baby.

After that, the lake trip became routine. A month or so later, Maude Blanford was walking up the hill to the road by herself. At home she had begun very slowly climbing the stairs, praising Jesus for each step attained. Or she would sit in a chair and dust a mahogany tabletop, saying, "Thank You, Jesus. Isn't this wood beautiful!"

Next she tried putting a small amount of water in a pail. Sitting in a kitchen chair, she would mop the floor in the area immediately around her, scoot the chair a few inches, mop again. "Thank You, Jesus, for helping me do this!"

Her daughter-in-law, who was coming over almost daily to clean house for her, asked one day in great puzzlement, "Mom, how is it that your kitchen floor never gets dirty?"

The older woman twinkled. "Well, I guess I'll have to confess—the Lord and I are doing some housework."

But their chief work, she knew, was not on this building of brick and wood, but on the house of her spirit, the house in her dream that had been roofless so long. Gradually, as her knowledge of Jesus grew, she sensed His protective love surrounding and sheltering her. Not that all pain and difficulties were over. She was still on pain-numbing narcotics, still experiencing much nausea as the aftermath of the radiation.

"The will to live is terribly important," she commented to me. "It takes a lot of self-effort just to get out of bed, to eat again after your food has just come up. This is when too many people give up."

One Saturday night, when the pain would not let her sleep, she lay on her bed praising God and reading the Bible. About two A.M. she drifted off to sleep with the Bible lying on her stomach. She felt that she was being carried to heaven, traveling a long way through space. Then came a voice out of the universe: "My child, your work is not finished. You are to go back." This was repeated three times, slowly, majestically, and then she was aware of her bedroom around her again.

The rest of the night she remained awake, flooded with joy, thanking God. When her husband woke up in the morning, she told him, "Honey, Jesus healed me last night."

She could see that he did not believe it; there was no change in her outward appearance. "But I knew I was healed and that I had to tell people."

That very morning she walked to the Baptist church across the highway from their home and asked the minister if she could give a testimony. He was startled at the unusual request from someone who was not even a member of the congregation, but he gave permission, and she told the roomful of people that God had spoken to her in the night and healed her.

A few weeks later she insisted on taking a long bus trip to visit her son in West Virginia. Still on narcotics, still suffering pain, she nonetheless knew that the Holy Spirit was telling her to rely, from now on, on Jesus instead of drugs. At five o'clock in the afternoon of April 27, almost two years from the first diagnosis of cancer, on the return bus journey, as she popped a pain-killing pill into her mouth at a rest stop, she knew it would be the last one.

So it turned out. In retrospect, physicians now consider this sudden withdrawal as great a miracle as the remission of cancer cells to healthy tissue.

It took time to rebuild her body-house, nine months for her bad leg to be near normal, two years for all symptoms of cancer to vanish. When she called Dr. Hayes over some small matter, he almost shouted in astonishment. "Mrs. Blanford! What's happened to you! I thought you were—"

"You thought I was long since gone," she laughed back.

"Please come to my office at once and let me examine you! I've got to know what's happened."

"But why should I spend a lot of money for an examination when I'm a perfectly well woman?" she asked.

"Mrs. Blanford, I promise you, this one is on us!"

What the doctor found can best be stated in his own words:

"I had lost contact with Mrs. Blanford and had assumed that this patient had expired. She appeared in my office two and a half years following her operation. The swelling of her leg was gone. She had full use of her leg; she had no symptoms whatsoever, and on examination I was unable to ascertain whether or not any cancer was left. . . .

"She was seen again on November 5, at which time her examination was completely negative. . . .

"She has been seen periodically since that time for routine examinations. . . . She is absolutely asymptomatic. . . . This case is most unusual in that this woman had a proven, far-advanced metastatic cancer of the cervix and there should have been no hope whatsoever for her survival."

No hope whatsoever. . . . No hope except the hope on which our faith is founded.

The miracle of Maude Blanford reminds me again of that scene on the night before His crucifixion when Jesus spoke quietly to His despairing disciples: "Ye have not chosen me, but I have chosen you" (John 15:16). He is still saying that to us today, while His Spirit, always working through human beings, sometimes confounds us, often amazes us and is always the Guide to the true Giver of health and strength.

SECTION
SEVEN

The Holy Spirit

The brief discussion Catherine and I had about the Holy Spirit early in our courtship was one of many to follow. The third Person of the Trinity was to become increasingly significant in our relationship and in every other aspect of our lives.

Here is how Catherine described her early experience with the Holy Spirit before we met; then His impact on our marriage, family members and friends in the 1960s and early 1970s.

Journey into Joy

t was during my college years and the early years of my marriage to Peter Marshall that I sensed something missing in my relationship to Jesus Christ. I had joined His church, I read God's Word regularly, I prayed to Him, but I sensed there was something more.

In 1943 tuberculosis sent me to bed 24 hours a day for an indefinite period.

Yet God brought good out of this seeming calamity. My search for health became a search for a relationship to God. One spring morning I knew it was time for the plunge—a quiet pledge to God, the promise of a blank check with my life. My healing began with that commitment.

A year or so after this commitment experience, I found myself with a lively curiosity about what seemed an odd subject—the Holy Spirit. Like most people, I had thought of the Holy Spirit as a theological abstraction, a sort of ecclesiastical garnish for christenings, weddings, benedictions and the like. As for the term *Holy Ghost*— that I regarded as archaic, if not downright eerie.

However odd the subject seemed, the fact remained that this was no passing curiosity. As is often the case when something is brought sharply to one's attention, everywhere I turned during those months I seemed to hear or read something about the Holy Spirit.

During our vacation on Cape Cod that summer, the church that Peter and I attended with Peter John included a talk for children as part of its regular Sunday service. The first Sunday we were there, the guest preacher gave as his sermonette an object lesson on the Holy Spirit as related to the Trinity.

Three glass containers had been placed on a table before the young preacher. One was filled with water, the second with ice, the third with what appeared to be steam, probably dry ice.

"Children," he began, "perhaps you've heard of the Trinity. *Trinity* means 'three.' When we speak of the Trinity, we mean the three Persons that go to make up God: God, the Father; Jesus Christ, the Son; and the Holy Spirit.

"Now look at these three jars. This one has water. This one has ice. And that one, steam. They all look different, don't they? Yet you know that ice is only frozen water. And when your mother boils water in a pan on the stove, steam rises from it. That means that water, ice and steam are really the same thing.

"Now, the same thing is true of the Trinity. Jesus Christ, the water of Life, is different from the Father—yet the same, too. The Holy Spirit, like the powerful steam that can drive an engine, is different from Christ and the Father, yet the same."

I listened, as interested as any of the children. What the young minister said that morning gave me a new concept and provided a background for approaching the subject that continued to occupy my mind.

About two months later something happened that took this interest out of the realm of theory and placed it on a personal basis. It was in the early fall of that year that my friends Tay and Fern told me of the experience of guidance they had had in Florida the previous winter.

I had known Tay for a long time. Often she had inner nudges and proddings of the kind would send her out to help a friend at a time of emergency that Tay could not, in any natural way, have known about.

Curiously I asked her, "How do you explain these intuitions?"

"Some people call them intuitions," Tay answered promptly. "But I prefer to call the help I get the direction of the Holy Spirit."

There it was again!

Tay was looking at me curiously. "What does the Holy Spirit mean to you?" she asked.

I remembered the sermonette at the Cape Cod church. "Oh, one of the three Persons of the Godhead, the third Person of the Trinity."

"But I sense something in the offhand way you say that—" She looked at me sharply. "Let me guess that in your mind the Spirit has an insignificant and unnecessary place. Isn't that right?"

I nodded. "That's right."

"But I know from personal experience that the Holy Spirit is just as great, just as needed as the other two Persons of the Trinity. Anyway, you still haven't answered my original question. What is He to you?"

Tay's intensity seemed to demand a candid reply.

"I've got to be truthful, Tay," I replied. "The Spirit is nothing to me. I've had no contact with it and could get along quite well without it."

Although at the time I believed my own statement, I was soon to find out that it was not so. As a matter of fact, I could not get along at all well without the Holy Spirit. Some searching in the Bible told me why.

Using a concordance and a notebook, I began methodically looking up all the references I could find on the third Person of the Trinity. Gradually I worked the findings into a logical outline in my notebook.

I learned that the Holy Spirit is not "an influence" but a Person; not "a thing" or an "it" but "He." In a sense, He is both the most basic and the most modest member of the Trinity, for His work is to reflect Christ and to glorify Him.

The obvious meaning of the word *glorify* is "to give homage to, as in worship." But there is a deeper meaning. Dr. Leslie Weatherhead in a 1952 Lenten sermon in the City Temple, London, brought out this richer meaning: "I would define glory as that expression of the nature of a person or thing which, of itself, evokes our praise."

Then the "glory" of a sunrise must be in the beauty of its delicate pinks and oranges reflected in the sky just before the sun itself appears. In this sense, the glory is in the qualities or characteristics of the sunrise that we can perceive.

The "glory" of Jesus Christ lies in the characteristics of His nature that make us want to adore Him. These traits are not kingly trappings or the halo placed around His head by medieval painters. Far from it! Men and women saw His glory in His humanity—His instant compassion, tenderness, understanding, fearlessness, incisiveness; His refusal to compromise with evil; His selflessness that culminated in His ultimate self-giving on the cross.

The apostle John puts it in unforgettable words: "And the Word was made flesh, and dwelt among us, (and we beheld his glory, the glory as of the only begotten of the Father,) full of grace and truth."

But then I found the New Testament declaring that these qualities of Jesus' nature are not apparent to us any more than a sunrise is apparent to a blind man. That is why we need the Holy Spirit— to make Christ's glory perceptible to us. It is as if the Spirit gives us a new way of seeing, with which we can perceive spiritual truth where all has been darkness before.

I found that Jesus had His own preferred names for the Spirit. Christ spoke in Aramaic, the tongue of His own people. This was the dialect of the bazaars and the seaside, replete with colorful idioms, metaphors and probably picturesque humor. There is good reason to believe that the tone of Jesus' speech was quite unlike the English of the King James Version of the early seventeenth century. The King James translators often rendered *the Holy Spirit* "the Holy Ghost." But Jesus liked to call Him "the Helper," "the Spirit of Truth," "the Teacher," "the Comforter," "the Counselor."

The Gospel of John was especially helpful in giving me more understanding about the Holy Spirit. In Christ's last talk with the eleven (Judas had already left the group), He made it clear that they were to experience Him through the Spirit. On that last night He had important things to say to His apostles, most of them concerning the Comforter.

The disciples knew that their Master was in imminent danger. They were frightened, sorrowful men.

"Do not be frightened about My leaving you," Jesus told them. And the future He promised to them, and to all believers, had these exciting components:

1. When He went away, He would send the Holy Spirit to be "poured out on all flesh," rather than (as in the Old Testament) on a few chosen people—prophets, priests, kings (Acts 1:4-5, 2:17).
2. He Himself would be the Giver of (or Baptizer with) the Spirit (Mark 1:8; Matthew 3:11).
3. His plan was that this Spirit would dwell actually within our bodies. This would be God coming closer to man than He had ever been before (John 14:17).
4. The apostles and all believers who would follow them down through the ages were, from the moment of Jesus' ascension, entering a new era—the era of the Holy Spirit. This would

last until Jesus' Second Coming in physical presence back to planet earth (John 7:39, 16:7).

5. The Spirit would make Jesus' continuing presence and His teachings real to us. He would always turn the spotlight on Jesus and glorify Him (John 15:26, 16:13-14).

6. The chief hallmark of the Holy Spirit would be power for service and ministry to others (Mark 16:15-18, 20, TLB).

7. The Spirit would be our Teacher, Guide, Comforter, Counselor, Prayer-Intercessor, Giver of joy, of freedom, of many spiritual gifts, of eternal life.

8. The Spirit would not ever be totally operative in an individual alone, but only in the fellowship of Christ's Body on earth—the Church (Ephesians 1:22-23).

9. The apostles and those who would come after must expect a degree of resistance, cleavage, even persecution and expulsion from their synagogues (or churches) because "the world cannot receive" the Spirit of truth (John 14:17).

10. After His resurrection and ascension the apostles were "to go into all the world and preach the Good News" (Mark 16:15, TLB). They were not to leave Jerusalem, however, or attempt any ministry of any kind until they had received the Holy Spirit (Acts 1:4).

11. Jesus promised that He would manifest Himself to us (John 14:21) and that the Spirit would lead us into further truth— all truth (John 16:13).

As I put all of this together back in 1945, it shed new light on the account of what happened next. That story is told in the book of Acts—really the Acts of the Holy Spirit. The Spirit's first great miracle was to transform the erstwhile timid, cowardly and contentious disciples into bold men moving with power and authority. Thus the infant Church was born.

Jesus' promise to lead us into further truth began to be fulfilled immediately. Old religious mores and set habit patterns had to be broken.

Virgin truth is always unexpected, often shocking. Though Jesus had spoken often of the Holy Spirit to the apostles, I could find no record that He had mentioned details of the Pentecost to come, such as the sound of a roaring wind or flames of fire, or the sudden speaking of languages they had never learned. Nor were the disciples prepared for the "further truth" that their Jewish food taboos were no longer necessary, or that the Gentiles were also beloved by the Father and chosen by Him to receive the Spirit.

In fact, it seemed to me that Jesus' promise of "further truth" gives us clear reason to believe that not all the truth and instruction Christ has to give us is contained in the canon of the Old and New Testaments. How could it be? He who is Truth will never find the people of any given century able to receive everything He wants to give.

Because the Holy Spirit is a living, always contemporary personality, down all the centuries there must be an ever-unfolding manifestation of Jesus, His personality, His ways of dealing with us, along with new, fresh disclosures of the mind of the Father. I found this concept endlessly provocative . . . and I still do.

At this point in my study some action on my part was clearly indicated. I had already summarized how we receive the Spirit:

1. By going directly to Christ for Him.
2. By asking for the gift of the Spirit.
3. By receiving the Spirit by faith (the only way to receive any gift from God).
4. By entering upon the discipline of hourly, daily obedience to Christ and the Spirit.

So very simply I asked Jesus for the gift of the Helper, thanked Him for granting this and entered upon that fourth step—the daily living out of this new relationship. I experienced no waves of emotion or ecstasy.

When I had asked myself, "Can we expect a manifestation of the Spirit?", I had little idea how to answer. Since the Helper is a Person, I reasoned, then of course He has personality traits, and presumably these traits will show themselves. How or in what way, I could not guess.

Manifest Himself He did, though not in a way I could have guessed. As I stepped out in faith back in 1945, listening day by day to the inner Voice for instructions, the first discipline He gave me was a leash for my tongue. For others the Spirit may give torrents of ecstatic speech; I needed the discipline of not speaking the careless or negative or discouraging word. For weeks I was put through the sharp training of opening my mouth to speak and hearing from the Teacher, *Stop! No, don't say it. Close the mouth.*

Many other experiences followed, such as the joy of discovering the Helper's concern with guiding us in the details of everyday life, the way He brings us to life at the emotional level. None of this I could have predicted. My experience was rather a solitary one. In 1945 I knew no one who was experimenting along the same line.

I realized that my husband, Peter, had already been given the Helper, along with the Spirit's gift of preaching. Unlike me, he had not been seeking the Spirit per se, rather what God's specific will for his life was. Probably the Helper had come to Peter at the time he was "tapped on the shoulder by the Chief," as he liked to put it, and told to emigrate to America to enter the ministry. Having long known the Spirit's presence and help in so many ways, Peter did not feel the need for conscious search that I did.

Later, at the time of my husband's sudden death, I shall be forever grateful that I was able to know the Spirit as Comforter. Without Him I might have survived, but only as a truncated person and without ever knowing the grace and splendor of the Comforter's presence on this, one of life's starkest frontiers. Not only did He comfort me, but in one practical step after another He showed me how to handle the devastation of widowhood.

By 1950 I was in need of another kind of help. I was under contract to deliver the manuscript of *A Man Called Peter* by May 1, yet had never had a single course in the craft of writing and had almost no practice except scribbling in personal diaries and journals. In that extremity, the Spirit became my Instructor in creative writing.

He took me by the hand, for instance, and showed me that the opening pages must present Peter Marshall in the framework in which the public knew him—through his Senate chaplaincy. Only then could I flash back (I did not even know the term *flashback*) to Peter's early life in Scotland and come forward.

I tried to outline the book and knew that it was not right. When I asked my Teacher the right way of outlining the book, I was told that Peter's biography would have no lasting significance apart from what his life demonstrated about God—His goodness, His revelation of truth, His ways of dealing with humankind. "Outline the book that way" was the instruction. I did, and the material fell into place.

My Teacher showed me how to construct a book, what to include out of the totality of one man's life, what to omit. All the way through He kept insisting on the importance of the light touch and humor as the way to emphasize greatness.

Now I experienced all the emotion I had not felt when I'd first asked for His presence—plus much, much more.

"No creative work," He told me, "has final impact unless it touches the reader at the emotional level." As I worked on the manuscript, He poured through me a stream of strong emotion, yet permitted me none of the sentimentality into which I was tempted to slip.

So functional and effectual was the Teacher's guidance that I had fewer editorial suggestions, less outside help with *A Man Called Peter* than with any book since, and I wrote it more swiftly.

The Jesus People

ittle did I dream that some ten years later I would see the rise of a major surge of the Spirit like a ground-swell across the world.

For me, it began with an encounter I had with John Sherrill, a top editor at *Guideposts*.

As with most of us, it was personal need that brought John to the point of commitment. My need had been a long illness. John's was a more immediate physical crisis. Two years before he had had a malignant mole removed from his ear that had been diagnosed as melanoma, one of the most vicious killers of all types of cancer. Miraculously, everyone felt, it had been caught in time. But now the doctor had discovered a small lump on John's neck that was suspect.

The details of the physical problem and the prayers for healing are not the point I want to make here. Suffice it to say that as soon as I heard about the situation, I knew that John's crisis was also my crisis, part of "my bundle" of responsibility, as the Quakers express it so vividly. Then: How were we who were so concerned to pray about John?

A series of thoughts kept pounding at me and would not be put aside: Healing is not an end in itself; it is a dividend of the Gospel. Physical health is but one part of total wholeness. Then came the inevitable question: Had John ever made an act of turning his whole being over to God?

Who was I to ask John a question like that? He was an intellectual—an editor and successful writer. Any emotional approach to Christianity, as well as the usual religious cliches and shibboleths, were repugnant to him. Considering all this, would not any question about his relationship to God be gross presumption on my part and anathema to him?

Still, time was running out. Only 24 hours remained until John would enter New York's Memorial Hospital for surgery. After all, what he thought of me did not matter at a time like this. The fact that a life was at stake gave me the courage to telephone John and tell him that I had to see him.

His wife, Elizabeth—Tib—came over with him. The three of us found a quiet room and shut ourselves in. There was no attempt at a subtle approach. I explained what had led up to my telephone call, what I had learned about the process of entering in, and why this seemed important as a foundation for any prayer for healing. My heart was in what I was saying, so that several times my voice broke.

When I had finished, John asked wonderingly, "Do you mean that I can just decide that I am willing for God to take over my life, and tell Him so, as blandly and matter-of-factly as that, and have it work?"

"That's right," was my reply. "Do it as matter-of-factly as you please. You do not have to have all your theological beliefs sorted out. Nor do you have to understand everything. You just come to Christ as you are—questions, complexes, contradictions, doubts, everything. After all, how else can any of us come? You make a definite movement of your will toward God. After that, the next move is up to Him. The feelings, the proof that He has heard and has taken you on, even the understanding, will come later."

At that point John and Tib had to rush away for their last hasty preparations for the hospital. It was not until later that I found out what happened immediately after they left me.

"After we told you goodbye and backed out of your driveway," John told me, "I did the simple thing you had suggested—just said yes to God while driving the car. I can show you the exact spot on Millwood Road where it happened, right by a certain telephone pole.

"Then, because it had been such a quiet, interior thing, I felt that I ought to go on record by telling someone. So I said to Tib, I suppose a bit ruefully, 'Well, I'm a Christian now.'

"And she asked curiously, 'Do you feel any different?'

"'Not a bit different,' I told her."

Yet John is different now—so different. That quiet transaction at that certain spot on Millwood Road launched John into a series of adventures with the Holy Spirit. But to finish this particular story, when the famous New York specialist operated on John, all he could find was a dried-up nodule, easy to remove. There was no malignancy.

Following his personal commitment to Jesus Christ, John discovered that as a reporter his story interests were switching from the practical and inspirational to the supernatural. That's why David Wilkerson intrigued him.

David Wilkerson was the skinny Pentecostal preacher from the boondocks of Pennsylvania who told his small congregation that God wanted him to go to New York and make the Lord Jesus real to teenage gang members in the inner city.

"But what can one country preacher do in that cesspool?" his church people asked.

David didn't know. He would trust God to show him. And God did. The Holy Spirit moved so powerfully among those teenagers through David's ministry that the media—and John Sherrill—were intrigued.

John proposed a series of articles for *Guideposts* magazine, but there was such skepticism among several editors over the dramatic conversions of tough, crime-addicted teenagers that John suggested that David himself come to the *Guideposts* office and tell his story. He did, and described effectively how the Holy Spirit transforms people. Still, not all were convinced.

Len, as the editor, had to make the decision. He didn't know at the time what a big decision it was. "Let's go with the Wilkerson series," he decided.

The articles had a huge impact on *Guideposts* readers; mail poured in, the great majority favorable.

A book publisher was interested. Both John and Elizabeth worked with David on *The Cross and the Switchblade*, a book that became a huge bestseller worldwide, was made into a successful movie and sparked the growing movement of the Holy Spirit.

John Sherrill was now a reporter on the trail of an even bigger story—the twentieth-century reenactment of the book of Acts. What about this "baptism of the Spirit"? What about tongues?

To a Full Gospel Business Men's meeting in Atlantic City, John came as a reporter. The sponsors asked John if he would like to be prayed for to receive the baptism. John was torn. The skeptical side of him said a firm no. The new believer side said, "Why not?"

He went to a hotel room with a half-dozen charismatic leaders, curious, open. The prayer began with several men laying hands on John. As John himself described it:

"The ceiling split open and this shaft of light poured through. I was thrown to the floor, my glasses flew off, joy welled up inside me. I laughed; I wept. Then I heard strange sounds pouring from my mouth."

Later that night John called Len and me from Atlantic City, urging us to drive down from Chappaqua to share his incredible experience. We couldn't. So a few days later John drove over to our house. He opened his mouth to describe what happened, said the word *Jesus* and began to weep. It was months until he could say the name *Jesus* without shedding tears.

John and Elizabeth had nearly completed a well-researched, objective and very arm's-length book about glossolalia—tongues. Now Len and I urged them to recast it as John's personal search. *They Speak with Other Tongues* captured the imagination of millions. By the late 1960s the Holy Spirit movement had the full attention of America.

Now came the big surprise. Young people who before had been indifferent or even hostile to religion groped their way—some of them through the jungle of drugs or the occult or Eastern religions—to become "Jesus people." They not only carried Bibles, they read them feverishly. They waded into the ocean or into backyard swimming pools to be baptized. All over the world they formed communities.

The Jesus Revolution was marked by highly charged emotionalism—hand-clapping, hugging, singing, religious rock music, exclamations of "Wow!" and "Far out!"

Some of these youthful experimenters, of course, were not serious and soon drifted away. Yet many had their lives turned right-side-up.

One night at the dinner table Chester was almost too busy talking to eat. He had flown in from Taylor University that afternoon, having just finished his freshman year.

Chester's voice was excited. "Pops, you wouldn't have believed the scene in the Notre Dame football stadium last weekend."

"Football in June?" his father asked quizzically.

"No—singing and prayer and praising the Lord, 25,000 people. It was fantastic!"

"What was the occasion?"

"A big meeting of the Catholic Jesus People. A bunch of us drove up from Taylor. Six hundred priests came pouring onto the field from where the players enter, singing, carrying banners. The whole place was clapping and cheering. I've never seen people so excited."

Later that week we read *Time* magazine's coverage of the event: First, men in business suits or sport coats carrying banners aloft, *The Spirit of Jesus Among Us* emerging from the football team's tunnel onto the Notre Dame field. Then the double line of priests in white robes and clerical stoles singing, their arms raised heavenward, hands open, palms up. The excitement of the crowd building, erupting into applause. As eight Roman Catholic bishops, followed by Cardinal Suenens of Belgium, resplendent in a brilliant red chasuble, came into view, the clapping exploded into a mighty roar.

To the crowd of 25,000 in the stadium, Cardinal Suenens said, "The Pentecostal renewal is not a movement. It is a current of grace . . . growing fast everywhere in the world. I feel it coming. I see it coming."

The seedbed of the Catholic Pentecostal movement was a group of four or five laymen (all members of the Duquesne University faculty) who had begun meeting together in the fall of 1966. A book that fell into their hands led them to ask for the gift of the Holy Spirit for themselves. Yes, it was David Wilkerson's *The Cross and the Switchblade* written by John and Elizabeth Sherrill. Two other books were also key to the movement: John Sherrill's *They Speak with Other Tongues* and Dennis Bennett's *Nine O'Clock in the Morning*.

Like most adults I have watched the Jesus Revolution among our young people with emotions ranging from delight to wonder to perplexity. Yet surely they have been saying something important that the rest of us need to hear: We could use more joy and more love in our spiritual lives. Perhaps we have become so occupied with worshiping God with our minds that we have forgotten that the rest of our beings, including the physical body, need to worship Him, too.

Self-forgetfulness, a sort of joyous, holy abandon, is indeed one of the Helper's trademarks. As Len and I became involved in the movement we formed a prayer group with the Sherrills that met weekly in our homes.

One evening Len shared with the group a problem he had at work and asked for prayer. Two women stood by his chair, rested their hands lightly on his shoulders and head, and prayed that the power of the Holy Spirit would free Len of resentments about the situation. He told me later that he felt warmth coming from their hands. The prayer ended, Len expressed gratitude and the meeting broke up.

Hours later, after we were in bed, Len spoke softly. "Catherine, I hate to wake you up, but I have the strangest feeling."

A little alarmed, I asked, "How do you mean?"

"There's this rushing, headlong joy inside me! It started in the pit of my stomach after I got in bed, then has kept bubbling up right into my head. I've been lying here thinking how silly it is to be so joyous when I should be asleep, but I can't control it. Catherine, I'd like to pray about it."

"Well, fine," I responded sleepily. "Go ahead—pray."

"But it isn't enough just to lie here. I'd like to kneel."

So both of us knelt beside the bed.

Len's prayer began quietly enough. First he expressed gratitude for the friends who had cared enough to pray for him. Then he thanked God for our life together. After that he expressed love for each member of our family, near and far. In between he kept telling the Lord how much he loved Him. Heartfelt love rose from the depths of his being for each person who had been a human thorn in Len's side. Afterwards he began God-blessing everyone he could think of, as if this love were so great it had to encompass the whole universe.

Always before Len's prayers had been short, even abrupt. Well thought out, words carefully chosen, quite unemotional. That night, in contrast, words poured from him lavishly, exuberantly repetitious, a geyser of deep emotion, unabashedly expressed. Like a bird uncaged, his emotions were darting, wheeling, soaring, wanting nothing so much as to keep on flying forever.

Minutes passed, half an hour, an hour, as love and joy kept pouring from Len. Finally, becoming aware of me kneeling there, too, Len interrupted himself long enough to say reluctantly, "This isn't fair to you, Catherine. I'd like to go on and on, but you need some sleep."

In the morning he reported, "It was the most cleansing experience I've ever had. I got to thinking it was almost like a car engine being overhauled. It's as though negative emotions—my frustrations and anger—had built up a residue in my body just as carbon deposits foul up sparkplugs. That love and joy pouring through me was like fresh, warm, sudsy water washing away the bitterness. This morning I have—I don't know—a scrubbed feeling."

Together we praised God for His answer to the prayer of the previous evening. As always He had done "above all that we ask or think."

Walk in the Spirit

In 1970 I received as a gift a very old copy of one of my favorite books, *The Christian's Secret of a Happy Life* by the Quaker Hannah Whitall Smith. As I eagerly turned the yellowed old pages of this 1885 edition—but what was this? A chapter on the Holy Spirit? I had many editions of this book in my library, knew this book practically by heart, and there was no such chapter.

Why the deletion? I wondered.

I couldn't wait to read the chapter. As usual, Hannah Smith turned to the Bible first to summarize what it taught about the Spirit, then took a middle-of-the-road position seasoned liberally with common sense. The gist of her conclusion went something like this. . . .

We make the mistake of looking upon the "baptism of the Spirit" as a single experience rather than a life, as an arbitrary bestowment rather than a necessary vitality. It is plain from Scripture that we cannot possibly enter into a new life in Christ without knowing the Holy Spirit.

There is a big difference, however, between being indwelt by the Spirit and being "filled" with His presence. For years, sometimes a lifetime, a Christian can keep the Spirit at a sub-basement level by the insistence on running one's own life. Then, through teaching or need or both, the person consciously recognizes his divine Guest's presence, opens the hitherto-closed doors into certain rooms in his being so that the Spirit can enter there, too. Thus the individual now deliberately abandons himself to the Helper's control.

"The result of this when done suddenly," Mrs. Smith explained, "is what many call 'the baptism of the Holy Spirit.' It can be, but isn't always, a very emotional and overwhelming sense of His presence."

Hannah Smith's words helped me to understand my own experience 25 years before when, after searching the Scriptures, I had asked God for the gift of the Holy Spirit and in faith thanked Him for granting this. Unlike Len's experience, I felt no waves of emotion or ecstasy. Later, too, when I was given the gift of a heavenly language, it was with no particular fanfare but as a divine quartermaster might casually hand out a tool for a job: "Here, you'll need this."

"In seeking for the baptism," Mrs. Smith continued, "it is not God's attitude toward us that needs to be changed, but our attitude toward Him. He will not give us anything new; rather, we are to receive in a new and far fuller sense that which He has already given at Pentecost. The Holy Spirit is the world's sunlight, its energy and power. Sunlight can be kept out only by erecting barriers against it. All we need do, then, is take down our shutters and barriers and walk out into the sunlight already given."

Though the experience may involve the emotions, Hannah Smith cautioned, it means more than that. "It means to be immersed or dipped into the Spirit of God, into His character and nature. The real evidence of one's baptism is neither emotion nor any single gift such as tongues, rather that there must be Christlikeness in life and character. By fruits in the life we shall know whether or not we have the Spirit."

Nor does this mean instantaneous holiness. The disciples had to learn that after Pentecost, and so do we. Ananias and Sapphira could still lie and cheat, and so can we. In practical fact, our life with the Spirit is a walk, a growth, an unfolding, as we learn to trust Him and open more and more of our being to His presence and control.

To me this seemed such solid teaching that I wondered all the more why the chapter had been deleted from all more recent editions of the book. Intent upon unraveling the mystery, I sought the story behind this chapter. These are the facts as I dug them out of Hannah Whitall Smith's letters and writings, and recent books about the Smith family.

Hannah was born in Philadelphia on February 7, 1832, into a Quaker family, eminently successful glass manufacturers. Though Hannah grew up a lively girl in a happy home, by age sixteen she was writing of "the aching void in my heart." This was in part adolescent drama, but the spiritual hunger was real, so much so that for the rest of her long life she was an eager, open-minded spiritual seeker.

Such eagerness might have led this Quaker girl straying down dead ends and onto paths of heresy. Fortunately she possessed qualities to balance her insatiable zeal—a thorough knowledge of Scripture and a high degree of common sense.

In 1865 Hannah and her husband, Robert Pearsall Smith, and their children moved to the village of Milltown, New Jersey, where Robert took charge of a branch of the family glass business. There Hannah met a group called "the Holiness Methodists." Some of the most penetrating and valuable parts of *The Christian's Secret*, a book helpful to generations of Christians, were to come from what Hannah learned from this group.

One summer the Smiths went to a ten-day Holiness camp meeting at a woodland campsite along the New Jersey shore. The purpose of these meetings, in Hannah's words, was "to open our hearts to the teachings of the Holy Spirit and His coming into seekers' hearts." But it was Robert rather than his wife who received an extraordinary emotional experience. As Hannah later reported it:

> After the meeting my husband had gone alone into a spot in the woods to continue to pray by himself. Suddenly, from head to foot he was shaken with what seemed like a magnetic thrill of heavenly delight, and floods of glory seemed to pour through him, soul and body, with the inward assurance that this was the longed-for Baptism of the Holy Spirit.
>
> The whole world seemed transformed for him; every leaf and blade of grass quivered with exquisite colour. . . . Everybody looked beautiful to him, for he seemed to see the Divine Spirit within each one. . . .
>
> This ecstasy lasted for several weeks, and was the beginning of a wonderful career of spiritual power and blessing.

Naturally this made Hannah renew her efforts to receive similar joy. She described how she "went forward" to the altar night after night in the meetings, then with a smaller group to one of the tents, where they spent hours kneeling in the dark, pleading and wrestling in prayer. For Mrs. Smith all this effort seemed of no avail. Not then or ever did she have an emotional experience of the type that had meant so much to her husband.

At first Hannah was disappointed. Then she realized that what had been given her was a "real revelation of God that made life to me a different thing ever since." She wanted emotions and was given conviction. She "wanted a vision and got a fact."

Later Mrs. Smith came to feel that the difference between her and her husband's experiences was largely a reflection of the difference in their natures: Robert was emotional, inclined to feel response in physical sensations; Hannah was more reserved and analytical.

A year or so later Robert traveled to Germany, where he held highly successful evangelistic meetings before large crowds, always in an intensely emotional atmosphere. "All Europe is at my feet," exulted Robert in a letter to his wife. When engraved pictures of him were offered for sale, eight thousand sold immediately.

Then the blow fell: gossip about Robert Pearsall Smith's improper conduct with female admirers. No one then or now knows the exact truth of the matter. The emotionalism so appealing to Smith had apparently gotten out of hand; Paul's instruction to "salute one another with an holy kiss" had been followed too eagerly.

The rumors got into the press. Meetings scheduled in England were canceled by their sponsors. Hannah stood quietly by her husband. She wrote a friend of the "crushing blow" that had befallen Robert.

And crush him it did. He gave way to discouragement, disillusionment and to a degree of cynicism. Robert sank into a joyless old age, while Hannah went on from strength to strength, her quiet, deep faith carrying her triumphantly over all sorts of trials and difficulties.

What can we learn from this for today? Each opportunity for Christian growth, each step forward, brings new temptations and dangers. In Robert Smith's case, tragedy resulted when he exalted personal experience instead of the Lord Jesus. With Hannah Smith, there was little ecstasy but a quieter joy from the fruitage of her convictions about God.

As for the missing chapter, clearly by the early 1900s editors had grown afraid of the subject. The Holy Spirit is fire. Hadn't Robert Smith been burned? Safer to omit all discussion of it.

As Len and I pondered Hannah's story, we agreed that the modern surge of the Spirit in America may stand poised at the edge of this same problem: too great a love affair with emotion, too little grounding in Scripture, too much wanting in garden-variety discipline, too small an emphasis on purity, honesty, morality—Christ's own life living in us.

What is needed, of course, is balance—plenty of solid teaching, but plenty of joy as well. Let's admit that overemotionalism is the last problem most of us face in our denominational churches. We shall achieve a proper mix of freedom and discipline, however, when we are truly led by the Helper, "always a Gentleman."

It may well be that the missing element in Robert Pearsall Smith's experience was a small corrective fellowship of other Christians like that of the infant Church in Acts 5. What was still missing in the late nineteenth century was a body of wisdom concerning the Holy Spirit movement.

Recent experience is teaching us that as we go adventuring in the Spirit, we must deliberately make ourselves subject one to the other, willing to be checked and corrected as well as encouraged and strengthened.

SECTION
EIGHT

Prayer Power

During our first date, that all-day trip along Virginia's Skyline Drive, I expected to find Catherine prim, super-spiritual, self-confident.

She greeted me wearing a casual blouse and a trim skirt that revealed two very shapely legs. More interesting disclosures were to come: She had recently learned to play bridge. She had taken ballroom dancing lessons.

"My life had become too one-dimensional," she admitted.

Most surprising to me: that what came through during our long talks that day was her sense of inadequacy. Despite ten years of success as a Christian writer and speaker, she had strong feelings of self-doubt as a mother and in social situations.

"That's why prayer is so crucial to me. When I go to Jesus with my helplessness, He hears me and responds. He is always adequate when I am inadequate."

After we were married I suggested Catherine write about some of her experiences with prayer for *Guideposts*. She did a series of articles that *Guideposts* eventually put into a booklet entitled *Adventures in Prayer*. Hundreds of thousands were distributed during the 1960s. Later the material was expanded into a book of the same title that has sold over a million copies.

Here are some excerpts.

The Prayer of Helplessness

When I lived in the nation's capital, I used to notice how often the Washington papers reported suicide leaps from the Calvert Street Bridge. This happens so repeatedly, in fact, that the site is often called "Suicide Bridge."

Sensing the human drama behind these brief notices—like the plunge of the Air Corps major's 31-year-old wife with inoperable cancer, or that of the elderly man whose wife had just died—I often thought there was probably a common denominator in all these tragedies. Each person must have felt helpless.

And I have thought, "If I could speak with such persons at the zero hour, I would try to stop them with the thought that helplessness is one of the greatest assets a human being can have."

For I believe that the old cliche "God helps those who help themselves" is not only misleading but often dead wrong. My most spectacular answers to prayers have come when I was helpless, so out of control as to be able to do nothing at all for myself.

The psalmist says: "When I was hemmed in, thou hast freed me often" (Psalm 4:1, Moffatt). Gradually I have learned to recognize this hemming-in as one of God's most loving devices for teaching us that He is real and gloriously adequate for our problems.

One such experience occurred during the writing of my first book under my own name. As the young widow of Peter Marshall, I was attempting what many felt was the rather audacious project of writing his biography. About midway through the manuscript, I received devastating criticism from one whose judgment I trusted. He told me bluntly, "You haven't even begun to get inside the man Peter Marshall."

And he was right, that was the sting of it. The realization of my inadequacy as a writer was not only an intellectual one. It was also emotional; there were plenty of tears. But out of the crisis came a major realization: In my helplessness, there was no alternative but to put the project into God's hands. I prayed that *A Man Called Peter* be His book, and that the results be all His, too.

And they were. I still regard as incredible the several million copies of *A Man Called Peter* circulating around the world. But numbers are of little importance compared to what I hear from time to time of individual lives changed through this book, of men entering the ministry through the inspiration of Peter Marshall's life.

Years later I saw the Prayer of Helplessness work in an everyday situation—the matter of household help. Before my marriage to Leonard LeSourd in the fall of 1959, I was full of trepidation at the thought of taking on the care of his three young children. My only child, Peter John, had been off at college for over three years, and I had involved myself with a writing career.

In his efforts to reassure me, Len was blithe with promises of household help. But the help situation in Chappaqua, New York, proved unbelievably tight. Months passed. One woman stayed a few weeks, then left. We tried the classified columns without success; persistent prayer brought us no nearer a solution. I finally decided I would have to do it all myself—take care of the family and meet my writing deadlines; but I soon found it was more than a full-time job running a lively household. Week after week I did not get near my desk.

So once again the old familiar pattern: the Prayer of Helplessness—the admission that I could not do everything myself; then the insight that my main responsibility was to our home. If God wanted me to resume my writing, He would show me the way.

After that admission of helplessness, Lucy Arsenault was sent to us. Lucy—steady, reliable, loyal, a marvelous cook, a great person.

Why would God insist on helplessness as a prerequisite to answered prayer? One obvious reason is that our human helplessness is bedrock fact. God is a realist and insists that we be realists, too. So long as we are deluding ourselves that human resources can supply our heart's desires, we are believing a lie. And it is impossible for prayers to be answered out of a foundation of self-deception and untruth.

Then what is the truth about our human condition? None of us had anything to do with our being born, no control over whether we were male or female, Japanese or Russian or American, white or yellow or black. Nor can we influence our ancestry, nor our basic mental or physical equipment.

After we are born, an autonomic nervous system controls every vital function that sustains life. A power that no one really understands keeps our heart beating, our lungs breathing, our blood circulating, our body temperature at 98.6 degrees. A surgeon can cut tissue but he is helpless to force the body to bind the severed tissue together again. We grow old relentlessly and automatically.

Self-sufficient? Scarcely!

Even the planet on which we live—we had nothing to do with its creation, either. The little planet earth is exactly the right distance, some 93 million miles, from the source of its heat and light. Any nearer and we would be consumed by solar radiation; any farther and we would be frozen to death. The balance of oxygen and nitrogen in the air is exactly right for the support of life, the elements in our soil and the water on which we depend, the creation of rare rock deposits. . . . All this goes on quite apart from man— little man who struts and fumes upon the earth.

Did Jesus have any comment about all this? Yes, as always He put His finger on the very heart of the matter: "Without me ye can do nothing" (John 15:5).

Nothing? That seems a trifle sweeping! After all, human beings have made great progress. We have almost eliminated diseases like smallpox, bubonic plague, tuberculosis, polio and most of the communicable diseases of childhood. We have learned to control our environment to quite an extent. We have put men on the moon. How can all that be helplessness?

Most of us do not enjoy that idea. The cult of humanism since the Renaissance has trained us to believe that we are quite adequate to be masters of our own destiny.

Yet not only did Jesus insist on the truth of our helplessness; He underscored it by telling us that this same helplessness applied equally to Him while He wore human flesh: "The Son can do nothing of himself, but what he seeth the Father do" (John 5:19). In this as in everything else, He was setting the pattern for imperfect humanity.

The Scriptures spell out for us point by point how helpless we are in relation to our spiritual lives as well as our physical ones. . . .

We feel an impulse toward God. We think we are reaching out for Him. Not so, Jesus told us. "No one is able to come to me unless he is drawn by the Father" (John 6:44, Moffatt).

We want eternal life and release from our sins. We think we can earn this salvation. No. The truth is, "It is the gift of God: Not of works, lest any man should boast" (Ephesians 2:8–9).

So far as the virtues and graces we long for in our lives—faith, joy, patience, peace of mind—there is no way we can work up such qualities. Paul tells us in Galatians 5:22–23 that these are gifts of the Holy Spirit; they can be had in no other way. "A man can receive nothing, except it be given him from heaven" (John 3:27).

This emphasis on our helplessness is found over and over in the writings of Christians in other eras. For instance, in that little jewel of a seventeenth-century book, Brother Lawrence's *Practice of the Presence of God*, helplessness was the hinge on which turned the Carmelite lay brother's relationship with God:

> That when an occasion of practicing some virtue offered, he addressed himself to God, saying, *Lord, I cannot do this unless Thou enablest me;* and that then he received strength more than sufficient.

> That when he had failed in his duty, he only confessed his fault, saying to God, *I shall never do otherwise if You leave me to myself; it is You who must hinder my falling, and mend what is amiss.* That after this he gave himself no further uneasiness about it.[1]

Though few of us have Brother Lawrence's maturity, nevertheless sometime in life every one of us finds himself out of control, caught in circumstances he is helpless to change. When this happens, welcome such times! Often it is only then that we lesser spirits enter into the truth of Jesus' statement "Without me ye can do nothing."

Dr. Arthur Gossip, who wrote the exposition on John for *The Interpreter's Bible*, has this interesting comment: "These are surely the most hopeful words in Scripture. . . . For it is on the basis of that frank recognition of our utter fecklessness apart from Him, that Christ . . . gives us His great promises. . . ."

1. Brother Lawrence, *Conversations: The Practice of the Presence of God* (Grand Rapids: Fleming H. Revell Co., 1973), pp. 15, 16.

Great promises! Like this glorious one, sweeping enough to make up a thousand times over for our helplessness: "With God all things are possible" (Matthew 19:26). He is telling us that an omnipotent, transcendent and immanent God is above all and through all, far more completely than we realize.

With helplessness alone, one would be like a bird trying to fly with one wing. But when the other wing of God's adequacy is added to our helplessness, then the bird can soar triumphantly above and through problems that hitherto have defeated us.

I have always been impressed by the story of Dr. A. B. Simpson, the famous New York preacher.[2] Poor health had haunted this man. Two nervous breakdowns plus a heart condition led a well-known New York physician to tell him when he was only 38 that he would never live to be forty.

The physician's diagnosis underscored the physical helplessness that the minister knew only too well. Preaching was an agonizing effort. Climbing even a slight elevation brought on a suffocating agony of breathlessness.

In desperation, sick in body and despairing in spirit, Dr. Simpson went at last to his Bible to find out exactly what Jesus had to say about disease. He became convinced that Jesus had always meant healing to be part of His Gospel for the redemption of man's total being.

One Friday afternoon soon after this revelation, Dr. Simpson took a walk in the country. He was forced to walk painfully, slowly, for he was always out of breath. Coming to a pine woods, he sat down on a log to rest. Soon he found himself praying, telling God of his complete helplessness with regard to his physical condition.

But to this helplessness he added his belief that God was "for health" all the way. It was that majestically powerful combination

2. A. B. Simpson, *The Gospel of Healing* (Harrisburg, Pa.: Christian Publications, Inc., 1915), p. 169ff.

again, "My total inadequacy, Your perfect adequacy." He then asked Christ to enter him and become his physical life, for all the needs of his body, until his life work was done.

"There in the woods," he said later, "I made a connection with God. Every fiber in me was tingling with the sense of God's presence."

A few days after that, Simpson climbed a mountain 3,000 feet high. "When I reached the top," he related joyfully, "the world of weakness and fear was lying at my feet. From that time on I had literally a new heart in my breast."

And so he did. During the first three years after this healing he preached more than a thousand sermons, conducted sometimes as many as twenty meetings in one week. His testimony was that never once did he feel exhausted. For the rest of his life he was noted for the amazing volume of his sermonic, pastoral and literary work. He lived to be 76.

Simpson's work, moreover, has lived after him. The Christian and Missionary Alliance, which he founded, is still a potent spiritual force today; his books are still being published and are blessing millions.

Why is prayer so startlingly effective when we admit our helplessness? First, as we have seen, because God insists upon our facing up to the facts of our human situation. In addition, this recognition and acknowledgment of our helplessness is the quickest way to that right attitude so essential to prayer. It deals a mortal blow to the most serious sin of all—man's independence that ignores God.

Another reason is that we cannot learn firsthand about God— what He is like, His love for us as individuals, His real power—so long as we are relying on ourselves and other people. And fellowship with Jesus is the true purpose of our life, the only foundation for eternity.

So if your every human plan and calculation has miscarried, if, one by one, human props have been knocked out and doors have shut in your face, take heart. God is trying to get a message through to you, and the message is: "Stop depending on inadequate human resources. Let Me handle the matter."

Here are three suggestions for presenting to Him the Prayer of Helplessness.

First, be honest with God. Tell Him you are aware of the fact that in His eyes you are helpless. Give God permission to make you feel your helplessness at the emotional level, if that is what is needed. Recognize that this may be painful! There is good psychological reason, however, why it may be necessary. Unless the power of our emotions is touched, it is as if a fuse remains unlit.

Second, take your heart's desire to God. You have accepted your helplessness. Now grip with equal strength of will your belief that God can do through you what you cannot. It may seem to you for a time that you are relying on emptiness, dangling over a chasm. Disregard these feelings and thank God quietly that He is working things out.

Third, watch now for opening doors. When the right door opens, you will have a quiet, inner assurance that God's hand is on the knob. That is the time of action for you, an opportunity for your creativity to join hands with His.

One sunny day in the future, you will look back and your heart will overflow with praise to God that He cared about you enough to shut you up to Him alone. Without that stringently kind providence, you could never have learned firsthand the amazing power of the Prayer of Helplessness.

Prayer: Where Are You, Lord?

Lord, I have been so defeated by circumstances. I have felt like an animal trapped in a corner with nowhere to flee. Where are You in all this, Lord? The night is dark. I cannot feel Your presence.

Help me to know that the darkness is really "shade of Your hand, outstretched caressingly";[3] that the "hemming in" is Your doing. Perhaps there was no other way You could get my full attention, no other way I would allow You to demonstrate what You can do in my life.

I see now that the emptier my cup is, the more space there is to receive Your love and supply. Lord, I hand to You this situation, _____, asking You to fill my cup from Your bountiful reservoirs in Your own time and Your own way.

How I thank You, Father in heaven, that Your riches are available to me, not on the basis of my deserving, but on the basis of Jesus and His worthiness. Therefore, in the strength of His name I pray. Amen.

3. Adapted from "The Hound of Heaven," from *The Complete Poetical Works of Francis Thompson* (New York: Boni and Liverright, Inc.), p. 93. The line of the poem reads: "Is my gloom, after all, Shade of His hand, outstretched caressingly?"

The Prayer That Helps Your Dreams Come True

t was from my mother that I learned about the Dreaming Prayer. She invoked it not only for her family but for neighbors, too—among them a young man from "Radical Hill," a rundown section of our West Virginia town.

Raymond Thomas, who lived with foster parents, had no idea who his real parents were. Dressed in working clothes and clod-hoppers, Ray often came to talk with my mother. Of a summer's day he would settle himself on the top step of our vine-shaded front porch talking . . . talking . . . while Mother sat in a wooden rocker shelling peas or stringing beans or darning socks. Mother enjoyed his boundless energy and fine mind.

On one particular afternoon there emerged from Ray the same inner longing I had had—to go to college. Once his dream was out in the open, shimmering, poised in the air, Mother was delighted to see the wistfulness in Ray's brown eyes replaced by kindling hope.

"But how can I manage it?" the boy asked. "I've no money saved. Nor any prospects."

Mother sensed that with Ray, the Dreaming Prayer should involve more than just college, a completely new approach to life.

"Raymond, whatever you need, God has the supply ready for you, provided you're ready to receive it. And ours is still a land of opportunity, Raymond. The sky is the limit! The money will be there for every dream that's right for you, every dream for which you're willing to work."

For a preacher's wife who had little enough herself, this was a doughty philosophy. But Mother believed it and had often proved it so. And these truths took root in Ray.

There came the day when Ray accepted Mother's philosophy so completely that she could lead him in the prayer that releases dreams to make them come true. Remembering how often she had voiced similar prayers for me, I can easily imagine how it was for Ray. . . .

"Father, You've given Raymond a fine mind. We believe You want that mind to be developed, that You want Raymond's potential to be used to help You lift and lighten some portion of Your world. Since all the wealth of the world is Yours, please help Raymond find everything he needs for an education.

"And Father, we also believe You have even bigger plans for Raymond. Plant in his mind and heart the vivid pictures, the specific dreams that reflect Your plans for him after college. And oh, give him joy in dreaming—great joy."

With a flat pocketbook but faith in his dream, Raymond Thomas got onto a bus and went off to college. How he made it is much too long to chronicle here. It involved Mother's finding a well-to-do woman to start him off with a loan; writing him encouraging letters; praying. And Ray himself accepting responsibility, developing initiative. In four years he had twelve jobs, budgeting time as well as money—so many hours for employer, classes, study, church work, recreation. It was a proud day for Mother when Ray received his bachelor of science degree, cum laude.

Twenty years later Len and I met Ray in Vienna, Austria, where he summed up how much of his dream had been realized: travel in sixty countries, his Ph.D. in physics (taken in German!) from the University of Vienna. Speaking Spanish, passable French, some Italian, Dutch, Swedish and a little Russian, he served his country through a job with the U.S. Atomic Energy Program in Europe.

A story like Ray's reveals the connection between constructive dreaming and prayer. For in a sense all such dreaming is praying. It is certainly the Creator's will that the desires and talents that He Himself has planted in us be realized. He wants us to catch from Him some of His vision for us. After all, this is what prayer is—human beings cooperating with God in bringing from heaven to earth His wondrously good plans for us.

Sadly, sometimes we fail to catch His vision for us because our capacity to dream has been atrophied by some condition that has given us a poverty complex. My first glimpse of this was in a former college friend who had suffered a poverty-stricken childhood.

Dot, as I will call her, was unable to visualize what she wanted in the vocational field. Yet she had come to Washington with idealistic ideas about a government job.

"I don't want just any job," Dot had explained to me soon after she arrived. "I go along with the idea that God has a plan for my life. Only I haven't yet found it, so how do I pray about this job situation?"

"What job would give you the most joy?" I asked her. "Usually that's a key to what one should do."

My friend merely looked puzzled and shook her head.

"Do you ever daydream?" I persisted. "Is there anything you've always longed to do?"

"No-o. Nothing."

The reason this particular girl could not dream constructively was that during financially difficult years, her widowed mother had taught her that those who hope for little or nothing will never suffer disappointment. Actually, this had been nothing less than excellent training in poverty expectation. Sadly I watched my friend fall into a routine government filing job that used but a fraction of her abilities.

I know now that there is healing for such a situation. When we become aware of such damaged areas in the unconscious, we can call on the power of the Holy Spirit. He can walk back with us into the past and drain out the poison, make the rough places smooth and create a highway for our God to march triumphantly into the present with His long-forgotten, oft-delayed plan for our lives.

In fact, there is no limit to what this combination of dreams and prayer can achieve. I have seen amazing results in many areas: finding the right mate or the right job, locating the ideal house, rearing children, building a business.

There are those who are wary of this Prayer That Helps Your Dreams Come True because they are dubious about praying for material needs such as bread, clothing, a catch of fish—or, to put it in modern terms, a parking place for a car. Rightly they also ask, "Isn't there the danger of trying to use God and spiritual principles for selfish ends?"

These are valid concerns that need to be addressed. As for whether God means for us to include material needs in our petitions, certainly Christ was interested in people's bodies as well as their souls. He was concerned about their diseases, their physical hunger. Christianity, almost alone among world religions, acknowledges material things as real and important—real enough that Christ had to die in a real body on a real cross.

And as for the danger that our dreams may spring from our selfish human will rather than God's will, there are tests we can give ourselves. Only when a dream has passed such a series of tests, so that we are certain our heart's desire is also God's before we pray, can we pray the Dreaming Prayer with faith and thus with power.

Ask yourself:

- Will my dream fulfill the talents, temperament and emotional needs God has planted in my being? This is not easy to answer. It involves knowing oneself, the real person inside, as few of us do without prayerful self-examination.

- Does my dream involve taking anything, or any person, belonging to someone else? Would its fulfillment hurt any other human being? If so, you can be fairly sure this particular dream is not God's will for you.

- Am I willing to make all my relationships with other people right? If I hold resentments, grudges, bitterness, no matter how justified, these wrong emotions will cut me off from God, the Source of creativity. No dream can be achieved in a vacuum of human relationships. Even one such wrong relationship can cut the channel of power.

- Do I want this dream with my whole heart? Dreams are not usually brought to fruition in divided personalities; only the whole heart will be willing to do its part toward implementing the dream.

- Am I willing to wait patiently for God's timing?

- Am I dreaming big? The bigger the dream and the more persons it will benefit, the more apt it is to stem from the infinite designs of God.

If your heart's desire can pass a series of tests like this, then you are ready for the final necessary step in the Dreaming Prayer! Hand your dream over to God, and then leave it in His keeping. There seem to be periods when the dream is like a seed that must be planted in the dark earth and left there to germinate.

But the growth of that seed, the mysterious and irresistible burgeoning of life in dark and in secret, is God's part of the process. The very moment a God-given dream is planted in our hearts, a strange happiness flows into us. I have come to think that at that moment all the resources of the universe are released to help us. Our praying is then at one with the will of God, a channel for the Creator's always joyous, triumphant purposes for us and our world.

Prayer: Give Me a Dream

Father, once—it seems long ago now—I had such big dreams, so much anticipation of the future. Now no shimmering horizon beckons me; my days are lackluster. I see so little of lasting value in the daily round. Where is Your plan for my life, Father?

You have told us that without vision we perish. So Father in heaven, knowing that I can ask in confidence for Your expressed will, I ask You to deposit in my mind and heart the particular dream, the special vision You have for my life.

And along with the dream, will You give me whatever graces, patience and stamina it takes to see the dream through to fruition? I sense that this may involve adventures I have not bargained for. But I want to trust You enough to follow even if You lead me along new paths.

I admit to liking some of my ruts. But I know that habit patterns that seem like cozy nests from inside may, from Your vantage point, be prison cells. Lord, if You have to break down any prisons of mine before I can see the stars and catch the vision, then Lord, begin the process now. In joyous expectation, Amen.

The Prayer of Relinquishment

ne kind of prayer I learned through hard experience. It is a way of prayer that has resulted consistently in a glorious answer, glorious because each time power beyond human reckoning has been released. This is the Prayer of Relinquishment.

I got my first glimpse of it in the fall of 1943 while bedridden with a "closed case" of tuberculosis. After reading the story of a missionary who had relinquished her own eight-year battle for health, telling God she wanted Him even more than she wanted healing, I did the same.

"I'm tired of asking," was the burden of my prayer. "I'm beaten, finished. God, You decide what You want for me."

Tears flowed. I felt no faith as I understood faith, expected nothing. The gift of my sick self was made with no trace of graciousness.

And the result? It was as if I had touched a button that opened windows in heaven, as if some dynamo of heavenly power began flowing, flowing. Within a few hours I had experienced the presence of the living Christ in a way that wiped away all doubt and revolutionized my life. From that moment my recovery began.

Through this incident and others that followed, God was teaching me something important about prayer. Gradually I saw that a demanding spirit, with self-will as its rudder, blocks prayer. The reason for this, I understood, is that God absolutely refuses to violate our free will; that unless self-will is voluntarily given up, even God cannot move to answer prayer.

In time I gained more understanding about the Prayer of Relinquishment through the experiences of others, both in contemporary life and through books. Jesus' prayer in the Garden of Gethsemane, I came to see, is the pattern for us.

Christ could have avoided the cross. He did not have to go up to Jerusalem at the festival season. He could have compromised with the priests, bargained with Caiaphas. He could have capitalized on His following and appeased Judas by setting up an earthly kingdom. Even in the Garden on the night of the betrayal, He had plenty of time and opportunity to flee. The next morning Pilate wanted to release Him, all but begged Him to say the words that would let him do so. Instead Christ used His free will to turn the decision over to His Father.

The Phillips translation of the Gospels brings Jesus' prayer into special focus: "Dear Father, all things are possible to you. Please— let me not have to drink this cup! Yet it is not what I want but what you want."

The prayer was not answered as the human Jesus wished. Yet power has been flowing from His cross ever since. Even at the moment Christ was bowing to the possibility of an awful death by crucifixion, He never forgot either the presence or the power of God.

There is a crucial difference here between acceptance and resignation. There is no resignation in the Prayer of Relinquishment. Resignation says, "This is my situation and I resign myself to it." Resignation lies down in the dust of a godless universe and steels itself for the worst. Acceptance says, "True, this is my situation at the moment. I'll look unblinkingly at the reality of it. But I'll also open my hands to accept willingly whatever a loving Father sends." Thus, acceptance never slams the door on hope.

Yet even while it hopes, our relinquishment must be the real thing; and this giving up of self-will is the hardest thing we human beings are ever called on to do.

I remember the agony of one attractive young girl, Sara B., who shared with me her doubts about her engagement.

"I love Jeb," she said, "and Jeb loves me. The problem is, he drinks. Not that he's an alcoholic or anything. But the drinking is a sort of symbol of a lot of ideas he has. It keeps bothering me— enough that I wonder if God is trying to tell me to give up Jeb."

As we talked, Sara came to her own conclusion. It was that she would lose something infinitely precious if she did not follow the highest and best that she knew. Tears glistened in her eyes as she said, "I'm going to break the engagement. If God wants me to marry Jeb, He will see that things change—about the drinking and all."

Right then, simply and poignantly, she told God of her decision. She was putting her broken dreams and her now-unknown future into God's hands.

Jeb's ideas and ideals did not change, and Sara did not marry him. But a year later she wrote me an ecstatic letter: "It nearly killed me to give up Jeb. Yet God knew that he wasn't the one for me. Recently I've met another man and we're to be married. Today I really have something to say about the wisdom and the joy of trusting God. . . ."

It is good to remember that not even the Master Shepherd can lead if the sheep do not follow Him but insist on running ahead of Him or taking side paths. That is the why of Christ's insistence on a very practical obedience: "Why call ye me, Lord, Lord, and do not the things which I say?" (Luke 6:46).

Obedience . . . trust . . . are all over the Gospels. The pliability of an obedient heart must be complete, from the set of our wills right on through to our actions.

When we come right down to it, how can we make obedience real except as we give over our self-will in reference to each of life's episodes, as it unfolds, whether we understand it or not, and even if evil appears to have initiated the episode in question?

This was the challenge to Mrs. Nathaniel Hawthorne, wife of the famous American author, as she wrestled in prayer in the city of Rome one February day in 1860. Una, the Hawthornes' eldest daughter, was dying of a virulent form of malaria. The attending physician, Dr. Franco, had warned that afternoon that unless the young girl's fever abated before morning, she would die.

As Mrs. Hawthorne sat by Una's bed, her thoughts went to her husband in the adjoining room and what he had said earlier that day: "I cannot endure the alternations of hope and fear; therefore I have settled with myself not to hope at all."

But the mother could not share Nathaniel's hopelessness. Una could not, must not die. This daughter resembled her father strongly, had the finest mind, the most complex character of all the Hawthorne children. Why should some capricious Providence demand that they give her up? Moreover, Una had been delirious for several days, recognized no one. Were she to die this night, there could not even be the solace of farewells.

As the night deepened, the girl lay so still that she seemed to be in the anteroom of death. The mother went to the window and looked out on the piazza. There was no moonlight; a dark and silent sky was heavy with clouds.

I cannot bear this loss—cannot—cannot. . . .

Then suddenly, unaccountably, another thought took over: *Why should I doubt the goodness of God? Let Him take Una, if He sees best.*

More than that: I can give her to Him! I do give her to You, Lord. I won't fight against You anymore.

Then an even stranger thing happened. Having made this great sacrifice, Mrs. Hawthorne expected to feel sadder. Instead she felt lighter, happier than at any time since Una's long illness had begun.

Some minutes later she walked back to the girl's bedside, felt her daughter's forehead. It was moist and cool. Her pulse was slow and regular. Una was sleeping naturally. The mother rushed into the next room to tell her husband that a miracle had happened.

In the realm of answered prayer, the progression of events in Una's recovery was not unique. For in the years since I first read the Hawthornes' story, I keep hearing of strikingly similar experiences from other mothers. The pattern goes like this:

In every case the mother wanted something desperately: life and health for her child. Each mother virtually commanded God to answer her prayer. While this demanding spirit had the upper hand, God seemed remote, unapproachable.

Then, through a combination of the obvious futility of the petition, plus weariness of body and spirit, the one praying surrendered to the possibility of what she feared most. At that instant there came a turning point. Suddenly and unaccountably, fear left. Peace crept into the heart. There followed a feeling of lightness and joy that had nothing to do with outer circumstances. And from that moment, the prayer began to be answered.

Now the intriguing question is: What is the secret or spiritual law implicit in this Prayer of Relinquishment?

Here is part of it. We know that fear is like a screen erected between us and God so that His power cannot get through to us. So, how does one get rid of fear?

That is not easy when the life of someone dear hangs in the balance, or when what we want most in all the world is involved. At such times every emotion, every passion, is tied up in the dread of what may happen. Obviously only drastic measures can deal with such a gigantic fear. My experience has been that trying to force it down by repeating faith affirmations is not enough.

Enter the Law of Relinquishment. Was Jesus expressing this law when He said, "Resist not evil"? Stop fleeing from and denying this terrible prospect. Look squarely at the possibility of what you fear most.

It seems to us at the time that this is the opposite of trust. "Lord," we are inclined to protest, "didn't You tell us to pray with faith? I'm confused. Does relinquishment mean that we can never be persistent about praying for any definite thing?"

To all such pleas for understanding, Jesus always, patiently gives the same answer: "Obey Me. Then—afterward, not before—you will begin to understand."

So we take the first hard steps of obedience. And lo, as we stop hiding our eyes, force ourselves to walk up to the fear and look it full in the face, never forgetting that God and His power are still the supreme Reality, the fear evaporates. Drastic? Yes. But it is one sure way of releasing prayer power into human affairs.

Sometimes the miracle of prayer gloriously answered takes place at that point. With other situations the Good Shepherd leads us from relinquishment on into knowing. Such knowing is different from trying to think positively or making affirmations. It is not our doing at all; it is the gift of God.

Sometimes the knowing is given to us through a verse of Scripture that leaps from the printed page or out of our remembrance and sets the heart afire. Or it may come from a self-authenticating, interior word from the Lord Himself about what is going to happen in our situation. On occasion God may tell us that He cannot return to us what we have relinquished, as in the case of Sara B. Obviously we have not really meant business about the Prayer of Relinquishment until we have faced that eventuality, too.

When, on the other hand, a loving Father grants our wish, gives us the thing we have ceased demanding, we understand that relinquishment and faith are not contradictory. The Prayer of Relinquishment is the child dropping his rebellion against being a child, placing his hand into the big, protective hand of the Father and trusting Him to lead even in the dark.

And if the darkness remains . . . if the cross cannot be avoided . . . our hand is still in His. Our heart is still obedient. But now a fresh revelation comes. We look into the Face beside us with a thrill of recognition: the hand of the Father is Jesus' hand!

All along, our heart told us it was so. Relinquishment? Faith? Just the certainty that Jesus is beside us, whatever comes.

Prayer: I Relinquish This to You

Father, for such a long time I have pleaded before You for this, the deep desire of my heart: _____. Yet the more I have clamored for Your help with this, the more remote You have seemed.

I confess my demanding spirit in this matter. I have tried suggesting to You ways my prayer could be answered. To my shame, I have even bargained with You. Yet I know that trying to manipulate the Lord of the universe is utter foolishness. No wonder my spirit is sore and weary!

I want to trust You, Father. My spirit knows that these verities are forever trustworthy, even when I feel *nothing*:

That You are there. (You said, "Lo, I am with you alway.")

That You love me. (You said, "I have loved thee with an everlasting love.")

That You alone know what is best for me. (For in You, Lord, "are hid all the treasures of wisdom and knowledge.")

Perhaps all along You have been waiting for me to give up self-effort. At last I want You in my life even more than I want _____. So now, by an act of my will, I relinquish this to You. I will accept Your will, whatever it may be. Thank You for counting this act of my will as the decision of the real person, even when my emotions protest. I ask You to hold me true to this decision.

To You, Lord God, who alone are worthy of worship, I bend the knee with thanksgiving that this, too, will "work together for good." Amen.

The Prayer of Joyous Blessing

Some years ago I knew of a home in Washington, D.C., that was full of tension because of an aunt's nagging faultfinding with the children. Ellen R., the mother of the family, did much praying about this situation, mostly that God would take away her aunt's hypercritical attitude. Nothing at all seemed to happen as a result, and Ellen became increasingly resentful of her aunt's attitude and presence in her home.

One afternoon Ellen, whom I had known for many years, dropped by our home to return a borrowed book.

"I know I must look a wreck," she apologized. "I feel like a ball knocked back and forth between the children and Auntie."

In the midst of discussing her problem, I had a sudden inspiration. "You've been asking God to change your aunt's disposition, and you say she's more faultfinding than ever. So why not forget about trying to change your aunt and just ask God to bless her, in anything and everything?"

Ellen looked astonished. "You mean I should ask God to bless Auntie whether she deserves it or not?"

Before I could answer, my friend had a counter-thought.

"I see it," Ellen said thoughtfully. "I guess none of us deserves anything from God, do we?"

"That's exactly my thought," I told Ellen. "Nothing we could ever do would be good enough to earn a scrap or rag from His hands."

"Then, Catherine, let's try your idea. But will you pray with me about it right now?"

"Of course. But remember, Ellen, when you ask God to bless someone, what you're really saying is, 'Make him or her happy.' That's the literal meaning of *blessing* in the Bible—happiness."

Ellen's prayer, as I recall, went something like this:

"Lord, I know it's Your will that we be happier in our house than we have been. And I know that can't happen while any one of us is unhappy. Bless Auntie now in whatever ways she needs. Give her the gift of happiness. Help the children to love and respect her, and show me how I can be kinder to her. Amen."

A week later Ellen telephoned. She said that day by day her prayer was being abundantly answered. "The atmosphere here at home is completely different. You know this blessing business is dynamite! But I still don't understand why that prayer was answered when none of the others were. Why would there be such power in wishing joy for someone?"

Perhaps one reason we are surprised when God moves to bless someone when we ask it is that we have thought of Jesus Christ as primarily "a man of sorrows and acquainted with grief."

But no man with an attitude of gloom could ever have drawn little children to Him. Only an enthusiastic man who went out to meet life with unflagging zest could have attracted rugged fishermen as His disciples. Sadness could not last long when a man threw away his crutches delightedly or a leper went leaping and singing on his way to show his clean new flesh to the priest. And don't forget that the Gospels record Jesus as breaking up every funeral He attended!

Certainly Jesus was unblinkingly aware of life's problems and disappointments: "In the world ye shall have tribulation," He promised His disciples. "But," He added, "be of good cheer; I have overcome the world." In other words: "Cheer up! The worst that the world can do is no match for Me."

The real source of Jesus' joy is given us in unforgettable words first spoken by the psalmist and centuries later by the author of Hebrews: "Thou [Christ] hast loved righteousness, and hated iniquity; therefore God, even thy God, hath anointed thee with the oil of gladness above thy fellows."

He who knew no sin and who is righteousness had a personality sparkling and overflowing with a degree of gladness none of us can match. How could it be otherwise!

That is why the Prayer of Joyous Blessing does not depend on our merit or lack of it. Jesus is the only righteous One; therefore, the only finally joyous One. But this joy He longs to share with all who will receive it.

Now we begin to see why my friend Ellen was on firm ground in not making her aunt's "worthiness" a condition for her Prayer of Joyous Blessing. She knew that Jesus told us, "Love your enemies, bless them that curse you." As soon as we begin to obey Him, we find that blessing those with whom we are having difficulties, and the answer to these difficulties, go hand in hand.

And contrariwise, our refusal to bless may impede God's saving intent. I had this dramatized for me some years ago when a woman came to see me, asking my advice about her marriage. Over a cup of tea she told me her problem. She had just had the hardest blow the feminine ego can sustain: Her husband had announced that he no longer loved her and was going to leave her.

Mrs. B. felt that their marital problems were her husband's fault and she was full of harsh criticism of him: He never went to church; he spent little time with their children; he was unfaithful. "Only God can save him," she intoned gloomily.

"Here's an idea how to pray for your husband," I suggested. "Ask God to rain His blessings—spiritual, physical and material—on him, and leave the rest to God."

My visitor sipped her tea, her lips pursed into a firmer line.

"My husband has prospered too much already," she said. "That's the trouble with him. The only thing that will ever bring him to his senses and back to God is trouble, and more trouble."

She left, saying she was going to pray that God would change her husband, make him good, then bring him back to her and the children. And her prayers fell to the ground. The husband eventually got a divorce and married someone else.

If you and I were running the world, probably we would not allow the wicked to prosper. But the simple truth is that often they do prosper. All through the centuries, this fact has bothered men and women. In what may be the oldest book in the Bible, Job wrestles with the problem. It is mentioned in psalm after psalm.

But Jesus was and always is the Realist. He simply took it for granted that because God is all love, the wicked will often prosper: "He maketh his sun to rise on the evil and on the good, and sendeth rain on the just and on the unjust."

"Therefore," Jesus was saying, "if you are going to be true sons of your Father in heaven, then you'll have to pray for the very best to happen to everyone you know, no matter how you personally may have been mistreated or hurt by them."

Is Jesus saying, then, that goodness or wickedness is of no consequence to God? Not at all! Sin is a serious matter, serious enough to have sent Christ to His cross and our world closer and closer to the brink of disaster. But the point is that self-righteous or accusing prayers do not change men and women from bad to good. Only joyous love redeems.

Long before Jesus' day, the ancient Israelites stumbled onto the truth that gladness is a key to God's empowering presence: "The joy of the Lord is your strength." "In thy presence is fulness of joy." "Serve the Lord with gladness."

Having so often seen the Prayer of Joyous Blessing gloriously answered, I have begun to wonder recently if here we do not have a key to world peace. Even for those who take prayer seriously, it is not easy to know how to pray for other nations. It is especially hard when their ideals are not ours and when they consider themselves our enemies.

Perhaps Christ would say to us, "The people of all nations are My children, too. The more violent, greedy men ignore Me and prey on My innocents, the more they need to be released to My all-encompassing love."

Now obviously, we cannot bless and pray for people who despitefully use others, or pray for people with whom we are at odds, unless we recognize that no self-effort can manage this and until we let Christ living in us love others for us.

But it may be that if even a handful of citizens could pray with that kind of joy for the people of "enemy" nations with the expectation of good, asking for God's all-abundant blessings on them in every sphere, tremendous results would be forthcoming.

Our first reaction to that suggestion may be exactly what Mrs. B.'s was: Too risky! Which of us wants other nations to pull out ahead of our own nation in the sciences, in the exploration of outer space, in military know-how, in the economic sphere?

But it is not a risky way to pray once we see that God's way is to make "his sun to rise on the evil and on the good," and that His sun of joy is the only power in the universe capable of transforming the hearts of men and women, no matter what their problems, their politics or their nationality.

Prayer: Bless Us, Father

Father, I cringe to see myself in that Pharisee in the Temple, for I have been believing a lie: That since I have tried to serve You, I have a right to ask for your blessings; but that _____, so unbelieving and uncaring about You, deserves the difficulties he/she has.

Now I understand, Father, that You must manifest love and joy to us, Your creatures, because You *are* love and joy; that You, as the Sun of Righteousness in whom no darkness dwells, shine upon us because it is Your nature to shine—not because a one of us is deserving of it.

I now release _____ from my judgment and I ask You to bless him/her abundantly in any and every way that seems good to You.

So live Your life in me, Lord, that from henceforward I shall desire as much good for others as I ask for myself; that I shall never again plead largess for myself and in my heart begrudge Your blessings for others.

Cleanse me of all selfishness and ungenerosity. And O Father, fill me up with the joy of Him who was anointed with the oil of gladness above us all. In His name I pray. Amen.

SECTION
NINE

Dark Night
of the Soul

From the beginning Catherine felt that she was to be fearless and selfless about revealing to readers her spiritual valleys as well as her mountaintops. Early in her career Catherine also realized that God often used her weaknesses more than her strengths as teaching points.

During the summer of 1971 and the months that followed, Catherine went through a dark night experience that shook her faith and tested all her resources. The following experiences led up to it:

1. MGM had paid handsomely for the rights to film Catherine's bestselling novel *Christy*, then shelved it.

2. After spending three years working on her second novel, *Gloria*, that, too, on the counsel of her editors and advisers, had to be shelved. This was her first editorial failure.
3. Catherine's relationships with me, with her son, daughter-in-law and stepchildren were strained.

Catherine's chief stumblingblock to marrying me was one she had never written about: my divorce. She had prayed about it and felt God telling her that He was in the business of redeeming and restoring broken situations and families, which she felt was a "yes" to our marriage.

Our first five years together in Chappaqua, New York, were creative and fulfilling. Then in 1964 Catherine began experiencing a recurrence of lung problems. When doctors suggested a warmer climate for her, we moved to Florida, with me commuting every other week to my job at *Guideposts* in New York City. By 1971 seven years of this week-at-home, week-away schedule was hurting our marriage.

On July 22, 1971, a third child was born to Peter Marshall and his wife, Edith. Amy Catherine was genetically damaged with cerebro-hepato-renal syndrome (brain, liver, kidney malfunction). Peter and Edith had lost their first child, a little boy, shortly after birth. Then they had a healthy little girl, Mary Elizabeth, now a lively three-year-old. The doctors gave this new baby six weeks at most.

For Catherine this was the worst blow yet—a baby named after her condemned to die. Rebellion exploded inside her as she issued a call to family and close friends to gather at

Cape Cod to pray for a miracle of healing for Amy Catherine. When sixteen of us gathered at Cape Cod, Catherine reported that the Lord had told her the baby would be healed.

An extraordinary week of prayer followed. There were healings, sure enough, among the sixteen who came to pray. God used baby Amy Catherine as a catalyst to touch many lives. Then, at exactly six weeks old, she died.

Catherine was devastated, felt betrayed by her Lord. Her dark night of the soul had begun.

These excerpts from *Light in My Darkest Night* reveal how Catherine emerged from the shadows.

The Clouds Descend

*atherine:* I believe that Satan won the victory last summer in the Amy Catherine situation. His handwork is all through it.

As I told the family the night before the funeral, there was a vast difference between the day of Amy Catherine's death and that of Peter Marshall back in 1949. I felt Jesus' presence in the room where Peter died. For a week after his death I walked in the glory of the Kingdom of God on earth.

At the time of Amy Catherine's death I could not feel Jesus' presence in her hospital room. On the contrary, I sensed evil there. We did not walk in any glory in the days following. Far from it! There was dissension, blame flung about, nitpicking over various decisions, a sense of failure.

Despite the good things that happened to some of the people who gathered to pray on Cape Cod, I have seen no good come from Amy Catherine's death itself, only misunderstanding and confusion. I have not understood why the results were so negative. I have not understood what was behind all this.

I dreamed last night that I was in my own home, though it was a larger house than our actual one, with several floors. Climbing to the top floor, I found to my surprise six people living there. They were not overtly antagonistic toward me but were obviously intruders; they had moved in secretly and were doing their housekeeping with inadequate equipment, a scruffy broom, etc.

Today, trying to interpret this dream, I sought the identity of my "squatters" so that they could be ousted. The first appeared to be *depression*, the second *unshed tears*, the third *grief*. That's all I've gotten so far.

The fourth one of the "squatters" in my dream of several days ago has to be *sleeplessness*. On the way to the airport to fly to New York yesterday, I realized that I had left my sleeping pills behind. So last night in the New York hotel I did my usual lying there, hour after hour, waiting for dawn. Just a bit of dozing the last few hours, from which I awoke with a raging headache. And still no feeling of Jesus' presence at all.

Yesterday I was struck by a phrase I read somewhere long ago: *We learn humility through humiliations.*

Having gone through a humiliation last summer, I should have much more humility today. Yet I don't feel that I've grown spiritually in this area. I don't feel that I've grown spiritually in any area these past months.

Humiliation. The dictionary calls it "a painful loss of pride, dignity and self-respect." I feel I represent every bit of that description and I don't like it at all.

My humiliation, of course, is a paltry nothing compared to the humiliation suffered by Jesus on the cross. Yet somehow Jesus and His suffering seem remote, unconnected with me and my present misery—that's all I seem to think about these days. I'm aware of a fatal self-centeredness here, but seem incapable of breaking free.

I woke up this morning with a Scripture passage running through my head: "No one is able to come to me unless he [or she] is drawn by the Father" (John 6:44, Moffatt).

Does that mean, I asked myself, *that I can't have a relationship with Jesus unless God instigates it?*

My mind whirled back through the years. Had God drawn me to Jesus as a child? Obviously so. The Father in heaven had drawn me to the Son. But now I feel no relationship with either Jesus or the Father. That seemed to end the day Amy Catherine died. So the Father must be blocking me from this relationship. Why?

I don't want to pursue it further. It's too painful. The hurt over my grandchild's death has to heal. I'm incapable of seeking understanding by going back over the events yet again.

So where does this leave me? Wallowing in my sin? Clearly this is so, but I feel helpless to do anything about it. I'm reminded bitterly of an article I wrote for *Guideposts,* "The Power of Helplessness." I sure don't feel any power in my present state of helplessness. Nor do I sense God coming to my aid. All above me, it seems, is a heaven of brass. My dreams recently have certainly reflected my state:

In one I was the preacher's wife in a church where an elaborate wedding required tickets of those invited. I seemed to have arrived late and not really dressed correctly. There was some discussion as to whether I was to be let in without a ticket.

Whatever was decided, I never saw the inside of the church in the dream. Instead, because something was missing, a whole group of us had to go and get it—whatever it was. As we went on this errand, I kept losing things. First my fur stole, then my gloves. The group grew angry at me; there were even physical threats. I woke with the sense of being odd-man-out, rejected by those who counted.

In another dream I was in an apartment where the plumbing was badly out of order and about to flood the place. I knew where the leak was, but instead of attending to it, I left the apartment to go to a meeting where President Nixon was speaking. I was seated in the front row. Since I had left the apartment while sorting the laundry, I still had in my hands a pair of my dad's old dirty work pants and two dirty socks.

During the meeting, I dropped the soiled laundry to the floor, and to my chagrin, the President came to where I was sitting, picked up the dirty work pants, looked at them wonderingly and handed them back to me. Though humiliated, even in my dream came the thought, *But they are not soiled in any shameful way, but through honest work!*

When I got back to the apartment, water covered the floor and the plumber had to be called immediately. Here the dream ended. Clearly the overflowing water from the neglected leak represented some situation that my subconscious knew to be wrong, which I was refusing to put right.

And still another dream: I was due to make an important speech, but had no time to go back to the hotel and change my clothes. I was told, "No, you'll just have to wear what you have."

This was dreadful because I had on an old skirt and ankle socks. Behind the stage at the auditorium I started to make up my face while several people watched me impatiently. By now I was acutely aware of an auditorium full of people waiting, too.

The makeup was a process of bungling and stumbling. I could not find a lipstick in the various cluttered purses I had with me. Finally I found it and with shaking hands tried to apply it, while trying to collect my thoughts about what to say in my speech. Thinking about the talk, I absentmindedly applied lipstick around my eyes. Those watching were startled. I tried to wipe off the lipstick, then apply powder on the area. *I'll go out there looking like an old hag,* I thought. There to my great relief the dream ended.

All these dreams have features in common: clutter, disorganization, unpreparedness, unacceptance of me by those around me, unhappiness with myself, a feeling of being threatened by circumstances and the critical attitudes of others.

And in them all—acute humiliation.

In the Valley

 *en:* I found Catherine sitting in her chair by the bed, looking listlessly through some catalogs. It was 11:30 A.M., a time when ordinarily she would be in her office hard at work on a manuscript. *How do I penetrate the darkness of her spirit?* I asked myself.

"We need to talk," I began.

"What about?"

"You cannot go on like this. We're all deeply concerned about you."

Catherine shrugged. Her eyes went back to her catalogs. My concern for her shifted to irritation. "How can you go against the warning you've so often given others about wallowing in self-centeredness?"

For a moment her eyes flashed. I welcomed this, preferring anger to apathy. The sparks quickly subsided, however, and she shrugged again. "Just say that I'm wallowing in my sin."

"You are doing exactly that, and what's more, you're enjoying it."

Catherine shifted about uncomfortably. "What do you want me to do?"

"Put the Amy Catherine matter to rest and get on with your life."

The pain inside suddenly shone through. "I can't put it aside."

"Why?"

"I keep seeing her little mouth crying out for help. I can still feel her body in my arms, wanting so much to be held and loved, yearning for health. Every time I try to do any writing, these images return to haunt me."

"Why don't we take off for a week? Go down to the Keys, perhaps, or to one of the islands."

Catherine brightened for a moment, then shook her head. "I don't think I'd be good company. It's my problem and I'll work through it." She thought for a moment. "What was the title of that *Guideposts* piece by Joe Bishop? 'The Way Out Is the Way Through'? Maybe I should read it again."

"The point of the article is that you don't duck a painful issue, you meet it head-on. Are you doing that?"

"I'm trying to." She paused for a long moment. "In some ways you know me better than anyone else in the world. In one area you don't know me at all."

"What's that?"

"There's a part of me, deep down, that since my childhood has belonged only to the Person of Jesus Christ. He and I have had some wonderful sharing times together. He has been with me in every crisis—until now." Her lip began to tremble. "Now He just isn't there anymore. Each morning when I awake, I seek Him, to no avail. I must have offended Him terribly this past summer."

I put my arms around her, feeling her pain, fighting back my own tears. "You've been through these dark times before, haven't you? What about those occasions during your widowhood when you felt estranged from God?"

"They were more like dry periods when I was simply unproductive. And they never lasted very long. Sure, I'd be sunk in self-pity for a stretch, but Jesus was somehow close to me even then. For months now there has been real darkness. I feel like I'm talking to the ceiling. And you know how listless my prayers have been."

I nodded. Listless was the right word. "When did you first feel this rejection—if that's what it is?"

For a while Catherine didn't answer. In fact, I had to repeat the question. Her thoughts seemed many miles away.

"I'm not sure," she said at last. "Probably right after Amy Catherine's death. Possibly after hearing about Virginia Lively's prophecy that Amy Catherine would not live. She heard correctly. I didn't."

"And that hurt your pride."

"She should have told me."

"If she had come up to you in Cape Cod and reported this revelation to you, you would have rejected it flat. I've never seen you so convinced, so determined about anything as you were about Amy Catherine's healing."

"I'll never go out on a limb like that again—for anything or anyone, ever," she snapped.

I took a deep breath. "I think it's your anger at God that has shut the door on your relationship with Him."

She shook her head vigorously. "I've been angry at Him before and He still comforted me. I believe God encourages us to be honest, to express anger when we feel it. So I don't think you're right, Len. Sure, I was angry when Amy Catherine died. Rebellious, too. . . ." She stopped, hearing her own words.

I voiced her unspoken thought. "There's a big difference between anger and rebellion. Feelings of anger are often justified, and usually subside fairly quickly. Rebellion is more long-lasting and destructive. Remember that Bible class we taught last year? How you kept stressing that it was the rebellion of the Israelites that kept them from the Promised Land?"

She nodded. "One's words can come back to haunt one, can't they?"

"Think about it, Catherine," I urged. "You're miserable without Jesus. Maybe you should go off somewhere alone and pray it through."

Catherine: Inside I am dry and lonely, unable to accomplish anything, really just going through the motions of life, and barely able to do that. It is more than a dry period. I've been through those before and did not lose the Presence. This is darkness. Deadness. Awful in the way it numbs you, makes you cold and indifferent. You do the very thing, say the very word, you know you should not. Frightening!

I must get down on paper some of the passages I've encountered this week in my reading of Scripture. Though my prayers are hollow and uninspired, I am receiving instruction from His Word. If the Lord will no longer speak to me directly, then I will go this route.

Here are some of the passages I have been led to:

When you spread forth your hands in prayer, imploring help, I will hide My eyes from you; even though you make many prayers, I will not hear; your hands are full of blood! Wash yourselves; make yourselves clean; put away the evil of your doings from before My eyes; cease to do evil.

> Isaiah 1:15–16, TAB

The Lord is far from the wicked, but He hears the prayer of the [consistently] righteous—the upright, in right standing with Him.

> Proverbs 15:29, TAB

You do ask [God for them] and yet fail to receive, because you ask with wrong purpose and evil, selfish motives. . . . You [are like] unfaithful wives [having illicit love affairs with the world] and breaking your marriage vow to God! . . .

> James 4:3–4, TAB

During my afternoon nap I had yet another version of a dream that has recurred over and over. I am always in a very large house. I go through corridors and rooms, from one floor to another. There are many people around but they pay no attention to me, and I have nothing to do with them, do not appear to know them. I am searching, searching for my own room, my own place, but cannot find it. I cannot even find which floor it's on. Fear is in the dream, building to panic. Sometimes, in exhaustion, I even stop in someone else's room to take a nap in order to get strength to rise and start searching again.

Usually I awaken from this recurring dream with my stomach hurting and symptoms of severe tension, probably with raised blood pressure.

"In my Father's house are many mansions. . . ." This passage used to comfort me because it promises a place for everyone. I do have a place in the universe. Why am I now so lost?

This terrible feeling of lostness, apparently deep in my subconscious, must reflect my separation from God. When one has lost one's way and can no longer feel the Shepherd's hand, when the Valley of the Shadow is dark, with the light of faith withdrawn, what does one do then?

Trust God in the dark and wait and hope and hang on as best one can, I suppose.

I have recently received some illumination about this shut-in place in which I have been so confined. It came from a section in *Mysticism* by Evelyn Underhill entitled "Dark Night of the Soul."

She explains that for those who have trod the Christian way for some time, a spiritual fatigue can creep in. In this state one knows anew the helplessness of the human condition. In fact, for a time we can be in a worse state there than at the beginning of our Christian walk.

The reason: When one first becomes a Christian there is, along with new awareness of one's frailty, the sure and wonderful knowledge of God's adequacy. In the darkness that assails the long-time Christian, the skies seem totally deaf; no light breaks through at all. Nothing, inside or outside, seems to work.

This is certainly my state at this time.

According to Evelyn Underhill, if one can ride it through on sheer, blind faith, just hanging onto the rock of salvation, then it has to pass, and we go on to a higher state in the spiritual life.

What was a fresh thought to me was that this dark state is necessary in our Christian growth. It comes when we've reached a kind of plateau of faith where nothing is changing, where certain areas of our life remain uncommitted to Jesus Christ, not being taken over by Him. So we have to find fresh truths in our helplessness and our need, become desperate in a new way, in order to get on with the next stage in our Christian development.

Even many great Christian saints went through a "dark night" experience, some pretty gruesome, according to Underhill, before they came out into the light again. This is encouraging for us ordinary strugglers!

More on "The Dark Night" from Evelyn Underhill: "The most intense period of that great swing-back into darkness . . . is seldom lit by visions or made homely by voices. . . . Stagnation . . . impotence, blankness, solitude, are the epithets by which those immersed in this dark fire of purification describe their pains."

I pause a moment to reflect. Am I being purified? I see none of that, at least not yet. There is stagnation, all right, more like sloth.

Len: After breakfast Catherine would go to her office to write. "How is she doing?" I would ask Jeanne Sevigny. Jeanne, by now a close friend as well as secretary and a participant in our ministry, would just shake her head. "Productivity about zero."

"Nothing at all."

"Nothing for me to type. She keeps reading over parts of the *Gloria* manuscript, but we all know that project is dead. A part of her seemed to die with it. We do get the mail answered, but I have to push and shove and prod her even with that."

"What's your diagnosis, Jeanne?"

"Grief and frustration. Anger, too."

"Aimed at whom?"

"God, mostly. And at us, too. All of us, even her mother."

"Buried anger, isn't it? She doesn't explode as she used to."

"You're right. I think the explosions were a lot healthier."

My efforts toward dialogue with Catherine were mostly unsuccessful. After receiving a series of one-word answers to my questions, I would usually back off. Yet I knew I had to keep trying. If only something would go right for her! The movie version of her novel *Christy* seemed permanently shelved, likewise her novel *Gloria*, though she kept pulling the manuscript from the file drawer and going through the motions of working on it. Amy Catherine had died. Her relationship to Peter and Edith was strained. In fact, none of her relationships was working very well.

The best news I had to give her was about Linda, who continued to astonish me with the changes in her life.

"Linda has found a most remarkable group of Christian friends," I told Catherine one day in our bedroom after I had visited Linda in Washington at the nonprofit organization Cornerstone where she worked. "In addition to her administrative responsibilities and leading a Bible study, Linda writes a newsletter. I think she has a gift for writing."

No response.

"Tell me something, Catherine. Why do you refuse to see the many positive results of Amy Catherine's short life? She was used in a mighty way, you know."

Catherine looked at me wearily. "I'm glad for Linda and for all the others who were helped. It's very self-centered of me not to be more grateful for this, I know. Forgive me."

"You say that, but you don't mean it. Words are coming out of you, but there's no emotion to back them up. It's as if the real you has gone somewhere else and I'm talking to a cardboard figure."

"Thank you for those kind words."

I shifted to another line. "You said several days ago that you felt you were moving about in a dark cage. Do you mean something like a prison?"

"That's pretty close."

"What are you doing to get out?"

"Not enough, I guess. I feel like a dead person. Abandoned."

"Not by those of us here in this house. We love you. We're praying for you."

"Thank you."

I sat down on the bed where she was sitting and reached for her hand. "I've heard you say many times that when a lot of things go wrong in a person's life, the Lord is trying to get that person's attention. I'm sure you've been applying this to yourself."

For the first time, Catherine's eyes met mine. "I sure have."

"What do you think He's saying to you?"

Long pause. "That I'm probably out of His will. That I may have been out of His will for some time."

There was sudden tension between us; a warning light within me cautioned me to cease the probing. Yet another part of me knew I must push ahead.

"How long do you think you've been out of His will?"

The question lay between us for a moment. Both of us knew where we were heading. Catherine's eyes left mine and her lip trembled.

"Since I married you," she finally said.

"You know and I know that everything hasn't gone wrong since we were married," I challenged her. "Forget all the books and articles we've worked on together and their impact on people. Look at the lives of our four children. Has our marriage made things better for them or worse?"

"Better, I guess. But I think you could have married any number of women who would have been better mothers to your children. I just think that I was supposed to stay single after Peter's death."

"And live alone in that comfortable sanctuary you were building, a snug retreat, well away from the action? That's not the guidance you got before we were married. After warning you that it would be difficult at times, the Lord nudged you to say yes to a new life with me."

Catherine nodded. "I remember. But I'm not at all sure about my guidance anymore. I thought I heard the Lord say He was going to heal Amy Catherine. Obviously I heard Him wrong. Maybe I heard Him wrong about us."

I sat there a moment struggling with a decision. How to reach Catherine? Gentleness and patience? Or confrontation? I made up my mind. "Would you like to hear my opinion as to when you began to move away from God's will?"

Catherine stared at me stonily. "Go ahead."

"It all began with the enormous success of *Christy*. I watched the change in you. It was gradual over many months. The plaudits, the adulation, the bestseller lists, the movie sale, all heady stuff. When we flew to New York for interviews, the publisher insisted on providing a limousine. We both loved it. Then came the bowing and scraping by the editors when you described your next book, another novel.

"What they were saying, essentially, Catherine, was that you could do no wrong. That's when the change in you really began. Deep down inside, you bought it. Every book you'd written, a major success. Magazines eager for articles."

I paused, watching Catherine's reaction. She didn't appear resistant, so I plunged ahead.

"It was at this point, Catherine, that I began to feel the arrogance. Before the success of *Christy* you had what I felt was a delightful sense of inadequacy, especially for one who had been so successful. It was this inadequacy that I related to when we first met. You needed God. Without Him you were incomplete. In a lesser way you needed me. We made a good team in both work and play. On your book projects you needed Tib. Then, after *Christy*, you changed. Ask yourself, Catherine: Did you come to a point where you felt you didn't need God anymore? Or me? Or anyone?"

Catherine flared. "I've always needed God."

"If you've always needed Him, why can't you reach Him now?"

A stricken look clouded Catherine's face. Tears welled up. I tried to embrace her, but she turned away. I patted her shoulder for a few minutes, then left her alone.

Catherine: I am forced to the conclusion that Len is right. I did become spiritually arrogant after *Christy*. I became selfish with the use of my time, not wanting to be bothered with people who bored me or disagreed with me. I forgot too easily what I owed to the skills of others.

God was right to discipline me. I deserved it. Len was right to correct me.

But did the punishment fit the crime? I now feel so completely abandoned, rejected. The pain of Amy Catherine's death still immobilizes me. It's so dreadful to be in a state of darkness that I can understand better the fear of hell. How awful eternal darkness must be!

Reading about the "dark night" in Evelyn Underhill's *Mysticism* both helps and depresses me. Her description of the pain and anguish suffered by St. Theresa of Avila, the sixteenth-century Spanish Carmelite, is agonizingly real to me. And Heinrich Suso's ten years of darkness—ouch!

Is there something inside those great saints that invites, even seeks this kind of suffering? The holy men and women of medieval times seem to have inflicted torture upon themselves as a way to subdue their flesh and thus come to know God better. I confess I'm baffled by this. Life is painful enough without making it more so. Some of these godly people make it sound as if the dark night experience should be deeply relished because it will end up being good for you.

In reading about these Christian saints and mystics, I'm reminded that though the way we talk about our faith changes, the basic truths of Christianity do not. Ego-slaying is a modern term for the process St. Catherine went through. It was a concept I thought I'd come to grips with in *Beyond Our Selves*. I'm forced to the conclusion now that though I may have assented intellectually to this principle, I have done little to live it out.

There are other popular phrases to describe it. "The cross life" is one used today in many Christian groups; "self-abandonment" is another. Whatever the words used, the underlying reality is the same: For there to be more of God in a person's life, there has to be less of self.

The suffering saints—and I should include Job here, too—make my troubles seem small and paltry indeed, but their ordeals continue to frighten me. Is this the kind of "cross life" the Lord wants all of us to live? If so, why does the Bible promise in so many places "good things" for those who love the Lord?

Did those saints have a certain kind of spiritual pride that the Lord found obnoxious and that needed to be demolished? More to the point, do I have this same kind of spiritual pride, and is my dark night experience His way of chastening me?

I find myself with many questions and few answers.

I have never had a problem facing up to the fact that I am a sinner. Since the fall of Eve in the Garden of Eden human nature has been sinful. Glibly I can repeat, "I am a sinner saved by grace."

By saying this, however, I place myself in a general category of sinners, enabling me to avoid facing up to the fact that I have committed, am committing, specific sins. It is much more comfortable to be general than specific. The other day I ran up against this phrase in *My Utmost for His Highest* by Oswald Chambers: "Sin is red-handed mutiny against God."

That hit me like a sledgehammer blow. I am in rebellion against God. I have been for many months now. I am in despair about it but cannot seem to change. All is darkness in my life. Nothing is working. I read books, I go to church, Len and I pray together, but Jesus is not in any of it. My sin is separating me from God—Father, Son and Holy Spirit.

Chambers also says, "If sin rules in me, God's life in me will be killed; if God rules in me, sin in me will be killed." How do I make that switch so that God again rules in me?

I do not want to go through a ten-year period of darkness, as Heinrich Suso did.

A Shaft of Light

*en:* One morning in the spring of 1972, two of Catherine's closest women friends, Virginia Lively and Freddie Koch, and I asked Catherine to join us in the living room of our Boynton Beach home. We were all struck by her joylessness, her heavy spirit and by the deep circles under her eyes. Sleeplessness was becoming more and more of a major problem for her.

We talked aimlessly for a few moments, then Catherine, always blunt, cut it short.

"You're here to confront me," she stated. "Let's get on with it."

"We've tried to be helpful to you several times since Amy Catherine's death," Freddie began. "You admit you're in trouble, we pray together and nothing happens. Why?"

Catherine shrugged, then waved her hand in a helpless gesture. "I wish I knew."

"Are you still angry at God?" asked Virginia.

Catherine hesitated a moment. "Who am I to be angry at God? He is our almighty Lord, who knows all, sees all and has His own ways that are mysterious and incomprehensible to us. It would be awfully silly for me to pit my puny anger against the Almighty."

"Yet that's what you've been doing for the past six months," I stated.

271

For a moment I hoped Catherine was going to deny it, argue back with her old zest. But she quickly subsided into passivity.

"What's happened in the past six months isn't as important as what happens in the future," Virginia enjoined. "We love you, Catherine, and it hurts us all to see you suffering."

Freddie Koch drew a deep breath and said, "Catherine, I feel the Lord is telling me something that He wants me to tell you. It's about your self-pity. You're neck-deep in self-pity."

Catherine nodded unemotionally. "I think that's probably right. I confess to being a mess. So how do I get out of this hole? I'm sick to death of the darkness in my life."

"You could really be sick to death unless you do something about it, Catherine," said Virginia.

"The first step is to confess the rebellion and self-pity to the Lord," I suggested softly. "Confession and repentance."

Catherine shrugged hopelessly. "I've already done this, again and again. I honestly have. It's the complete lack of response that confounds me. I've never, ever lived in this kind of vacuum before. I talk, I pray. Nothing. For most of my life I've felt God's presence, heard His voice, received thoughts that I knew came from Him. No more. He's gone from my life. I know I offended Him terribly last August. I guess I offended almost everybody. But I was so totally caught up in the Amy Catherine battle. It was all-out warfare, you know. Nothing ever like it."

Tears began spilling out of her eyes. "What's destroying me is that I understand nothing about it, nothing about anything that happened. What's wrong with going all-out for something you believe in? God likes single-eyed people, doesn't He? It says so in Scripture. Well, I've always tried to be one hundred percent in everything I do. And always before God honored my efforts. Why not this time? Why have I been flattened so completely?

"I know it's happened to others. Great saints have gone through dark nights a thousand times worse than mine. But they almost seemed to ask for it, seeking some higher plane of spirituality. I didn't ask for anything for myself, only that a tiny baby be healed; and God not only refused that request but turned His back on me. I don't understand."

"Maybe it's that insistence on understanding that's the problem, Catherine," suggested Virginia.

Catherine stared at Virginia for a moment with a hint of surprise in her eyes.

Something stirred in me. Had we made a small breakthrough in Catherine's impenetrable shell?

When the session broke up after a prayer time, I was still not sure.

Catherine: Something happened to me yesterday when Virginia, Freddie, Len and I met. For a moment a shaft of light seemed to break through the darkness. When I awoke this morning, however, the darkness still surrounded me. My prayers still seemed to bounce back from the ceiling.

Then for the first time in months, a new and gentle thought came to rest on my mind: *Read Isaiah 53.* It didn't come from my thoughts, nor would Satan likely be sending me to Scripture. With a surge of hope, I knew it had to be from the Lord.

I read the 53rd chapter of Isaiah eagerly, struck anew by this foretelling of how Jesus would suffer hatred and rejection, of how alone He would be on the cross. These passages leapt out at me:

He was oppressed and he was afflicted, yet he never said a word. . . . He was buried like a criminal . . . but he had done no wrong. . . . Yet it was the Lord's good plan to bruise him and fill him with grief.

Isaiah 53:7, 9-10, TLB

I had read this passage many times before, even since Amy Catherine's death, but it had not affected me as it did now, particularly the tenth verse. God made His own Son suffer, but it was a "good plan." More than "good," it was perfect, as only something from God could be. It was terribly important to the future of the human race that Jesus Christ have His dark night experience on the cross. Yet what a desperately dark night it had to be for Him, a time of despair and abandonment, for Him to have cried out, "My God, my God, why hast thou forsaken me?" (Matthew 27:46).

Suddenly I was overwhelmed with feelings of remorse, embarrassment, gratitude and relief, all mingled together. Reading about the saints and their trials had not touched or enlightened me the way this sudden realization had. For reasons of His own, God had allowed Amy Catherine to be born genetically damaged. Her death served God's purposes, fulfilled His plan in some specific way not revealed to us, just as Christ's death on the cross baffled and dismayed His disciples at first, but did not destroy their faith.

I heard my own words, "What's destroying me is that I don't understand." I, from my tiny human vantage point, demanding to see into the secrets of eternity!

Virginia had challenged me on it: "Maybe it's that insistence on understanding that's the problem, Catherine."

How many others had tried to caution me? Linda, reading from Isaiah: "Maybe we aren't supposed to understand why God does certain things." Tib, with one of the best minds I know: "Just because I don't understand something doesn't mean it isn't so."

What about the weeks after Peter's death when my plea for understanding was met with something infinitely greater?

Instead of feeling rejected and abandoned, I suddenly felt ashamed. When Amy Catherine died, I demanded that God explain Himself to me, and when He didn't, I proceeded to sulk like a child, a petulant child who had failed to get her own way.

Now, day after day in our Florida home, I shut myself away with my Bible and notebook to work through my new discoveries, seeking a new relationship with my Lord.

Again and again I have read the crucifixion account, feeling the aloneness, the agony, the abandonment Jesus must have felt. I am there in the crowd, looking up into His face.

Flooded anew by contrition one afternoon, I burst into tears and stumbled to my knees. "Forgive me, Lord. Forgive me for my rejection of You, too."

Then came this revelation: When life hands us situations we cannot understand, we have one of two choices. We can wallow in misery, separated from God. Or we can tell Him, "I need You and Your presence in my life more than I need understanding. I choose You, Lord. I trust You to give me understanding and an answer to all my why's, only if and when You choose."

Understanding. That seems to be the key word in my difficulties. I have sought it from the Lord most of my life and in His gentle tenderness He has often provided it. So often, in fact, that I had begun to take it for granted, assumed I had a right to understanding. What arrogance! What presumption!

Then a new thought hit me like a thunderbolt: Presumption was my sin. During the prayers for Amy Catherine, I took the lead in telling God what He was to do about Amy Catherine: "Thank You, Lord, for healing this tiny, precious baby." Had I really heard Him say what His plan was for her? Or had I wanted the healing so badly I simply imagined that He must, too? Presumption. I had assumed something I had no right to assume. God will always be God. We will never fathom His ways, but I presumed to try. "O Lord, forgive me for my presumption."

Then still another thought struck me. Worse than my presumption, even, is the fact that with Amy Catherine I had really wanted to play God, to be God in her life. Appalled, I tried to

detach myself from this sin. There was no detachment. I tried to
usurp the power of almighty God. "O Lord, can You forgive me
for this abomination?"

And He answered me. At long, long last, I heard the Voice that
had been silent for so many months: *I, your God, am in everything.
The baby died, but Amy Catherine is with Me. And while she lived, she
ministered to everyone who prayed for her. You alone, Catherine, were
too stubborn to see it.*

> After this first glimmer of light, Catherine began a disci-
> plined early morning program of a 6 A.M. arising, with Scrip-
> ture reading, prayer and a focus on praise. It was months before
> Catherine was ready to resume her writing ministry. When
> she did, seasoned by her dark night experience, ten of her most
> productive years followed.

SECTION
TEN

The Intercessors

As the editor of *Guideposts* from the 1950s into the 1970s, I worked on many prayer articles. The term *intercession* was familiar to me—"praying for others." I remember suggesting once to another editor, "Intercession doesn't exactly roll off the tongue. Wish we could come up with a simpler word for it."

After my marriage to Catherine in 1959, when we joined two broken homes, there were so many prayer concerns in our family that we set aside that early morning hour for prayer. I began listing the specific people and situations, the date we prayed and when and how the prayers were answered. Soon I had a prayer log that served as the basis for a book called *Personal Prayer Journal*, which Catherine and I published in 1978.

By now the word *intercession* had a more familiar ring. Scripture passages using the term were meaningful.

Then one morning early in 1980 Catherine felt led to go off alone to her office to pray. She knelt in front of her reading chair, opened her Bible on the seat of the chair, placed her hands on it and prayed, "Lord, do You have a special word for me today?"

Sometime later Catherine sought me out. Her eyes were shining. "I had an incredible time with the Lord this morning," she began. "He showed me that I knew almost nothing about intercession. Then He gave me a vision for a new ministry."

The pages that follow contain Catherine's description of how the Breakthrough intercession ministry started, plus excerpts from some of her teachings in its newsletter.

The Vision

have never known a time of such burgeoning need as in our world today. Not just in the lives of those who have never received Christ, but even in Christian families. With so many frantic requests in my mail each day, I ask myself continually, How is it possible to respond adequately?

My mind turns to several organizations that handle such requests by mail or phone. But, my thoughts protest, these groups usually respond with a single prayer petition offered for each need presented, probably with little sacrifice of thought or time given. Surely such a one-time intercession falls far short of the sustained prayer needed.

Then I remember how I was first taught about the awesome power released when a group of people covenant together to pray about a specific need for a stipulated length of time.

On November 10, 1953, I was to leave for Hollywood for two months of daily script conferences as Twentieth Century-Fox began making *A Man Called Peter* into a motion picture. On November 1 I sent a letter to 1,800 friends who had written me after reading the book, asking them for two months of specific prayer that this movie would be protected from "Hollywoodizing" and would be God's project all the way.

The response was overwhelming. I heard from almost everyone who received the letter. And this wave of prayer was gloriously answered! Hollywood proved no match for our sovereign God. *A Man Called Peter* was not only Fox's biggest box office picture for 1955; more important were the lives inspired, even turned around by this movie. For me, this experience was an unforgettable lesson in the power of concerted intercessory prayer.

As I prayed about many concerns one morning, a vision began taking shape in my mind. One part of the vision was a picture of a growing number of Christians—among them the elderly, the handicapped and those in institutions of some sort—dissatisfied with their present level of service.

In the letters I receive, such people ask, "How can I make my life count for more? I'd like to serve Jesus in some way but I'm so limited in movement." Or, "With small children at home, how can I get out where the need is?" Or, "So many appeals come from our church and I have so little money to give."

Recently two parts of the vision began coming together. On the one hand there are His hungry, thirsty, needy sheep who are reaching out, asking frantically for prayer. On the other hand are all those Christians whose intense heart's desire is to be of help, but who are seeking the practical means.

In the vision I saw need and supply coming together. A third part of that vision—a physical location to serve as a coordinating center, to receive the prayer needs and pass them on to intercessors—was already in place in a remodeled school building here in Lincoln, Virginia, currently serving as a publishing headquarters but soon to be vacated.

The passion of Jesus' heart has always been "Feed My sheep." Those asking for prayer often feel so lonely and isolated. They have such a desperate need of knowing that somebody, somewhere cares about them. On the other side are people with time on their hands and untapped potential—time to care, time to write letters, time to pray.

During this same period, certain books and pamphlets have come into my hands stressing the fact that intercessory prayer is the most important work there is in the Kingdom. So important, in fact, that the Pioneer and Captain of our salvation, Jesus Christ Himself, "ever liveth to make intercession" for us (Hebrews 7:25).

Having accomplished our redemption on His stark cross, the glorified Lord's chief work before the Father's throne is to intercede as our perfect High Priest (Hebrews 2:10, 17-18). But to complete His work, He also needs some of us on earth to share His concern, His passionate caring, to be His hands, His feet and His voice in co-intercession. Only then is the circle completed from heaven to earth and back to the Father's throne again.

But let's admit it, intercession *is* work. It means caring about others as much as ourselves, sacrificing time and energy to their well-being.

And if I am anything like the typical Christian, I know all too little about the how of praying for others. So in my vision I saw that some teaching about intercessory prayer would be necessary, including the sharing of fresh insights and discoveries as we made them. All of that would, in turn, take regular communication through something like a periodical newsletter.

"It seems like a big order, Lord," I protested.

"Are not My dreams always big ones?" came the gentle reply.

And being His dream, it would not go away, but caught fire with others. An article was published in the magazine *Charisma*, inviting people to become intercessors for the non-profit organization Breakthrough that was formed to do this work. Hundreds responded.

[Editor's note: To learn how you might get involved in this intercessory prayer work, see the Appendix on page 349.]

"Old Warhorse"

s we took the first steps toward setting up the mechanism to do the work of Breakthrough, I remembered a chapter in Betty Malz' book *Prayers that Are Answered.* She described one "prayer warrior" nicknamed "Old Warhorse Buckland" as the person her family called on for prayer help in every emergency. As a young girl, Betty had never seen "Old Warhorse," but she imagined him to be a seven-foot giant of a man with booming voice and flashing eyes.

One day Old Warhorse came to dinner, arriving by car. Betty's dad hurried down to the street to help *her* out of the backseat and guide her tottering steps to the house. She was small, stooped, plainly dressed.

Betty was terribly let down until she looked into Mrs. Buckland's face. Gray hair; firm, resolute chin; patrician nose; character lines creasing her forehead like rivulets. But it was her eyes that held Betty. They flashed determination, tenacity, power. Flecks of fire seemed to emanate from the gray irises of her eyes.

The elderly woman's voice, however, was gentle. She told Betty that as a girl she had been plain; she could not sing, play an instrument or even sew very well. She was too small for sports. But she did love to read.

Stories of courage had fascinated her. She fantasized about riding horses to battle. As an American Joan of Arc, she vanquished the forces of evil in every skirmish. When she became an all-out believer, she transferred her battle to the spiritual realm. And then came the discovery: God had given her the gift of prayer power for others! She rode figurative horses into battle as she fought the forces of Satan.

Her prayers were not loud, but intense and prolonged—in fact, unceasing. As she prayed for people in crisis, she put on the whole armor of God, claimed the power of Jesus, mounted her horse and went "against the rulers, against the authorities, against the powers of this dark world and against the spiritual forces of evil in the heavenly realms."

Old Warhorse did not need to leave her house to wage these battles. Instead, she called upon God to send His ministering angels into action.

This "little" woman did not stop her prayers even when the enemy was in retreat. She kept praying after the victory was won, only too aware that the enemy will return if given a chance.

We need people like Old Warhorse Buckland who know some of the secrets of intercession. We need those who have the willingness and the heart's desire to tithe some time each day for prayer effort on behalf of His lost, hurting sheep. All of us agree that our world is at a crisis stage. Why should we Christians lie down and allow a massive assault of evil to invade our families and our society?

God has given us the total victory of the power of the cross through the weapon of prayer. Isn't it time that we covenant together to pick up that awesome weapon and use it to His glory?

Why Answers Can Be Delayed

hose of us involved with intercession learn patience. If we do not, we are in constant turmoil, railing against the inscrutable quality of the Almighty.

A friend tells me, "For eight years I've been praying that my son John will become God's man. I know that what I'm asking is His will. And John's three children need a Christian father. So—why such a long-delayed answer to prayer?"

Another friend writes me, "Ted's affair with that 'other woman' still goes on. I love my husband and this is devastating to our teenagers. I've prayed every way I know to pray and God doesn't seem to hear me. How long will this misery last?"

Is there in your life a cherished desire taken to God over and over in prayer, yet still unfulfilled? Then link hands with my two friends, and with the rest of us, and with all prayer warriors across the centuries! No wonder Jesus had so much to say about persistence in prayer (Matthew 7:7–11, 15:22–28; Luke 11:5–10).

Jesus' actions were consistent with His teaching. As in the story of Lazarus.

We read about it in the eleventh chapter of John. The first few verses set the scene: Lazarus' home in the village of Bethany, less than two miles from Jerusalem. It was the Master's favorite retreat spot where He could relax with His friends Martha and Mary and their brother Lazarus, all three dear to Him.

One day the sisters sent an urgent message to the Master: "Lord, he whom you love so much is desperately ill. Please come quickly."

As I read this story one morning, the transition word between verses 5 and 6 all but leaped off the page: "Now Jesus loved Martha, and her sister, and Lazarus. When he had heard *therefore* that he was sick, He abode two days still in the same place where he was."

Verse 5: He loved this little family especially.

Verse 6: *Therefore* He delayed going to them in their distress.

How odd! Why?

Martha and Mary did not understand either. For as Jesus waited, Lazarus died. Separately each sister verbalized the same thought: "Lord, if You had been here, our brother would not have died. You could have prevented it."

Distressed by their grief to the point of tears and groaning, Jesus gave two reasons for His deliberate delay: First, this experience was going to increase their faith—that is, their ability to trust Him in the midst of seemingly impossible circumstances; and second, they were to have an even greater firsthand demonstration of the glory of God.

The Lazarus story has a message for you . . . that Jesus loves you especially. You are His special friend. *Therefore* He delays. The *therefore* has wrapped in it the limitless love of God, with Jesus experiencing to the full, along with us, our concern, our agony of spirit and sorrow.

Meanwhile, where do we get the needed patience? When the situation shows no change or even grows worse (as with Lazarus), how do we hang onto the faith that God's love is working out our problems?

Marge, a dear friend of mine, was shown how. She and her husband had just learned that he had Parkinson's disease. The entire family gathered, anointed their father and husband with oil, asked the Lord for His healing, then made a deliberate act of turning the situation over to Him.

But Marge's heart questioned, "Until such time as our family sees this prayer answered, how can I keep enough peace of mind not to let worry and fear destroy me?"

God answered her question in an experience Marge had aboard a plane bound for Cleveland, waiting for takeoff. As she settled into her seat, Marge noticed a strange phenomenon. On one side of the airplane a sunset suffused the entire sky with glorious color. But out of the window next to her seat, all Marge could see was a sky dark and threatening, with no sign of the sunset.

As the plane's engines began to roar, a gentle Voice spoke within her.

You have noticed the windows, He murmured beneath the roar and thrust of the takeoff. *Your life, too, will contain some happy, beautiful times, but also some dark shadows. Here's a lesson I want to teach you to save you much heartache and allow you to "abide in Me" with continual peace and joy.*

You see, it doesn't matter which window you look through; this plane is still going to Cleveland. So it is in your life. You have a choice. You can dwell on the gloomy picture. Or you can focus on the bright things and leave the dark, ominous situations to Me. I alone can handle them anyway. And the final destination is not influenced by what you see or feel along the way.

Learn this, act on it and you will be released, able to experience the "peace that passes understanding."

Marge's sharing is helping me to handle my "meanwhiles." Not one of us finds it easy to put our problems into His hands that completely. But only in that way can our trust in Him grow and our prayer life mature.

The Waiting Prayer

Over the years Catherine learned a lot about patience in prayer, particularly with her son, grandchildren and three step-children. Here is a petition she offered up regularly.

ord Jesus, You want honest words on my lips; no thought of mine is hidden from You anyway. I am puzzled about the Father's timing.

You know how long I have been praying for _____. I have tried to be patient about the answer.

I know that the seasons come and go in majestic sequence. The earth rotates on its axis in a predetermined rhythm. No prayers of mine could change any of this. I know that Your ways are not my ways; Your timing is not my timing. But Lord, how do I, so earthbound, come to terms with the pace of eternity?

I want to be teachable, Lord. Is there something You want to show me, some block You want removed, some change You want in me or in my attitudes before You can answer my prayer? Give me the gift of eyes that see, of ears that hear what You are saying to me.

Come, Lord Jesus, and abide in my heart. How grateful I am to realize that the answer to my prayer does not depend on me at all! As I quietly abide in You and let Your life flow into me, what freedom it is to know that the Father does not see my threadbare patience or insufficient trust, rather only Your patience, Lord, and Your confidence that the Father has everything in hand.

In Your faith I thank You right now for a more glorious answer to my prayer than I can imagine. Amen.

The Mercy Prayer

When you spend a great deal of time praying for others, there is much to learn. Like the Mercy Prayer.

It was my Florida friend Betty who taught me about this way of praying. She had been attending a baptism in an Episcopal church. The baby being christened was not only crying but screaming his lungs out.

"I could see how embarrassed the infant's parents were and I felt such compassion for them," Betty said. "But then the thought dropped into my mind that there was no way I could possibly be feeling more compassionate than Jesus. So I simply prayed, 'Lord Jesus, have mercy on that baby and his father and mother.'

"Catherine, it was remarkable. The crying stopped as if a faucet had been turned off."

Betty went on to explain that she had first "discovered" the mercy prayer when her husband had undergone surgery for cancer. His recovery had seemed threatened some months later when his doctor suspected a return of the cancer.

"It was a time of great agony," Betty told me. "All my praying, hours of it, finally jelled down into a single heartfelt plea: 'Father in heaven, will You have mercy on us simply for Jesus' sake?'"

The result? The finest cancer specialists at Duke University pronounced it a false alarm. There was no return of the cancer.

Since talking with Betty I have spent several of my morning prayer times asking the Lord for insights about the Mercy Prayer. Passage after passage of Scripture was brought to my attention. I saw that many of Jesus' healings, as recorded in the Gospels, came as the result of a prayer for mercy by some sufferer.

There were, for instance, the two blind men sitting by the side of the road one day as Jesus was leaving Jericho (Matthew 20:29-34). Hearing that this was Jesus passing by, the two men cried out, "Have mercy on us, O Lord, thou Son of David."

The crowd following the Master rebuked the men, telling them to keep quiet. But the blind men were so desperate they only cried the louder: "Have mercy on us, O Lord, thou Son of David."

And Jesus, standing still and giving the men His full attention, asked what they wanted of Him. When they begged Him to open their eyes, He had compassion on them, touched the eyes of both men, and immediately each received his sight.

Then there was the time Jesus encountered ten lepers (Luke 17:11-14). Since lepers were ostracized from public gatherings, these ten men stood at a distance crying almost in unison, "Jesus, Master, have mercy on us."

The Master did not question each man about how well he had kept the Law or how righteous he was. Out of Jesus' overflowing, compassionate love, He healed all ten on the spot. "Go at once, and show yourselves to the priests for proof of your healing," He told them. "Your faith has already made you clean."

Faith in what?

The connecting link is our belief that God loves each of us far more than does the most warmhearted person we know; that He heals simply out of that all-encompassing love. "I will have mercy, and not sacrifice: for I am not come to call the righteous, but sinners to repentance," Jesus said (Matthew 9:13).

The apostle Paul expressed the same truth: "Blessed be the God and Father of our Lord Jesus Christ, the Father of mercies and God of all comfort, who comforts us in all our affliction" (2 Corinthians 1:3-4, RSV).

"So then [God's gift] is not a question of human will and human effort, but of God's mercy" (Romans 9:16, TAB).

You and I are altogether dependent, in other words, whether we recognize it or not, on His love and mercy.

From earliest times the liturgical church has incorporated this reality into its essential act of worship, the sacrament of holy Communion:

> Lord, have mercy upon us.
> Christ, have mercy upon us.
> Lord, have mercy upon us.

Cruden's *Concordance* provides an extensive list of Scripture references to the word *mercy*. Alexander Cruden's original words of description set down in 1769 are rich food for thought: "Mercy signifies that the essential perfection is in God, whereby He pities and relieves the miseries of His creatures." And, "'Grace' flows from 'mercy' as its fountain."

The resounding validity of the Mercy Prayer all through Scripture is meant for everyone: "The Lord is good; his mercy is everlasting; and his truth endureth to all generations" (Psalm 100:5).

The Servant Role

The message I am getting today from Jesus is the servant role that He wants to play in the lives of every one of us. Scriptures that affirm this include Matthew 20:28, TAB: "The Son of man came not to be waited on but to serve, and to give His life as a ransom for many"; and Luke 22:27, TAB: " . . . I am in your midst as one who serves."

When Jesus wrapped a towel around His waist, poured water into a basin and began to wash His disciples' feet (see John 13:4-5), Simon Peter objected that this was beneath the dignity of the Master. I want to insist along with Peter that we, as His disciples and intercessors today, are to be the servants.

But Jesus answered him, "If I do not wash you, you have no part in me."

This is a stunning and stupendous thought. Unless I can believe in this much love for me, unless I can and will accept Him with faith as my Servant as well as my God, unless I truly know that it is my good He seeks, not His glory (He already has all of that He can use for all eternity), then I cannot have His companionship.

What an amazing revelation!

Freedom from Bondage

esterday as I was praying and lifting up certain people who had written to me of their needs, I was suddenly aware that there had been a gradual change in the type of problems presented in my mail. More and more people seem to be in bondage to something: alcohol, drugs, sex, gambling, money, careers.

Then I was given a fresh viewpoint of what a difficult time the Lord must have had in freeing Saul of Tarsus from his bondage to the Jewish law. For Saul (who became Paul) was a legalist and all-out persecutor of Christians because they were violating the Law.

Yet as we read Paul's letters, we see evidence over and over of how total his freedom became. Paul berates Christians for even considering the need of circumcision, for instance, the very foundation of Jewish Law.

How was Saul freed so totally of his bondage?

The key might well be in the words Saul heard on the road to Damascus: "Saul, Saul, why are you persecuting Me?"

If Jesus considered Himself to be the One persecuted and sinned against, more so even than the Christians Saul had killed or thrown into prison, then is not Jesus the central figure in our present-day problem with bondages?

And if so, then during the period I was in bondage to sleeping pills, I was offending and grieving Jesus more than I was hurting myself.

When our neighbor down the street beats his wife because of his bondage to alcohol, he hurts his wife, but his greatest offense is to Jesus.

When any of us allow ourselves to be in bondage to the things of this world, we offend and grieve Jesus.

So turn the coin over for the answer. Jesus is saying to us:

Why do you grieve Me with your dependency on alcohol, pills, sex or sweets? Look to Me for freedom from these bondages. I am the Healer and the Restorer. I am the One to set you free.

Jesus, and Jesus alone, is the Teacher and Corrector and Deliverer from any bondage. Then the old Saul in me, my dependence on [name your bondage], is dead.

Thank You, Lord Jesus, for life and freedom in You.

Pulling Down Strongholds

s lust one of the strongholds in your life? Is it envy? Or greed? Whatever has a grip on you, know that the Lord is ready to help you be freed. Hold onto this promise:

(For the weapons of our warfare are not carnal, but mighty through God to the pulling down of strongholds;) Casting down imaginations, and every high thing that exalteth itself against the knowledge of God, and bringing into captivity every thought to the obedience of Christ.

2 Corinthians 10:4–5

In intercession the picture often comes to my mind of a strong, fortified castle-fortress atop a steep hill with precipitous cliffs all around. Deep inside a man or a woman is held in chains, a prisoner. Armed guards patrol the area. This is Satan's stronghold. But the above passage tells us that the weapons of our spiritual warfare are able to demolish even such seemingly impregnable bastions.

For Scripture also tells us that Satan's strongholds are delusions, unreal, lies, just as everything he says is a lie and everything he tries

to persuade us is real is not real at all. The only real Stronghold is
Jesus Himself and the Truth that He is and stands for:

> For You [Lord] have been a stronghold to the poor, a stronghold
> to the needy in his distress, a shelter from the storm, a shade from
> the heat; for the blast of the ruthless ones is like a rainstorm against
> a wall.
>
> Isaiah 25:4, TAB

> The Lord is good, a strength and stronghold in the day of trouble;
> He knows—recognizes, has knowledge of and understands—those
> who take refuge and trust in Him.
>
> Nahum 1:7, TAB

Our refuge, no matter what the assault, is in the light of Jesus'
presence. In it we see His truth; in it Satan's lies stand exposed.

SECTION ELEVEN

The Flood

Of all the hundreds of writers I have worked with, Catherine had perhaps the most total absorption with the literary process. As soon as she learned to read, she fell in love with books; they were best friends. As a teenager she began to write poetry. She loved research and always overdid it, whether in a term paper or a novel!

She had researched *Christy* for a year when I married her, having spent weeks in the Great Smoky Mountains, talking to the mountain people, recording dialect and figures of speech and spending countless hours in North Carolina and Tennessee libraries. One reason it took her nine years to write *Christy* was her perfectionism over the small details.

So it was with her novel *Julie*. On three occasions we drove four hundred miles from our home, Evergreen Farm, to Johnstown, Pennsylvania, to research the big floods of 1889 and 1934, the operation of a big steel mill, the inner workings of a weekly newspaper.

Facts and details—Catherine loved to track them down. And she was great with descriptions, character development, bringing out spiritual truths. I loved dialogue, confrontations, plotting the action. With both *Christy* and *Julie* we used our trips by car to talk through the characters, plot the action and suspense.

While the model for nineteen-year-old Christy had been Catherine's mother, Leonora, Julie was eighteen-year-old Catherine herself with her passion for causes. As a reporter for the weekly *Sentinel*, Julie could take on corrupt capitalists, battle for oppressed workers and be delighted and confused by the attentions of three suitors, one of whom was from Great Britain.

And when the big flood occurred, she was right in the middle.

*S*aturday, September 21, 1935, began in such a normal way.

There had been heavy rain across western Pennsylvania on Friday as predicted. It rained especially hard north of Alderton between midnight and six A.M.

When we gathered for breakfast, Mother outlined for Anne-Marie and me some chores she wanted done.

"They're expecting me at the Fleming farm this morning. Queenie's about to have her puppies," Anne-Marie protested.

My father sighed. "Call and ask if you can come out after lunch. If not, then I guess you can do your chores this afternoon."

Anne-Marie was soon back to report that she was needed this morning. Dad capitulated and agreed to drive her to the farm in the Willys. As Anne-Marie skipped out the front door, she winked at me. I was not amused. I was needed at *The Sentinel*.

Life and death for everyone in Alderton that day hung on such small decisions as to where they would be in the early afternoon.

I carried my lunch to *The Sentinel*, planning to work through the afternoon. When I arrived, Emily Cruley was already there, poring over the subscription list, her black leather case open on her desk with the ledger planted in front of her. She announced self-righteously that it would take her all day to bring it up to date.

Dean Fleming was due in the office after lunch to work on the Goss press.

At 11:30 Rand phoned, very agitated. "Julie, I need to see you. Are you free this afternoon?"

"I'm here all day."

"I'll be there shortly after one."

"Is something wrong?"

"Yes. Things here are in a fright. After he sacked me, Old Man McKeever told me to stay until the club was closed up. But since that official from the railroad stopped by to see him yesterday, he has been in a towering ill humor. This morning he called and told me to clear out by noon today. All my things are in the boot of my car."

"Did you know he is suing *The Sentinel* for two million dollars?"

There was silence, and then a whistle at the other end of the line.

"He's lashing out at everyone in sight," I added.

"The Old Man's not there now, I gather, or you wouldn't be talking so freely."

"He's at the *Vulcania*. But you never know when he'll show up. Can't wait to get out of here. I'll see you in about two hours."

At 12:30 Rand called again. "Julie, I'm not sure when I can make it. The rain last night was so heavy that the lake is rising very rapidly. We've opened the spillways, but it looks as if there'll be an overflow. I'll ring you up later."

Rand telephoned me a third time while I was eating my sandwich. His voice was tense. "I'm leaving right now to see you."

"Is the dam all right?" I asked.

"I can't tell. A lot of men are there working on it."

When he hung up, I had an eerie feeling that I should call him back and ask him to meet me at our home instead. How silly!

When Rand arrived, he walked swiftly back to the editor's office. As he closed the door and turned to me, I was astonished at his appearance. His hair was tousled, his face flushed, his shirt rumpled. I had never seen him so wrought up.

"Dean just called," I said. "Worried about the dam. He's coming down to grease the press. Thinks we ought to clear out."

Rand nodded, flicked a shock of red hair out of his eyes and grinned at me.

"May I kiss you?" he asked.

The look in his eyes made me tremble. "Why so sudden?"

He pulled me to my feet. "No reason. I've been wanting to kiss you for two weeks now—no, three—no, it's closer to four."

I started to resist, but his lips closed over mine. His intensity so overwhelmed me I could scarcely breathe. When we broke apart and I caught a breath, his lips found mine again. Moments later I pulled away and sat down numbly in Dad's chair.

"Rand, please."

He shook his head, sat down beside me and began to stroke my hair. Then he drew my face toward him and kissed each eye and the tip of my nose before he reached my mouth again.

The telephone rang. I was so weak I could barely lift the receiver. "Hello."

A strangled voice spoke, one of Dean's friends. "Get out quickly! The dam broke! A wall of water is heading for Alderton."

Rand saw the fear on my face and grabbed my hand as we ran out of the office toward the front door.

"The dam broke!" I shouted at Emily.

As we reached the door, two people from the street had pushed it open from the outside.

"Too late!" one shouted. "You can hear the water coming. To the top floor!"

We all turned and scrambled frantically up the stairs.

There is no way I can describe the mammoth tragedy of that Saturday, except to put together chronologically the graphic details given me over a period of months and even years afterward by my family and friends, as well as other survivors.

The heavy rain of Friday night covered all of western Pennsylvania. In the mountain area just north of Kissawha Dam there was a torrential downpour that totaled nearly fifteen inches in a three-hour period. The runoff into the lake from the two feeder streams, Bear Creek and Smather's Run, began about 6:00 Saturday morning.

One viewer described these streams at 9:00 A.M. as "going berserk." Smather's Run, seldom more than ten feet wide and two feet deep, was nearly fifty feet wide and stripping branches off trees five feet off the ground.

At 10:00 A.M. a resident of the Hunting and Fishing Club climbed into his small outboard and chugged around the side of the lake.

"The meadowland was underwater in spots almost three hundred feet from the edge of the lake," he reported. "Debris everywhere, mostly logs washed down from a sawmill miles away. The lake was a mass of junk."

All available manpower had been gathered by 11:00 that morning as the lake rose and threatened to spill over the dam. The sluice guards and spillways were opened wide. Then one group of men began to pry away the drift guards and tear up the road to get at the heavy iron gratings in the spillway that kept fish from escaping down Brady Creek.

The panting, gasping workers encountered iron grids rusted and wedged in by years of overgrowth. The heaviest crowbars wielded by the strongest men could not budge them.

By 1:00 P.M. logs, tree branches and other flotsam flowing into the lake from the two feeder streams had reached the dam, adding to the pressure on it. Suddenly workers were horrified to see several large concrete blocks loosen, then tumble thunderously into the stream below. A geyser of water shot thirty feet into the air.

At this point the workers made a final effort to slow the overflow by pouring wheelbarrows full of rocks across the road atop the dam. The heavy rocks were washed off like pebbles.

At 1:30 dam erosion had created a V-shaped notch about six feet wide and two feet deep in the breast of the dam. As it continued to widen and deepen, the workers knew the dam was lost and began a retreat toward the club. Suddenly a big chunk of the roadway over the dam collapsed and was washed away.

Within minutes the opening was so large a yacht could have cruised through it. A sheet of water nearly sixty feet wide was now pouring over and through the opening. So far the concrete buttresses had easily diverted the heavy overflow away from the Sequanoto River into Laurel Run. Onlookers then witnessed an awesome sight. The main part of the earthen dam and the road above it did not burst or crumble, it just moved away. The water, treetop high, exploded over the dam like a living force, sweeping everything before it: trees, other vegetation, rocks, concrete.

The onslaught of water hit the new waterway area with the roar of an express train. Cement retaining walls crumbled, then dissolved into hundreds of missile-like objects and became part of the roaring torrent that joined the Sequanoto River as it thundered toward Yancyville.

It was 2:10 P.M.

It took only 27 minutes for Lake Kissawha to empty more than five hundred million tons of water into the valleys below. Engineers later estimated that 118 tons of water per second pounding away at the dam wall had pushed away 90,000 cubic yards of earth and stone, which went tumbling downstream.

The workers watched, incredulous as the water snapped century-old four-foot-thick trees as if they were twigs and propelled them forward like matchsticks in the swirling torrent. The growing mass of water tore huge boulders from the stream banks and rolled them over and over as if they were marbles.

What had been lake bottom was now eight hundred acres of brown ooze, separated here and there by a few small streams flowing quietly in the direction of the dam. Black bass, pike and trout flopped about in the mud at the bottom of the reservoir basin.

The course of the floodwaters was strangely selective, though it mostly followed the Sequanoto River bed, which flowed through Yancyville, Mills Ford and then into Alderton. Yancyville was the first hit.

Anne-Marie, who had stayed through lunch, was in the kitchen of the farmhouse with Hazel Fleming when she observed Queenie behaving strangely. The usually placid dog, heavily pregnant, was dashing about the yard whining and whimpering. Suddenly the collie sped up the hill toward the small cabin as if in great pain. Anne-Marie, who could not stand to see any animal hurting, hurried after Queenie to see what was wrong.

From her position on the hillside beside the cabin, Anne-Marie heard the flood coming before she saw it. "It was like the roar of a fast freight train," she said later. The noise was obviously painful to Queenie's sensitive ears. Whimpering even more, the dog crept close to Anne-Marie's legs for protection.

Now the booming freight train sound was closer, just around the bend in the river. Anne-Marie stood rooted by the cabin, craning her neck to see. Her first impression was that a dark mist was rolling in. Then she saw a fifty-foot-high wave of debris hurtling forward. She watched in horror as the wall of junk slammed into the right side of the farmhouse. Above the sound of splintering wood and crashing glass, her own screams seemed disembodied.

The roof of the farmhouse tilted sideways. The trunk of a large tree tore through the second-story window above the porch, leaving half of the tree hanging grotesquely outside, swaying in the air. Then the whole building dissolved and was sucked up into the dark mass.

Behind the mountain of trash came the water: huge, churning waves over 75 feet high, carrying along on their swirling surface cows, horses, pigs, trees, sections of fences, boulders.

And, yes, human bodies. A woman's long hair floated on the water. Then the heaving waves thrust a man's body halfway out of the water, only to suck him under again.

Sobbing, Anne-Marie turned her head away. A thunderous crash drew her gaze back. A second wave of water, equally high and spread over a wider front, had crushed two walls of the big red Fleming barn. The ripping, tearing sound of wood, plus the terrified squeals of the animals, sickened her. Just a half hour before, she and Hazel had gone to feed the two Guernsey cows, the riding horses and the beloved old swayback Shorty.

The flow of water continued for about twenty minutes, then stopped abruptly. Because the log cabin had been built on an elevation, the raging water had missed it and Anne-Marie. In fact, the cabin was standing there serenely intact, as though viewing with equanimity the total annihilation of the farmhouse, its mistress and the barn.

Dazed, blinded by her tears, Anne-Marie made her way back down the hill. What had been a gracious dwelling minutes before was litter-strewn ground: a piece of brass, fragments of glass, a kitchen knife, a dented pot, several broken springs, fragments of wood and metal. That mighty body of water had swept away everything else.

Half of Yancyville was demolished by the flood, half was spared. Those farms, houses and stores on the west side of Seven Mile

Mountain Road were swept away. Buildings on the east side, on higher ground, suffered only minor damage.

Just below Yancyville the steel bridge over the Sequanoto River took the full brunt of the waters. Said one observer: "The bridge squirted into the air in a crazy L-shape, then exploded into pieces and was gone."

Mills Ford was the next target.

At 2:11 the Allegheny Local, an eight-car passenger train that serviced some twenty stops between Altoona and Pittsburgh, stopped at Mills Ford to discharge and take on passengers, mail and freight. The exchange usually took five minutes.

At 2:13 the railroad clerk received a frantic call from the Yancyville station. He listened for less than ten seconds, then raced outside, shouting at the conductor: "Get the train out of here! The dam broke and the water is heading this way!"

A whistle blew, the loading of freight was stopped and the train pulled out of the station, building up momentum slowly, one minute ahead of the water. A mile south of Mills Ford the tracks turned from the riverbed and climbed to high ground. Would the train reach this spot in time?

With a grade crossing three hundred yards ahead, the engineer pulled the cord of his locomotive whistle. He never let it go for the next two and a half minutes.

The first wall of water hit Mills Ford at 2:16. Warned by the train whistle and shouting word-of-mouth, over half the population had scampered to higher ground. The station clerk, who fled with the others, later described the approaching mass as "a brown hill a hundred feet high rolling over and over."

A flour mill, five stores, eight houses and the railroad station were obliterated by the first onslaught of water. Pieces of railroad track were spinning and flying about "like someone had rained down a shower of steel spikes from above."

The second wave of water collected three more houses, a wooden church and a warehouse. As the roof of one of the houses disappeared down the valley, a naked man was seen on top of it, holding frantically to what remained of the chimney.

Ahead of the water the engineer of the Allegheny Local had pushed his throttle as wide open as he could. But before the life-saving high ground could be reached, the track bed ahead made a sharp turn around a bend in the river.

A truck driver on Seven Mile Mountain Road several hundred feet above the railroad tracks saw the train's race against death. The water, a tumbling, foaming, debris-clogged mass, closed the gap quickly as the train made its circuitous turn around the bend in the river.

A hundred yards was the difference. The engine had reached high ground, but the rolling water thundered into the last five cars and sucked them up like pieces of kindling, sending them tumbling and bouncing until they broke apart. The engine and three other cars were yanked sideways and flipped over.

In the seconds that passed before the second wave of water struck, seven people scrambled from the first three cars of the train and reached high ground. Then the second force surged into the helpless and prostrate train and lifted up its parts as an ocean wave picks up driftwood along a beach.

The last view the truck driver had was of engine and cars cartwheeling down the floor of the riverbed like a toy train bouncing down a flight of stairs. Death had won the race.

As the first body of water approached Alderton, the weight of its accumulated debris—trees, buildings, automobiles, trucks, railroad cars—slowed it down. At times it appeared to be an almost solid mass, giving out logs, hunks of metal, bodies and boulders along the way. The second body of water caught up to the first about a quarter-mile north of the turnoff road to McKeever's Bluff.

When the second mound of water hit the first, there was a thunderous roar, as though a bomb had gone off. The whole mass seemed to explode into a thousand multicolored pieces. The rays of the afternoon sun revealed one section of the mass as emerald green, another jet-black, still another an oily brown, while pieces of metal caught the sunlight in a weird pinwheeel effect. Then, for no discernible reason, the watery ball veered to the right and ripped a gaping swath through the wooded area behind McKeever's Bluff.

Several viewers lived to describe what then happened to the wealthy steel magnate's private railroad car. "Like a scene in a movie spectacular," said one. "As though the god of water picked up the *Vulcania* like a small toy and threw it over the cliff."

Another said, "It looked from a distance as though the water just nudged the *Vulcania* over the cliff. The *Vulcania* seemed to struggle for a moment as if clawing for its life, then it fell."

The car twisted completely around before tumbling the first hundred feet, where it hit a clump of trees. For a few seconds the *Vulcania* hesitated, then spun, pirouetted and plunged forward end over end.

"It crashed, bounced, slammed into the ground, bounced again as if it had been a pogo stick," reported one witness. "I think it did that four or five times."

At the last crashing impact, a burst of flame shot out one end of the car. Then the *Vulcania* began a slow, rolling, bouncing fall the last few hundred yards down to the outskirts of Alderton. It was a flaming torch when it finally came to rest at the bottom of the hill. Then a wall of water rolled over the *Vulcania*, dissolving it and the hated McKeever inside into a thousand fragments.

When the dam waters hit Alderton, they were about thirty feet high, five hundred feet wide and two miles long.

The time was 2:19.

It takes a moment to react to crisis. When the cry came, "To the top floor," I darted about *The Sentinel* office looking for my sweater. Rand's shout brought me to my senses. He grabbed my hand and fairly propelled me up the stairs. Out of the corner of my eye I saw Emily just behind us, subscription case held tightly to her bosom.

At the top of the stairs I heard a shout and turned to see Dean Fleming coming through the front door. He gave a quick look about and scurried jerkily after us, his bad leg hardly slowing him down at all. In addition to the six of us who raced upstairs from *The Sentinel* office, five others had scampered up the staircase from the side entrance.

The view out the north window of the second floor was frightening. Panicky people were scurrying about in a state of confusion, some heading one direction, some another. The din was growing: dogs barking, women screaming, men shouting, whistles blowing, church bells ringing.

Two comparable scenes flashed through my mind. The first was a picture I remembered in an old religious book of confused people running about on the Day of Judgment. The second was a sight that had turned my stomach as a little girl in Timmeton: a hen flopping around this way and that after Dad had chopped her head off.

Suddenly we saw the reason for the pandemonium below. A dark, misty wall of water was bearing down upon us, one block away. The sound that preceded it was like rolling thunder.

"Upstairs!" The order came from Dean Fleming.

My last glance at the dark mass revealed all sorts of objects swirling in it: an automobile, a bicycle, a push-cart, street signs, bodies.

Rand held my hand as we rushed up the twisting stairs to the top floor; behind us came Dean and Emily, who still clutched her black case. The third floor contained trunks and boxes scattered about. Old-fashioned clothes trees stood upright, sporting costumes and uniforms.

Rand pulled me aside, placed his mouth close to my ear. "Whatever happens, Julie, I love you."

Grinding, buckling noises shook the floor; the entire building groaned. Rand and I fell onto the floor as the bodies of a brown dog and a half-clothed man burst through a window. Our screams were drowned by awesome noises all around us.

How can I find the words to describe the sounds and sensations of a building breaking up? Swirling waters were hurling assault after assault at the foundation. Timbers cracked, then splintered, mortar crumbled, entire walls heaved and buckled.

A rain of dirt and small particles showered us from the ceiling. When the building suddenly tilted, costumes flew in every direction. Rand and I were back on our feet, arms around each other. Dean was next to us, protecting Emily with his body. I heard him murmur these words:

God is our refuge and strength. . . . Therefore we will not fear. . . .
Though the waters roar, though the mountains shake. . . .

Abruptly the floor under us split in two. Next, the seams at the top of the gabled roof ruptured and we could see daylight just above us. Water was pouring through the openings as the floor began to sink under us.

Numbly I stared at the opening above us. Then I found myself thinking that clambering through that space would take no more agility than climbing the cherry tree in our backyard. I jumped on top of a nearby trunk. Rand leaped up beside me, grabbed me with his sinewy arms, strengthened by years of rowing, and propelled me toward the light above.

Desperately I clutched the broken edge of the roof and pulled myself on top. Then I turned to give Rand a hand. He was gone.

The building seemed to explode underneath me. The mass of water catapulted my roof-perch forward as I clawed to keep my handhold. It was tipped at a crazy angle and spun around several times, banging into logs and bales of wire. Dazed, I coughed up brown fluid and clung to a slab of roofing.

Twice my raft almost spun over as I found myself on the crest of a river of debris, cruising through downtown Alderton as buildings on either side of me crumbled. The rushing floodwaters had been slowed by Alderton's stone, brick and wooden structures; we were moving no faster than fifteen miles per hour.

I knew I would not survive on such a wobbly raft. The nearly intact roof of a small house swirled by. In desperation I leaped toward it. My feet went into the water, but miraculously I was able to pull myself up. Then that rooftop was struck by the crest of a wave and began to buck and lurch like a wild bronco. On hands and knees, scrambling and clawing, I clung frantically to it.

I had just a moment to wonder about Rand, Dean and Emily when the branches of a tree swung by and knocked me off my rocking rooftop. Down I plunged into darkness. "This is death," I told myself with surprising calm as blackness settled over me.

Next instant I was catapulted up to the surface. I reached out and grabbed a sodden canvas awning dangling off a piece of house siding. I tried to pull myself up but could not. All strength seemed to have drained from my arms and hands. There was no way I could hang on.

The words Dean Fleming had muttered came back to me: "God is our refuge and strength. . . ."

"Lord, if You have anything for me to do in this life, please save me," I pleaded.

For years afterward I would have the same dream: I was hanging, dangling, gripping that canvas with my fingernails, spitting out putrid water, flinging heavenward my stumbling prayer, knowing that soon my grip would loosen and I would sink down, down. . . .

I felt something brush by. A large tree, torn out by the roots, nuzzled me. With a sudden infusion of strength I pulled myself into the branches and then onto the large tree trunk. Wonderful, protective trees! How I have always loved you!

As I lay there on my stomach, I was able to stare out at scenes all around me—an immense steel girder poking up through the muck; a woman's body clutching a baby and turning over and over in the water; one of the store dummies floating by serenely, hardly distinguishable from other bodies; an entire family—father, mother and two little children—kneeling on the siding of a house. As the current quickened, speeding by me went one dead cow, the bodies of two riding horses, the back of a haywagon and a school of rats swimming smoothly behind a staircase that could have come from our office building.

One hefty woman covered with tar was riding astride a barrel that kept rolling from side to side while she screamed in terror. A man rode past me standing on a large garage door. It was Salvatore Mazzini, the Italian shoe repair man, all alone and totally naked; he raised one hand toward heaven in supplication.

Aware that I was shivering, I looked down and made a shocking discovery—all my clothing had been torn off. I, too, was stripped bare. "Please, let this be a bad dream," I heard myself saying.

But it was not a bad dream. I was astride a large tree, bruised, naked, terrified, as the flood debris merged into one body moved along the riverbed. My tree had slowed down so that instead of holding onto the branches with all my strength, I could sit up a bit and look forward. What I saw was not reassuring. Dead ahead, about three hundred yards, was Railroad Bridge, that stone relic from the past century. People had called it ugly, too small for modern traffic and a transit hazard for all except the smallest boats. It was built to last centuries.

Much of the flood had rushed over, under or around the bridge, which had resisted an immense tonnage of water power. It had remained firm when assailed by logs, trees and pieces of housing. Trucks, railroad cars and whole houses had not budged it. When a locomotive smashed against two stone pilings, bystanders later reported that the bridge trembled but held.

All these big objects blocked up the passageways underneath the bridge, creating a pileup that had quickly reached the top of the bridge and was backed up hundreds of yards in an area as wide and long as three city blocks.

Then came the most terrifying sight of all. Fire suddenly shot out of a small house that had crunched up against the left side of the bridge. As I watched, the flames leapt high, obviously fed by oil or gasoline. With a brisk breeze now blowing, the entire mass backed up behind the bridge could turn into a fiery torch.

What escape was there? The water had slowed down enough that for a desperate moment I considered swimming for the bank. But it was too far off and the water was churning with debris. Could I steer the tree away from the fire? Several kicks in the water quickly showed me the futility of that approach.

Despairingly I looked behind me for help. Dirt-colored water extended as far back as I could see, floating the wildest collection of objects, living and dead, swimming and drifting, all heading for Railroad Bridge. And all set to pile up on top of me, I thought with horror. I wanted to scream, shout, cry, but to whom? Everyone around me was either dead, seriously hurt or struggling to survive. At least I was astride something unsinkable.

I prayed again, "Lord, are You there?" It was a pathetic plea, a bare whisper, as though I were ashamed to call attention to myself in my nakedness. How ridiculous! I'm about to die and yet still concerned about how I look. Have I always been this vain? Then I laughed. The whole thing was ludicrous. I was stripped down to nothing. I came into the world with nothing on; I was going out the same way. Why was I ashamed of being the way the Lord made me?

The thought freed me. I straightened up, realizing that in my hunched-over state, I had assumed an almost fetal position. I was certainly not ashamed of my body; in fact, in the privacy of my room I had admired it. I looked around me again. Then I stood up to see better.

The sun had gone. The sky was overcast and drops of rain pelted down. I liked the feeling of the rain on my body. I looked up and let it wet my face. Tears came; I don't know why. They poured from my eyes and mixed on my face with the rain.

A new, tingling sensation flooded me. It seemed to start in my feet and work upward. How to describe something I had never felt before? Exhilaration. Joy. Elation. Warmth. A combination of all. But something more, too. Caring. No, stronger than that. Love.

I was being suffused with love. Washed in it. It penetrated every cell in my body. I was being totally, completely loved. By whom? By Someone I did not know, but wanted to know very much.

I stood as straight as I could and reached for the invisible sun.

Nineteen minutes had passed from the time the dam was breached until the wall of floodwater smashed into the outskirts of Alderton. North Bridge took the full impact. Three cars were crossing the bridge at the time; the cars pinwheeled and somersaulted into the air like toys, then were swallowed up. The asphalt surface on the bridge simply disappeared, leaving the bridge skeleton tilting at a grotesque angle.

The wave of water then separated. One mass roared southwest into downtown Alderton. The other veered to the east side of the Sequanoto River and bore down on the Lowlands.

The first building hit in Alderton was the one-story brick dwelling and office of dentist Harry Froehling. It was smothered by the thirty-foot-high mass of watery debris. Only the foundation was left. Harry had dashed to safety only minutes before.

Next struck was a vacant two-story wooden structure that had once been used as a stable. It exploded in a shower of kindling.

Jordan's Hardware was obliterated before the mass bored into our three-story Sentinel Building. Observers seemed to agree that this structure put up a fight. The dark, broiling wall broke around the building, causing it to shudder violently. As the follow-up waters continued to cascade into it, *The Sentinel's* home began to totter and tilt. The roof split with a shriek, part of it torn away. People were seen spurting out of the top, spinning, whirling, scrambling, clutching at anything for support.

Then, slowly, the whole building broke apart, floor by floor, and was swept away. Dean Fleming held onto Emily Cruley as they were propelled through the opening in the roof. He managed to get Emily up on a piece of roofing before a tumbling beam knocked him unconscious and he was sucked down into the torrent. Emily was later pulled from the waters, still alive and still clutching her black leather subscription case.

Rand was catapulted into the turgid water and, being a good swimmer, tried to keep himself afloat. Bruised and buffeted, he grabbed a heavy beam as it sped by and hung onto it grimly until his legs were smashed by the pileup at Railroad Bridge. It took rescuers several hours to pry him loose from the debris; by then he was near death from loss of blood.

Of the seven others who scrambled to the top floor of the Sentinel Building with us, only one survived—a woman who was rescued from the tangle at Railroad Bridge.

After conquering the Sentinel Building, the floodwaters roared into the heart of Alderton, looking for bigger challenges. Salvatore Mazzini's shoe repair shop was no obstacle. It was swept up like a piece of flotsam as the old man leapt onto a garage door that was spinning by. Mazzini's body was recovered later, burned almost beyond recognition by the fire.

Onlookers thought that surely the six-story Haslam House Hotel, a solid brick structure, would withstand the roiling waters. At first it seemed to. As the first wave crashed into the brick building, it trembled but held. It resisted the following assaults, too, until a tumbling locomotive gashed a deep hole in the west side of the building at the second-floor level. Waters rushed into the wounds, causing the hole to widen.

Screams poured from the guests as the top floors began to settle. The relentless, flowing mass of debris ricocheted through the hotel, smashing doors, splitting seams, breaking furniture. When the third and fourth floors on the west side collapsed, the whole building shuddered, bobbled, groaned and then broke apart.

I have two vivid memories from the moments just before plunging into the mess in front of Railroad Bridge. One is of the roaring fire about twenty feet to my left and the hideous screams coming from it. The other is of the huge black horse on my right. He kept popping up out of the water, then disappearing into the muck, only to reappear once again like a monstrous rocking horse. I knew he was dead because his hindquarters had been severed.

As we jolted to a stop I burrowed into the tree branches. Then it seemed as if a whole mountain landed on top of me.

Some time later the shouts of rescuers revived me. "There's one under that dead horse!"

Grunts. Curses. "One big heave. Now!"

The weight lifted. Two men pulled me up. A blanket was thrown around me. Someone brought a makeshift stretcher and I was placed on it. The fire was so near I could feel its heat.

Through pain and shock I dimly remember being carried off the bridge. There I was placed beside the road with other wounded. When I tried to test my body, a spasm of pain shot through my back. Better lie still until a doctor could examine me.

Meanwhile the ambulance shuttled back and forth, taking the injured and burned to the hospital. It was getting dark now, and all about me was turmoil and confusion, groans of pain, sobbing, frantic people searching for relatives. I wondered where my parents were. Anne-Marie? Rand? Dean? Spasms of fear shot through me.

The ambulance was back again. A man stood over me, saw my eyes were open. "How bad you hurt?" he asked.

I just shook my head. He called another man and they lifted me into the ambulance. At the hospital I was carried inside and placed on a mattress on the floor of a hallway already lined with injured. An hour must have passed.

"Julie!"

I looked up to see my father. His face was contorted with a mixture of anguish and joy. Then he was kneeling beside me, clutching my hand, his eyes brimming with tears.

"I think I'm all right, Dad. I was knocked out. My back hurts, but I can move my legs O.K." Sobs choked me.

My father sat down beside me, still holding my hand. "We'll have to wait our turn. Only a few doctors here. So many hurt and burned."

"Mother? Anne-Marie?" I asked.

"Your mother and I were home when the water hit. It missed our house. Anne-Marie was at the Fleming farm." He stopped, his eyes full of pain. "You're the first one we've found."

My head fell back and I closed my eyes to digest this news. My little sister. . . .

"Rand?" I whispered. "He saved my life when the building collapsed."

"Rand's here in the hospital."

Joy and fear jumbled together. "He's badly hurt, isn't he?"

Dad nodded. "Left leg crushed."

"What about Dean? Miss Cruley?"

"Emily's all right. Dean's—" Dad's voice broke. "Dean drowned, Julie."

"No, no." Tears filled my eyes. If only Rand and Dean hadn't come to *The Sentinel*. . . . If only I had followed through on that inner nudge to have Rand meet me at home.

A harried doctor began checking over the patients on the hall floor. He tested my reflexes, then had me wheeled to the X-ray room. Not until the X-rays proved to be negative was I given a hospital gown and allowed to get on my feet. "Slight concussion, bad bruises and twisting of the lower lumbar region," was the diagnosis. "Keep her here overnight."

I learned of Anne-Marie's rescue when Dad returned to the hospital later that night. Meanwhile, makeshift wards were set up in every available space; I was moved into the nurses' off-duty room along with seven other women, mattresses lined up on the floor for us to sleep on.

When I questioned medical personnel about Rand, they just shook their heads. There had been no time yet to chart patients by name. Was he still alive? Was this all a bad dream?

No, the moans of the wounded, the sounds of weeping and the hurrying figures in white made it only too real. It was a miracle that I was alive. How had I survived?

Then I remembered. Those last moments before I hit the bridge, something important had happened. I had called out to God and He had responded. Not by voice, but by His presence. The memory stirred me and my lips began to move.

"Please, Lord, help Rand!"

Tears began to roll down my cheeks. So many people drowned. I closed my eyes and sleep came.

Early next morning my father reappeared. I stared at his face, looking for a sign.

"Rand is still in critical condition. He lost a lot of blood, but the doctor thinks he'll make it."

When I walked into Rand's hospital room later that morning, he was asleep. I stood by his bed silently, not wanting to wake him. The gray color of his face frightened me.

Rand stirred and his hand fell off his chest. Timidly I reached over and touched his fingers. Then I cradled his hand in mine; a tear rolled down my face and splashed onto his hand.

I looked back into Rand's face. His eyes were open and his lips slowly spread into a smile.

"We made it, didn't we?" he said.

SECTION
TWELVE

Facing Death

One morning late in our marriage Catherine admitted to me that she feared death.

"But Catherine, all you've written on that subject. . . ."

"I'm not talking about immortality," she interrupted. "I believe everything Jesus had to say about the resurrection and life after death."

"Well, death is simply the doorway to all that."

"I know that, too," she said, her voice tinged with impatience. "But it's all in my head, not in my emotions. Somehow, somewhere back in my childhood, a feeling took root inside me that death is the enemy to be hated and fought every step of the way."

"Catherine, we've been married almost twenty years. Why have you kept this hidden?"

"I guess I was ashamed to admit it."

As we prayed together about it, we saw again how Satan uses fear as a weapon to weaken our faith. I had become the spiritual head of our family years before. Now I knew that I needed to go a step further as head of our home and wage all-out spiritual warfare against the enemy.

Though Satan was assaulting us and our family, we were not defenseless. He hates prayer. Our intercession ministry had shown Catherine and me that a wave of prayer renders him ineffective.

Early in 1982 Catherine realized her time on earth was limited. The emphysema in her lungs had been slowly sapping her vitality. Walking up a flight of stairs was a major undertaking. Talking to people, meetings, shopping drained her.

Saddest of all was how her growing breathlessness affected her mornings—the time for the manuscript work she looked forward to so much. I would watch her go resolutely into her office at 9 A.M. Forty minutes later I would hear her return to our bedroom.

Once I confronted her there as she lay listlessly on the bed.

Tears welled up in her eyes. "The inner drive is gone. I don't have it anymore."

Then she railed at herself for being a quitter, got up and tried again.

My dilemma was: Should I prod her into doing what was painful and hard or let her drift into invalidism?

The answer soon became clear. Catherine's basic competitiveness, her battling nature, her spirit of adventure and her curiosity about life could not, should not be allowed to die. Catherine would never have forgiven me if I had encouraged her to let go of all this.

So we waged spiritual war against the forces of darkness and the enemy's subtle enticements to give in to weakness. We ended each day in prayer, when I anointed Catherine with oil, taking a stand against ill health, asking for sharpness of thinking and healing of body and spirit.

Here are some of Catherine's journal entries during her last days.

His Unfinished Work in Me

reamed last night about death. I don't relish putting this one on paper, but since it has to be worked through with the Lord, I suppose I must.

I was in a country where certain citizens were being exterminated by order of the state. One got one's notice and came to a special "office" in which were three booths, side by side. In one of these you were given a shot, like a dog being "put to sleep." Afterwards you were carted off to a back room where the bodies were stacked.

Apparently my number had come up. When I got to the office, I noticed that there were stacks and stacks of dirty dishes in the three booths. I sought to stall my death by offering eagerly to wash all the dishes. The attendant said, "Sure, go ahead. I don't blame you. Just don't tell any of the others that I agreed."

I started to wash a stack of plates, saying to myself, "There's always the chance of something happening to intervene, a national emergency or something." Then I woke up.

So now that I have put this dream on paper, Lord, what does it mean—and what do I do about it?

As I waited for some response, a name came to mind—John Wesley. Tuttle's book on Wesley was in the stack of unread volumes on my night table. I picked it up and soon discovered that Wesley and I shared a dread of death as the great enemy.

Wesley's fear surfaced dramatically in 1735 during a crossing of the Atlantic to Georgia. There were heavy storms at sea and the small wooden ship at times seemed doomed. Most on board, including the crew, were terror-struck. The only ones who remained calm were a group of German Moravian Christians.

Seeing the strength of these believers as they faced death, Wesley knew he must work through his problem. In reviewing his walk of faith, he realized he had espoused a life of asceticism that took four forms:

1. Self-denial (he lived frugally in order to give money to the poor)
2. Solitude
3. Works of charity (including visits to the terrible prisons of the time where he prayed with condemned men)
4. Interior prayer life

Wesley had to admit that while each of these disciplines have a place in the Christian life, not one of them dealt with his fear of death. Finally he began to see that this fear was not from God, but from Satan.

Soon after these discoveries, John Wesley had his personal experience of the Holy Spirit at Aldersgate. He was back against the basic New Testament proposition: There is no road to God except by faith in the finished work of Jesus Christ on the cross. Joy flooded in and gradually his fear of death dropped away as the Spirit brought alive these triumphant words of Jesus:

In My Father's house there are many dwelling places (homes). If it were not so, I would have told you, for I am going away to prepare a place for you. And when (if) I go and make ready a place for you, I will come back again and will take you to Myself, that where I am you may be also.

John 14:2–3, TAB

I know that the Holy Spirit has much unfinished work to do inside me about my attitude toward death. I need this, and I will myself to desire it.

Body Language

I beseech you therefore, brethren . . . that ye present your bodies a living sacrifice, holy, acceptable unto God, which is your reasonable service.

Romans 12:1

eading the Bible yesterday afternoon, I felt an inner nudge to stop and reread the above verse. I was conscious that I resisted this idea of offering my body as a sacrifice. Why? Because I suspected it could mean more speaking and traveling, more stress and pressure, with consequent loss of sleep at night and no chance to recoup with daytime naps.

What is so bad about this is that it is not really trusting the Lord with my physical body, and that's an awful confession. God expects His followers to be willing to be expendable; I have been circling around this point of total trust in a kind of spiritual holding pattern, unwilling to lay down my body as a living sacrifice. I am constantly protecting myself, succumbing too quickly to the temptation to stop my work and lie down for a while.

The conviction then came that I must be willing—and tell God so—to have the self I call "me," the particular bundle of talents, predispositions, preferences, tastes, all that constitutes myself, nailed to the cross with Jesus, to actually die and be buried with Him.

But, a voice inside me argued, didn't I do just this when I became a Christian? Jesus assured me, however, that this was a new step of dying to the self that so loves body comforts and beautiful things, that longs to escape the demands and entanglements of other people.

Much of that self I dislike (Romans 7:15-25). But a lot of what constitutes "me" I like very much. I have been "me," lived with "me" and put up with "me" a long time. To lay this self on the altar would indeed be a death.

I remembered Jesus' words about "counting the cost" (Luke 14:28). Was I really willing to take myself to the cross, die and be buried, not having any idea what sort of person would rise with Jesus on the third day?

I went through agony thinking about this, with a lot of tears.

Scripture says that Jesus resolutely and willingly turned His face to the cross for "the joy that was set before him" (Hebrews 12:2).

I finally told Jesus that I was going forward with this because I knew He was going to have His way with me, now or in the next life.

I got down on my knees in my office by the daybed at 4:40 P.M. and offered up my body to Him as a living sacrifice.

As a result, I must now be obedient hour by hour, day by day, and not hold back. This means seeing the indwelling Spirit so residing in my mortal flesh that I am willing to spend myself totally for others, as He did. It means letting all selfishness go, everything in my desire world, whenever it cuts across His higher priorities.

No wonder we can do no mighty works until the surrender is this complete! Until Jesus has been allowed to come and make His home in me like that, I will be praying for others, doing His work, in *my* name and in *my* nature rather than in His.

The apostle John puts it this way:

> . . . He laid down His [own] life for us; and we ought to lay [our] lives down for [those who are our] brothers [in Him].

> 1 John 3:16, TAB

Self-Pity

his morning I took to the Lord a matter that has been troubling me lately: sudden tears. I have never been a person who cries often. I generally keep my emotions in check, perhaps more than I should. Recently, though, bouts of unpredictable weeping.

The Lord has graciously shown me this morning the why of tears being just under the surface these past weeks—self-pity. In reality, I am weeping for myself.

I weep because of what is happening to me physically. First, my energy level has again dropped to such a degree that it is literally a chore to put one foot before the other. Added to that, worse breathlessness than I have ever known. Sometimes even sitting or lying in bed, I wonder if I am going to be able to take the next breath. This makes the stairs and hills at Evergreen Farm an agony.

Most puzzling, after years of battling sleeplessness, suddenly I can hardly stay awake. I must check out with the doctor whether this is an overreaction to the new arthritis drug they are giving me.

Or is it possible that, through lack of oxygen to the brain, I am coming into early senility? Hideous thought! For the first time since early girlhood I have no desire to read at night. During church yesterday, I could scarcely keep my eyes open.

Lord, help!

I am led to this verse:

> I know . . . Him Whom I have believed . . . and I am [positively] persuaded that He is able to guard and keep that which has been entrusted to me and which I have committed [to Him], until that day.
>
> 2 Timothy 1:12, TAB

Since self-pity is a sin, then clearly it has to be dealt with as a sin. It is a sin because since I belong to Jesus, it is He who has control over my life. Thus He overrules everything that He "allows" to happen to me—overrules it for good.

My part is to trust Him as a loving heavenly Father in each of these adverse circumstances. I am to watch expectantly for the "good"—the new adventure He has for me, the open door I am to go through toward the better way to which He is leading me.

So, given all that, what is there to have self-pity about?

I see that there is a self-discipline to practice during the days ahead: Each time I am tempted toward despairing self-pity, I am to rebuke it, reject it and turn immediately to praise.

Crucified with Jesus

On July 9, 1982, Catherine was so weak we had her taken by ambulance to the local hospital. When tests showed an alarming carbon dioxide content in her body, she was placed in the Intensive Care Unit with respirator tubes through her mouth to her lungs. The prognosis for her recovery was not good. She could not speak but she could still write in her journal.

n many ways my 32-day stint in the Intensive Care Unit of Bethesda Hospital was a crucifixion experience. Soon after I arrived there, the Lord reminded me of the act I had performed (through Romans 12:1) of offering my body as a living sacrifice on His cross.

While lying on my back hour after hour, unable to read or talk, I had plenty of time to reflect on the study I did a while ago on the humanity of Jesus. Through it I saw that His humanness for 33 years on earth was real; that He was as helpless, as "out of control" of circumstances, as we are. All this was in order for Him to be the Way-Shower, the true and very practical Captain of our salvation.

I also perceived that during His earthly walk, the guiding principle of Jesus' life was "never what I want to do but what pleases My Father in heaven."

In the intervening months since I made this study, several things have been happening:

1. The Holy Spirit has been doing a steady softening and melting process within me. This has meant that the plights of other persons presented to me, mostly through correspondence, have been laid on my heart with a new urgency.
2. During this same period my own circumstances have not only been taken out of my control, but also have gone in directions contrary to anything I would wish.

At what point in the Christian walk are we actually "crucified with Him"? At what point is the mortal self dead on His cross and buried with Him?

In my case, I concluded, dying to self has been going on for some time. For me it has been a slow, torturous, lingering death indeed— no doubt because I have been resisting all the way. I am reasonably sure that it need not be this drawn out and painful if the believer really understands what is going on and why and assents to it in his will. Yet I do think it is something we have to walk through all the way and feel. Death on a cross hurts.

Early the morning of July 24, fifteen days after entering the hospital, the climax came for me. I was in a semiconscious, dreaming state when I felt myself literally hanging on the cross with Jesus. There was no pain from nails in my hands or feet, only a suffocating, crushing weight on my chest as my entire body dragged downwards. I knew I was close to death, but strangely I had absolutely no fear.

As the weight on my rib cage grew unendurable, however, I was aware of a dark presence, as well as that of Jesus. A fierce struggle with some evil force ensued. Again and again I rebuked the dark power and ordered him to be gone. He didn't leave easily, but leave he did at last.

Then, so gently, Jesus picked me up and removed me from the cross. As He did so, three words came to me: *the great exchange*. Later I realized this is what theologians call "the substitutionary atonement," meaning that every sinful thing in our lives was dealt with in Christ's finished work on His cross and exchanged for something wonderful—righteousness for sin, health for sickness, life for death. At the moment I knew only that the crushing weight had lifted from my ribs.

I awoke the next morning very excited, feeling that a miracle had taken place in my body. This is the note I wrote to the nurse, saved by Len:

Please grant me this one request! I want to see my family, now! My husband first. Please call him. 732-6352.

My husband, my son Peter, my son Jeffrey. I want all of them. I want no medication before they get here. I'll "calm down" to suit you.

When Len, Peter and Jeffrey arrived, I told them through notes about my "death"; that at one point in my struggle with that dark force, it had seemed that my body parts were burnt up and lying in pieces around the room. The turning point came when way down deep I cried, "Jesus! Lord. My Lord." And He came and was with me. And He healed me.

My family was very responsive, but I think they wondered if it was a hallucination brought on by low oxygen levels in the brain. The key would be the next blood gases test.

When the doctor arrived at my bedside the next day, he was all smiles. "The carbon dioxide is way down!" he reported.

And then we all celebrated! On August 11 I was moved out of the Intensive Care Unit. On August 26 I was allowed to go home.

What transpired on the cross two thousand years ago has taken on sparkling new meaning for me. We are accustomed to thinking that Jesus carried only our sins on the cross, but Scripture makes it equally clear that He bore all our sicknesses and diseases there, too.

> When evening came they brought to [Jesus] many who were under the power of demons, and He drove out the spirits with a word, and restored to health all who were sick; and thus He fulfilled what was spoken by the prophet Isaiah, He Himself took (in order to carry away) our weaknesses and infirmities and bore away our diseases.
>
> Matthew 8:16-17, TAB (see Isaiah 53:4)

Len asked me the other night what I considered the chief significance of my crucifixion experience.

"I'm not sure yet," I replied. "I was close to death and the Lord returned me to life. He must have had a reason."

"Do you know what that might be?"

"There are a number of things I'm supposed to do, especially work on some bruised relationships." Then it struck me. "I've had a crucifixion, but not a resurrection."

Len wouldn't accept this. "You emerged from a dark valley into the light. Wasn't that a resurrection?"

"Not entirely. My breathing was restored to what it was last spring, but that's far from normal. My lungs have still not been completely healed."

"Consider this, Catherine," Len replied. "You've operated with little more than half your normal lungpower for almost forty years.

But look at all you've accomplished. Maybe, like Paul, God's given you a thorn in the flesh for a reason."

Lord, how much more I have to learn!

This morning I had this word from the Spirit. He tells me to praise and rejoice. He brings to mind the Scripture song we have sung so often at church: "Rejoice in the Lord always; again I will say, Rejoice" (Philippians 4:4, RSV).

Rejoice!

That I can enjoy music again through my stereo record-player. I actually got up and played the piano a bit—"Breathe on me, breath of God. . . . ."

Rejoice!

I telephoned T. and confessed my lack of love and understanding about several matters. A time of renewed fellowship and reconciliation.

Rejoice!

For patient Len and faithful family . . . for the Intercessors . . . for all who prayed . . . for my doctors and the hospital personnel.

Rejoice!

Linda and I are so close now. She drove down to be with me for a week, bringing a gift of four placemats and four napkins for the dining room table. "Use them," she urged. The point is that Len and the doctor have insisted on my getting out of bed and eating at the table.

Rejoice!

Praise You, Lord, for Pastor Bob Bonham giving up half of every Saturday to be with me.

Praise You, Lord, for bringing out all the fears that are clinging around the fear of death, so that I can deal with them.

Praise You, Lord, for allowing me to have those experiences in Intensive Care, and for pulling me back from death.

Receiving Love

od continues to heal me here in our Florida home. This morning He gave me a walloping message about the fact that I have not always been able to receive other people's love and so cannot receive Jesus' love. This revelation was sparked by a hassle with Len last night in our bedroom when I was complaining about members of the household who are shielding me about family situations, finances and decisions that involve my manuscripts and affairs.

Len became quite agitated. Finally with tears in his eyes he said, "Catherine, the doctors have told us that you need time to recover from being at death's door. What we're doing is for your protection, out of our love for you. Don't you realize we almost lost you?" With that, his voice broke with a show of emotion such as I have rarely seen in our marriage.

This morning I awoke with the full impact of Len's deep feeling sweeping over me. How often, I wondered, do men in our society shortchange themselves and their families by letting a "macho" front cover up a sensitive nature underneath?

The conviction came, too, though, that I have not been open enough to love. I have often had trouble accepting the feelings Len did express. The affection and gratitude of friends and readers, too.

Read 1 Corinthians 13, the Spirit nudged.

Those verses lay it out for me even more stringently than Len did last night:

> Love is patient, love is kind. It does not envy, it does not boast, it is not proud. It is not rude, it is not self-seeking, it is not easily angered, it keeps no record of wrongs. Love does not delight in evil but rejoices with the truth. It always protects, always trusts, always hopes, always perseveres.
>
> 1 Corinthians 13:4-7, NIV

I see further that, while my act of laying my body on the altar as "a living sacrifice" was a good first step, it was not enough: "If I . . . surrender my body to the flames, but have not love, I gain nothing" (verse 3).

Now comes further revelation, even as I write. Following the 1944 experience of Jesus' healing presence in my room after I had been bedridden for almost three years, I nevertheless lacked something. I have always supposed it was sufficient faith to make the healing complete.

But suppose it was love that was missing, not faith. Oh, obedience was not altogether there either, but obedience would have followed love.

Lord, I rejoice. Lord, I capitulate. Lord, let Your love—and Len's, and the love of those around me, each member of my family, and all the love of far-flung friends through my books—take over.

Keeping My
Eyes on Jesus

Fell on my face yesterday. Breathing was laborious. Did very little walking. Could not do the exercises. Was discouraged and disheartened and bored.

I knew the cause of all this. A letter came from my doctor, putting names and tags to my "chronic" illness for use in Medicare forms. It sounded so final that I began looking at this, accepting it, settling down to it.

I also opened the door to fear. Not so much fear of death, because I have actually, finally worked through that. This time it was a fear that I would let down the readers of my books who expect me to be an example of victorious faith.

In my session with Bob Bonham I traced the roots of this fear of letting people down back to my childhood. What came out was that my father's praising me so highly when I played the piano for his prayer meetings, or made top grades in school, eventually created in me the feeling that I had to achieve in order to have his love.

As the years passed, this feeling was extended to other members of my family, to friends, even to God. Added to this was my belief that because I have been so public in my life as a Christian, if I did not measure up to what Jesus expected of me, I would not only let Him down, but people "out there" would think less of Him; that Jesus' reputation would actually suffer.

Put in so many words, this is obviously ridiculous! But that's what came out. So yesterday was a total setback for me.

This morning I sought the Lord's forgiveness and was told some-thing like this, most emphatically:

Catherine, take your eyes off yourself, off your symptoms, off your fears, and center your attention on Me. Look at Me. Keep looking at Me.

Allow Me to be your Doctor. This is My will. I do know how to give you health. I made you. I know how to mend you.

Why do you think I healed everyone who came to Me in the days of My flesh? Out of overflowing mercy. I had only to see any human being blind or crippled or sick or in pain to want to set the wrong situation right as quickly as possible.

I have told you in My Word (Hebrews) that as man's High Priest I am able—and want—to run to the assistance of those who cry to Me.

In my answering prayer I said, "Lord, I do cry to You. I give You permission to change me on the inside, to strengthen my flabby spiritual muscles, to reverse the direction of my gaze, to make me eager to look at You only.

"I know You want a resurrection thrust inside me and an end to my doubts and negative thinking. In the wake of this will come new life and health. If not on this earth, then I will go into the next life with the differentness that You want for me."

Then Jesus led me to the sixteenth chapter of John where I was stopped by this magnificent verse:

> . . . It is profitable—good, expedient, advantageous—for you that I go away. Because if I do not go away, the Comforter (Counselor, Helper, Advocate, Intercessor, Strengthener, Standby) will not come to you—into close fellowship with you. . . .
>
> John 16:7, TAB

These are the blessed functions of the Holy Spirit promised by Jesus:

Counselor—He gives wisdom to the simple
Helper—He lifts us over every obstacle
Advocate—He is our personal lawyer to plead our case
Intercessor—He stands before the throne of grace
Strengthener—He gives us vitality and courage
Standby—He is always at our side

How can a one of us get along without any of those things!
Then glorious verse 33:

I have told you these things so that in Me you may have perfect
peace and confidence. In the world you have tribulation and trials
and distress and frustration; but be of good cheer—take courage,
be confident, certain, undaunted—for I have overcome the world.—
I have deprived it of power to harm, have conquered it [for you].

Resurrection

Thanks to her pastors George Callahan and Robert Bonham, plus loving friends and family, Catherine made good progress during 1982. Thanksgiving and Christmas involved healing times with family members.

At the beginning of 1983 Catherine set several goals for herself. An 800-page draft of the novel *Julie* had been completed, but months of work were needed to sharpen characterization. She wanted to resume writing for *The Intercessors* newsletter and do an article about her mother for a *Guideposts* series on aging.

At the end of January she underwent a cataract operation. From her journal:

*ebruary 9:* I am staggering under what the eye surgeon said to me yesterday during a routine checkup following the cataract surgery: "You are sick from head to toe." I did not have to accept this verdict, but I did. Now I really have to ditch it—with the Spirit's help and by God's grace. This verse has truly helped me:

If the Spirit of Him Who raised up Jesus from the dead dwells in you, [then] He Who raised up Christ Jesus from the dead will also restore to life your mortal (short-lived, perishable) bodies through His Spirit Who dwells in you.

Romans 8:11, TAB

February 24: Have hit a new low. I am quite out of breath—indeed, gasping for air—just in walking from room to room. My doctor could find no obvious cause for the trouble yesterday. Today it hit me: Once again the doctors know neither what is wrong nor how to help me. So . . . I am backed up against Jesus' help.

March 9: In my quiet time, this thought: My hospital experience of the crucifixion was centered on the matter of breathing. This morning the Holy Spirit reminded me once again: *Jesus took your breathing problem into His own body on the cross so that from henceforth He is your life-breath.*

Here is Catherine's last journal entry made from the hospital where she was undergoing tests:

March 12: The blood test yesterday showed the carbon dioxide level in my blood too high, but not dangerous; not enough oxygen in the blood, however. Another problem seems to be anemia.

This morning Jesus told me once again: *Keep your eyes off yourself and look steadily at Me. I love you. I know how to mend you.*

Shortly after midnight on March 18, Catherine's heart stopped beating. The Lord had come to take her with Him.

Afterword

n the hours and days that followed, the Lord seemed to place all of us in the family under His special love and protection, plus a necessary degree of numbness. The calls, letters, cards, flowers and food that flowed in warmed and nourished us.

Two triumphant occasions followed:

The burial service at National Presbyterian Church, Washington, D.C., conducted by its pastor, Catherine's close friend Dr. Louis Evans, Jr., and her son, Peter John Marshall.

And the memorial service at the New Covenant Presbyterian Church, Pompano Beach, Florida. Pastor George Callahan and Dr. William Earnhart (church elder and Catherine's personal physician) shared their memories of a great lady.

Robert Bonham, the pastor who for so many hours ministered healing to Catherine, spoke these words at this same service:

> During Catherine's funeral in the National Presbyterian Church, my eyes went to some beautiful stained glass windows through which the sun was shining. I thought of Jesus telling His disciples,

"You are the light of the world." Catherine as a twentieth-century follower put her light on a lampstand so that all might see.

I looked at the glass in those windows and thought about all the pieces therein. There were dark pieces and light pieces, all kinds of colors blended together. I thought about the suffering experiences Catherine had early in her life and recently in the hospital. These were deep, deep colors. Her body never was able to keep up with her mind and her spirit. It always hauled her back.

There were, of course, the brighter colors, the rose tints of love and warmth—the giving of her heart to those in her family and to everyone she touched. Those colors went out across the United States and throughout the world.

There were so many pieces in her life—the books she wrote, the articles for *Guideposts* and other magazines. She wrote nothing that did not have all of her heart and mind in it, as well as the heart and mind of Christ.

Starting the Breakthrough intercession ministry not long ago, she and Leonard mobilized prayer warriors across the nation to bring help to many people. The members of her family represent warm, glowing pieces of glass in the mosaic of her life.

A surprising thing about a stained glass window is that when the light is not shining through, it comes across as dull. Have you ever looked at a stained glass window when there is no light behind it? You cannot see what is in it. Catherine always had Christ's light shining through her life. As the light of Jesus radiated through the stained glass mosaic of her life, all of us who were within sight of it got blessed.

When the sun goes down, the horizon stays bright for a long time. There is going to be a long afterglow to Catherine Marshall LeSourd's life. The books that were written will go on to become classics in Christian literature. The articles will go on helping people. There are things she has written that will yet find their way into print to bless us. Her touches on our lives will live on, ministering to our children, our children's children.

In the last page of her book *To Live Again*, Catherine wrote these words as she faced life without her husband Peter:

"At moments when the future is completely obscured, can any one of us afford to go to meet our tomorrows with dragging feet? God had been in the past. Then He would be in the future, too.

"And with His presence had always come an end to tasteless living. Always He had brought adventure—high hopes, unexpected friends, new ventures that broke old patterns. Then out in my future must lie more goodness, more mercy, more adventures, more friends.

"Across the hills light was breaking through the stormclouds. Suddenly just ahead of the car an iridescent rainbow appeared—hung there—shimmering. I hadn't seen a rainbow for a long time.

"I drove steadily into the light."

Catherine is doing that right now—moving steadily into the Light.

APPENDIX

How the Breakthrough Intercessory Prayer Ministry Operates

It begins with the scriptural promise that the Lord's joyful task as our High Priest is to make intercession for us before His Father's throne.

The prayer needs of individuals are sent to

Breakthrough
The Catherine Marshall Center
Lincoln, VA 22078

Prayer requests for governments, causes or special works are handled occasionally by Breakthrough, but more often forwarded to other groups like Intercessors for America, which specialize in this kind of petition.

Intercessors are the "supply" people who have volunteered to tithe their time to pray for the needs of others. Their names and addresses are known only to the Breakthrough administrators.

Need and supply meet in this way: A summary of each person's need (first name only) is sent to five or more intercessors who have committed themselves to pray for each request for a three-week period. At the end of this time the prayer-requester may ask for an extension of this commitment.

The anonymity of both parties is kept so that the ministry can focus on prayer and not get into personal counseling, which the intercessors are not equipped to do.

When a prayer insight (often a revelation from God) is received by an intercessor, it is forwarded to the prayer-requester via the coordinator in the Breakthrough office.

When an answer to an intercessor's prayer is received by letter or telephone at the Breakthrough office, there is a joyful time of praise.

The Breakthrough newsletter circulates regularly to provide teaching on intercessory prayer and reports on the results of the work. It can be obtained free of charge by writing to the above address.

Excerpts are taken from the following books:

AMERICA'S MOST INSPIRATIONAL AUTHOR

BEYOND OUR SELVES
72202-X / $8.00 US/ $10.00 Can

TO LIVE AGAIN
72236-4/ $8.00 US/ $10.00 Can

A MAN CALLED PETER
72204-6/ $9.00 US/ $12.00 Can

SOMETHING MORE
72203-8/ $8.00 US/ $10.00 Can

THE HELPER
72282-8/ $8.00 US/ $10.00 Can

CATHERINE MARSHALL'S STORY BIBLE
69961-3/ $10.95 US/ $13.95 Can

Coming Soon
THE BEST OF CATHERINE MARSHALL
72383-2/ $9.00 US/ $12.00 Can